CELTIC
WARRINGTON
& OTHER
MYSTERIES

VOLUME TWO

WARRINGTON EAST TO SOUTH

MARK OLLY

CHURNET VALLEY BOOKS
© Mark Olly and Churnet Valley Books 1999
ISBN 1 897949 57 X

TO MY LONG-SUFFERING WIFE HEATHER ELIZABETH OLLY:
WHO HAS SUFFERED ENDLESS DAYS OF LONELINESS & WILD CHILDREN
WHILE I SLAVED IN ISOLATION OVER OBSCURE BOOKS & MANUSCRIPTS OR
WAS ABSENT ALTOGETHER 'ON SURVEY'. THANK YOU FOR CORRECTING MY
LINGUISTIC BLUNDERINGS & MAKING THE ENTIRE CELTIC WARRINGTON
PROJECT POSSIBLE.

TO THE GODDESS FROM THE HAWK OF MAY

ACKNOWLEDGMENTS

A BIG THANK YOU TO: Many people have helped greatly in the project & the production of this book, especially: Mum & Dad, Heather Olly, Lesley Lowery, Miles Fordham, Bill & Sarah Griffiths, Sue, Audrey & Linda at Supersnaps Warrington, Neil and Linda Skellan, Mike Nevell at The University of Manchester & Greater Manchester Archaeological Units, Martin Patch at The Manchester Museum, Jill Collens at Cheshire Sites & Monuments, Alan Leigh & the staff at Warrington Museum & Library Services, Derek Pierce & all at South Trafford Archaeological Group, Robert Woodside for the National Trust Dunham Massey Survey, Oliver Knapp for Tatton Park, Charles Foster for Arley Hall, Judy Popley for High Legh, Joe Griffiths for Lymm Historic Society, Dr. Rodney Baguley, Harry Richards, Scott Lloyd, Diana Bennett & Family, Andrew Sim, Wayne Percival, Doug & Hilary Pickford, Steff 'Farinda' Else, Debbie Acton & Family, Mr & Mrs Harrison & family at Barley Castle Farm, Dr. Paul & Mary Cottrill at Lymm Hall, all at 'The Door' Histories, Mysteries & Discoveries Group. Special thanks to 'Ulfhadnir' especially Andy Von Kiesel (alias Sir Gawain) on the book cover. Celtic Warrington Exhibition thanks to: Lorraine Hall & all at Salsa Warrington, Stephen Broomhead & Leo Kolassa & all at Warrington Borough Council, Anthony Potts, Business Connections 97, Fon Matthewes & Mathrafal (Wrexham Celts), Ruth, Ian & Jenny (Warrington Celts), Paul Rice at 'Warrington Now' for sponsorship, Suzanne Lightfoot & all at the Warrington Guardian for continued support.

All Photographs by Mark Olly & Lesley Lowery unless otherwise stated. Illustrations drawn or adapted from ancient celtic manuscripts & archaeological publications. Victorian copper-plate engravings, wood-cut prints & maps drawn or adapted by Mark Olly.

IN SEARCH OF ENGLAND:

YOU WILL REMEMBER, LADY, HOW THE MORN
CAME SLOW ABOVE THE ISLE OF ATHELNEY,
AND ALL THE FLAT LANDS LYING TO THE SKY
WERE SHROUDED SEA-LIKE IN A VEIL OF GREY
AS, STANDING ON A LITTLE ROUNDED HILL,
WE PLACED OUR HANDS UPON THE HOLY THORN.

DO YOU REMEMBER IN WHAT HOPEFUL FEAR
WE GAZED BEHIND US, THINKING WE MIGHT SEE
ARTHUR COME STRIDING THROUGH THE HIGH, BRIGHT CORN,
OR ALFRED RESTING ON A SAXON SPEAR?
AND AS THE COLD MISTS MELTED FROM THE FIELDS
WE SEEMED TO HEAR THE WINDING OF A HORN.

YOU WILL REMEMBER HOW WE WALKED THE VALE
THROUGH MEARE AND WESTHAY UNTO GODNEY END;
AND HOW WE SAID: 'TIME IS AN ENDLESS LANE
AND LIFE A LITTLE MILE WITHOUT A BEND
BEHIND US WHAT? BEFORE US, IF WE RAN,
MIGHT WE NOT BE IN TIME TO SEE THE GRAIL?'

"IN SEARCH OF ENGLAND" (1927) H.V.MORTON.

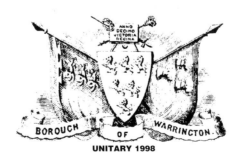

UNITARY 1998

FOREWORD

This series of books (of which this is the second) is intended as a practical tour guide to actual sites which can be visited out in the region at this time, as well as giving basic background information required to view these sites from a more informed perspective. With this in mind, this book is arranged in the order best suited to a circular, clockwise car journey through the areas covered, with a few relevant detours.

Technical information will only be included if it is important to the story in hand and all archaeological information has been summarised to make it more readily understandable. I do not intend this series of books to be factually exhaustive, the majority of people simply want to experience the existence of local history on a 'first hand' basis, without losing the joy of discovery.

The books are primarily a guide, secondarily a collection of useful or mysterious information otherwise hard to find, and thirdly the start of a greater system of mysteries which surround the town and go back into very ancient history. In the final book of this series I hope to look at the full mystery of the town that is Warrington, a mystery which still lies partially veiled to me, at this present time.

Once again, my apologies if you know something I have left out or if I make a few mistakes along the way. I always appreciate anyone dropping me a line to the address at the end of the contents page with any further information that I have missed or to correct any errors. This is how the Celtic Warrington Project has developed over the last few years and has encouraged more people to search for history in their own neighbourhoods - even if nothing of historic importance has ever been thought to previously exist there. Have a look - you never know what you might discover! Seek and you will find.

Mark Olly. May 1999.

CONTENTS

CHRONOLOGY OF PRINCIPLE TIME PERIODS IN THIS BOOK

FOR BIBLIOGRAPHY SEE BOOKS ONE AND THREE

MARK OLLY

CELTIC WARRINGTON AND OTHER MYSTERIES

INTRODUCTION

A heart-felt Celtic welcome to all those who join me in searching the mysteries of the ancient settlements which make up Warrington.

Without a doubt this present volume has been the hardest written-material I have had the task of assembling since I began writing in 1984. From an early and mistakenly preconceived idea that only a small selection of Celtic material would be available for the East to South area, the book grew and grew, as a vast sea of complex data gradually accumulated. I can heartily agree with Philo of Alexandria when he wrote in *On the Contemplative Life*: *"Ancient history is like a night-landscape, over which we grope, vaguely discerning a few outlines in the general gloom, and happy if here or there the works of a particular author or a ruin or work of art momentarily illumine, like a lightning flash in the dark, the particular field which we are exploring."*

Add to this several changes of office, the availability of thousands of unpublished old photographs, a very wet summer unsuitable for field work, the extra work generated by the promotion of book one and associated exhibition, and you have even more chaos than otherwise exists in a book project of this kind.

Through all of this, I can only hope that I have succeeded in providing a Celtic guide at least as acceptable as volume one. I hope that it is revealing and useful to those of you who wish to seek out the diamonds of Celtic history and wisdom; those things which have remained so well embedded in the rocks of our region for so long, which are now being carved out, and are presented here.

In response to several requests, I have chosen to add some more background information on Celtic culture where it applies to those things found in Warrington. I have also had to stray from our present day geographic divisions back to those which have existed in past times. For example, this is the reason why information relating to Wilderspool, Latchford and Walton can be found mixed with the section on Stockton Heath. The areas of Thelwall, Grappenhall and Appleton also overlap. The book has also had to reach far and wide in order to begin to cover the subject of the River Mersey.

I have added a little more of my own personal comments and a greater selection of, previously unpublished, local history photographs where relevant. While not always Celtic in nature, these Victorian photographs add a valuable insight into the region before industrialisation gained a real foothold at the start of the twentieth century, sweeping away the quiet farming economy which had remained largely unchanged for a thousand years.

It would be of great help to the reader to buy the four relevant Ordnance Survey maps covering Warrington in the 'Pathfinder' series, numbers 722, 723, 739, 740 and/or the Geographer's A-Z street plan of Warrington. A new, updated range of maps by the OS are in production but are not yet available for our areas. These will prove useful when available, as will any map showing the course of the River Mersey, while reading certain sections of this book.

As before, in terms of time, the Celtic period can be taken as emerging from the mists of the Late Neolithic Period or New Stone Age around 2500 years BC and developing into distinct Celtic cultures about 1000BC, through the Bronze & Iron ages, fading out at some point after 900AD with the establishment of early Christianity in Britain and the invasion of the Angles, Saxons, Danes, Norse and, finally, the Normans in 1066AD.

Some authorities maintain that the Celtic period continued right up to 1200AD and beyond, but a better term for this period would be 'Early Medieval' (although 'Celts' may still survive in Ireland, Scotland and Wales in some form even to this day). With this in mind, the reader should excuse the odd drift into Medieval or even later times should the subject matter dictate. There are also some 'Other Mysteries', which I may explore along the way, which are relatively recent but have definite Celtic origins and connections, or are important folklore associated with the sites in question.

The second step in the voyage of discovery is to choose a method of travel appropriate to the trip. In this case I have chosen to divide Warrington into a 'clock' with 12.00 set at North, 3.00 at East, 6.00 at South and 9.00 at West with Bridge Street and the 'River of Life' sculpture in the present Warrington Town Centre as the central point.

So great is the quantity of information, that each quarter will be dealt with in a separate book of similar length, culminating in the 'Grand De-Coda', a final volume written to summarise the whole. This present volume is book two in the series and deals with sites in a clockwise direction starting at the banks of the River Mersey and Manchester Ship Canal at Stockton Heath. It then heads east out of Warrington (3 o'clock) as far as the village of Dunham before turning back through Knutsford and High Legh, ending just east of the A49 Roman Road south out of Warrington (6 o'clock) at Appleton Thorn, with all areas in that quarter included and found on Ordnance Survey Pathfinder 740. The furthest reaches of this quarter are defined by the estates of Dunham Massey, Tatton Park and Arley Hall.

The third and final requirement to any voyage of mystery is a certain aptitude for the unseen, a sort of 'sixth sense' awareness of the stars, nature, magic, belief, etc. To this end I have included a small element of the more esoteric such as ley lines, geomantic details, underground water sources, star alignments and sacred sites as well as the recognised sciences of archaeology, cartography, geology and palaeontology.

In 1927 H.V. Morton took to the roads to write one of the very first car-orientated tour books based on a circular driving route round England. He called it *In Search of England*, and chose to come through Warrington painting a picture of the town which has pretty much 'stuck' ever since. He says:

I was passing between Liverpool on the left and Manchester on the right, and about sixteen miles from both cities. Far off to the left I could see the Mersey estuary, with red smoke stacks rising above the flat lands by the sandy shore. To the right there was an ominous grey haze in the sky which meant Manchester.

For months I have motored through a green England which might never have known Industrial Revolution .... yet how difficult it is to kill an English field, to stamp out the English grass, and to deform the English lane! Even here, within sixteen miles of the two great giants of

the north, men were raking hay in a field within a gunshot of factory chimneys.

At Warrington I heard the clap-clop of clogs; at Warrington I saw mill girls with shawls over their heads; at Warrington I smelt for the first time the characteristic aroma which permeates the industrial towns and villages of Lancashire - fried fish and chips.

The only consolation is that these monster towns and cities of the north of England are a mere speck in the amazing greenness of England: their inhabitants can be lost in green fields and woodland within a few minutes. London is much more distant from a real wood than Warrington.

And so may it always remain.

A POSTCARD FROM THE HOXNIAN INTERGLACIAL!

It has long been assumed that our 'ridge and valley' region of north Cheshire spent the vast majority of the Ice Ages under the ice. I say 'Ice Ages' (plural) as the prevailing opinion of our day is that there were several long breaks in the Ice Age during which our climate improved sufficiently to allow for human habitation and that a single Ice Age did not occur as such.

If we could travel back in time we would not find ice threatening Cheshire until the Devensian period beyond 10,000BC, but this mild situation only lasted for about 20,000 years. Go back further to 150,000BC and ice would be covering Cheshire for the 50,000 years of the Wolstonian 3 period, then again at 280,000 to 320,000 during Wolstonian 2, and at 350,000 to 380,000 during Wolstonian 1. At this mind-bending point in prehistory comes the last warm spell, before the 100,000 years of the Anglian Ice Age arrives and destroys plants and animals only found now as fossils.

This gap 380,000 to 400,000BC is known as the Hoxnian Interglacial and now represents the oldest recorded visit of Homo Erectus, or very early Stone Age man, to north Cheshire.

On the 29th September 1998 myself and photographer Lesley Lowery were surveying a ploughed field, looking for pottery fragments on the ridge behind a Tudor building, Denfield Farm, Millington, when she picked up a medium-sized flint pebble which had obviously been shaped to form a primitive tool. Further investigations revealed a scatter of seven other flint pebbles within a radius of about 60 feet (19m), three of which resemble small tools. The remaining four resemble 'pot boilers' which were heated in a fire and then put into water in order to heat it - there were no heat-resistant containers at this time which could be put over a fire.

Research has revealed that these finds come from the Hoxnian Interglacial dating them to between 380,000 and 400,000BC.

These could be the oldest site finds in Cheshire and raise some important questions for local and national archaeology. For help in understanding the historical chronology contained in this section please refer to Chronology of Principal Time Periods Listed, at the end of this book.

HARVEST TIME ABOUT 1910 AT STOCKTON HEATH IN THE AREA
NORTH OF CHESTER ROAD AND (AT BOTTOM LEFT) AN INTERESTING
GATHERING OUTSIDE GRAPPENHALL CHURCH

It has always been thought that the Mersey Valley spent most of the Ice Ages under the ice, but the pebble-tool and associated flints indicate the location of at least one tool-making hunter here during this period. Evidently the north Cheshire ridge overlooked a much flooded Mersey valley as the ice sheets retreated north.

Tools of this kind are common in the South especially on the Downlands, Suffolk, Kent and Essex, like the site at Clacton-on-Sea where they have been found in the gravels underlying the golf course. All of these sites are waterside settlements and no Hoxnian cave sites are known. Northern cave sites of great age have been found at Pontnewydd in North Wales and Creswell Crags in Derbyshire but these are much more recent than the Ice Age hunters, who used open hunting camps. These camps are virtually unheard of north of Oxfordshire and The Wash on the East Coast. Certainly I can find no hunting camps recorded in Cheshire. Flint is also not a material native to Cheshire so must have been brought here by these hunters. Two distinct types of 'axe' tool were in use during the Hoxnian period and are regarded as the oldest definitive identifiable tools of early man:

Type 1 is thought to be the older hand-sized 'chopping tool' which does not appear again after the Hoxnian period and of which we found a fine example at Denfield Farm.

Type 2 is the larger 'pear-shaped' or 'tear-drop' hand axe - one of which was reported in the Northwich Guardian (16/9/98, p.9) just three days before our discovery. This axe had been found 25 years earlier in 1973 by Jennifer Ritchie (then Jennifer Cule aged 17) in a garden in Mobberley Road, Knutsford, but had only recently been handed in to Tatton Park who sent it to the British Museum. The lady who took the axe to London informed me that their initial estimate placed this somewhat damaged example at 250,000BC (Ilfordian) and they thought it had possibly been carried to Knutsford from Yorkshire, Lincolnshire or the South-east. It has also been water-worn by river gravels. I venture

MILLINGTON
HOXNIAN 400,000 BC

KNUTSFORD/TATTON
ILFORDIAN 250,000 BC

STOCKTON HEATH
STONE AGE 12,000 BC

to suggest that this find is also a relic from the same hunting activities of the Stone Age visitors to Warrington who came in the days of wild bear, rhinoceros, sabre-toothed cats, elephant, deer and bison.

I have this impression of a skin-clad hunter wearing his antlered head piece, standing on a grassy tundra ridge, gazing across a rushing torrent in the floor of the Mersey Valley and outlined against a huge wall of glacial ice just to the north. This sheet is about to return for Wolstonian 1. The climate changed and the animal species, and the hunter culture that hunted them, died out.

MESOLITHIC MAN 10000 BC - 5000 BC

"For many centuries after Britain became an island the untamed forest was king. Its moist and mossy floor was hidden from heaven's eye by a close drawn curtain woven of innumerable tree tops, which shivered in the breezes of summer dawn and broke into wild music of millions upon millions of wakening birds; the concert was prolonged from bough to bough with scarcely a break for hundreds of miles over hill and plain and mountain, unheard by man save where, at rarest intervals, a troop of skin clad hunters, stone axe in hand, moved furtively over the ground beneath."
From Trevelyan's History Of England Part 1.

In our area, and those areas surrounding the Pennine foothills, it has been established through archaeological endeavour that the Stone Age 'Sauveterre Culture' (which takes its name from the distinctive settlement site of Le Martinet Sauveterre at Perigord in France) reached the Mersey Valley between 7600 and 6800 years ago (5700-4900BC).

These very early settlers hunted in local forests which were comprised mainly of oak with wych elm, English lime and hazel, and completely surrounded the Mersey valley at that time. Like their Hoxnian forefathers they preferred to settle in sandy places by water during the summer as they had no permanent 'houses' (unless a cave was available nearby for convenient use). The winding, sandy curves of the Mersey with its fertile flood plains and wooded hillsides would have provided a perfect settlement area for these first Stone Age immigrants from France. It is worth noting that throughout the Bronze Age and Celtic periods, little or no distinction was made between Britain and France and the English Channel was regarded more as a 'big river' than as the sea.

Although 'Sauveterre Man' is only known by his flints (most noticeably found locally at Alderley Edge and Frodsham Hill), it is likely that he was the ancient ancestor of the original Mersey Valley inhabitants found here during the later Bronze Age. All the areas of Bronze Age settlement from 3000BC onwards had previously been areas of Mesolithic occupation which also serves to demonstrate the earliest evidence for a connection between cultures existing in Ireland, The Isle of Man, Anglesey, The Wirral and the Mersey Valley, which are all surrounded by the Irish Sea.

In *Cheshire Before The Romans*, W.J. Varley makes the observation that: *"On the banks of the River Bann in Northern Ireland there lived a Mesolithic community of salmon fishers and makers of a very distinctive broad-tanged flint blades. A radio-carbon date for them of 5290 BC (+-100 years) makes it quite certain that they were separated by the Irish Sea from both Man and England. Yet they made the crossing. Professor Clark drew attention to Bann flakes in the Isle of Man. They also figure in the collection of objects recovered from the Meols shore (Hoylake, Wirral) housed in the Grosvenor Museum, Chester. Here is proof of inter-connection between opposite sides of the Irish sea at the end of the Mesolithic period (5000-4000BC)."*

From these earliest connections in France and Ireland developed the Mersey Valley culture which produced a prolific spread of Stone Age flint finds (the largest site of which is dealt with under the section on Tatton).

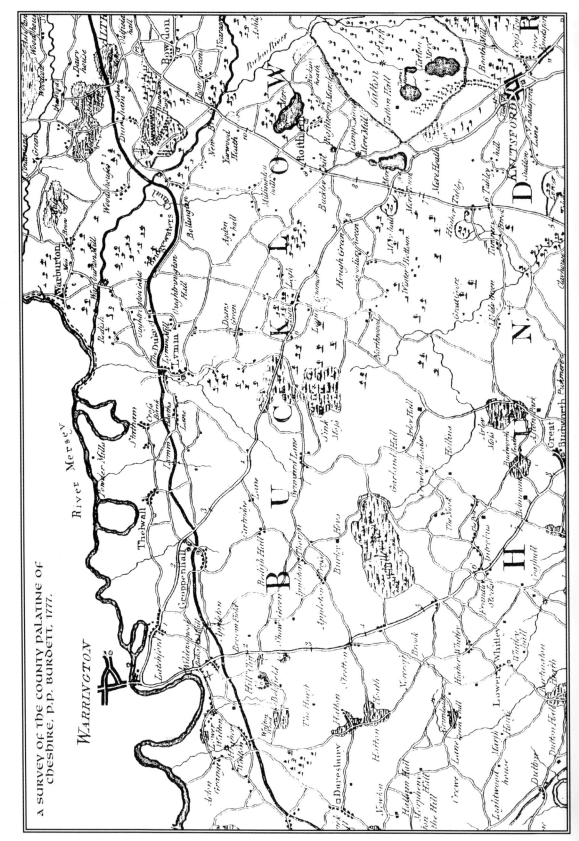

A SURVEY OF THE COUNTY PALATINE OF CHESHIRE, P.P. BURDETT, 1777.

STOCKTON HEATH

LATCHFORD

WILDERSPOOL

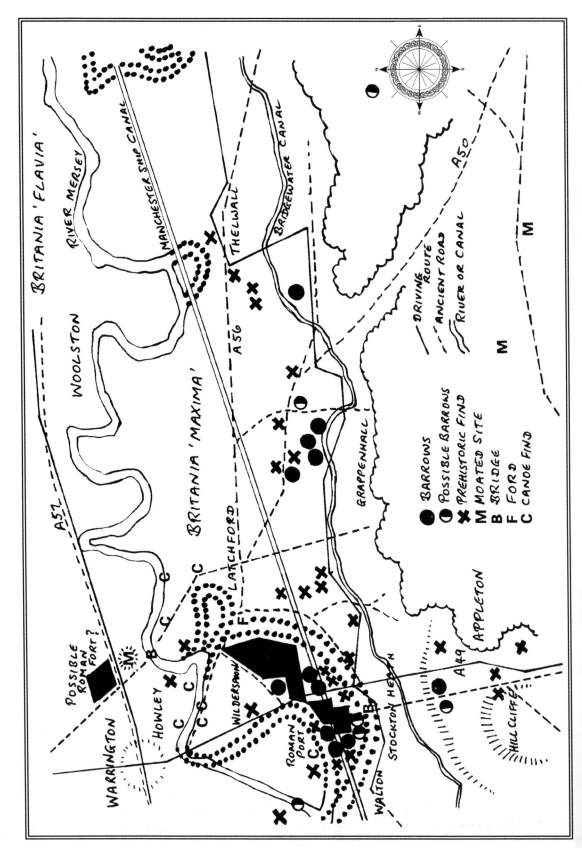

STOCKTON HEATH

Stockton Heath lies just over a mile to the south of Warrington town centre along the A49 London Road between the Manchester Ship Canal and the Bridgewater Canal; two industrial enterprises from very different times but with the same end in mind, to transport goods by water to and from Manchester. Now most of the transport development here is concerned with people in cars, and the large area covered by this book demands that we choose this mode of transport for our explorations once again. But don't be too eager to move on. There is much to read about here in the south east quarter of Warrington and the sacred Celtic River Mersey looms large over our shoulder through the first half of this book as far as Dunham Massey. (A map showing the Mersey would be useful from this point on).

Our journey begins in the busy Victoria Square, centre of the village, where there is ample evidence of development over the last two centuries, before which time the few buildings on this spot would barely have qualified as a hamlet.

THE STONE AGE HUNTER'S CITY

The most ancient finds to come to light in Stockton Heath result mainly from the development of the area during the end of the nineteenth century and early twentieth century, so details are often badly recorded (if at all) and the sites of the finds have been continually destroyed at the hand of the developer. It is obvious, however, that the area now occupied by Stockton Heath constituted the nearest thing to a Stone Age 'City' to be found in the north Cheshire/south Lancashire area.

The number and type of finds indicate a concentration of activity between the sandstone outcrop of Hill Cliffe and the River Mersey at Wilderspool and Latchford. This indicates the vast age of settlement here, over which later cultures added their progressively more developed and Celtic identities. It should also be remembered that the trees we now see covering the Hill Cliffe escarpment were three plantations artificially introduced in the late eighteenth century (1750 to 1800). Archaeological activity in the area of this escarpment is sadly lacking.

I shall now attempt to reconcile the various prehistoric find accounts to form a fairly comprehensive list, with locations where available. Several Neolithic 'Stone Age' axes and hammer heads have come to light.

The first recorded was found in the area of the village main street south of Victoria Square in 1902 and is described as a *"flaked grey flint axe with a polished cutting edge"*. This was accompanied by a flint flake with a worked edge and a flint nodule but the date of this find is not recorded in the Cheshire County Treasures Record.

Another polished flint axe head was recovered from the Roman levels of Thomas May's excavations between 1895 and 1905, probably from the temple area close to Roman Road. Warrington Museum are currently displaying a white, polished flint axe head simply recorded as found on the "Roman Site - Wilderspool" (Find No. 222'06) which may be the one found by Thomas May.

Next to be found in 1926 come three Prehistoric stone hammers which are recorded in 1976 in *The Archaeology Of Warrington's Past* as being found east of Ackers Pits between Ackers Road, Chester Road and Montclare Crescent. These may relate in some way to the later Bronze Age burial site found further along Chester Road at Euclid Avenue, Grappenhall.

In October of 1934 Mr A.L. Armstrong exhibited a Neolithic axe hammer at a meeting of the Society of Antiquaries of London, said to have been found 4ins (10cm) below sand somewhere near Stockton Heath. Mr Armstrong's collection was eventually presented to Warrington Museum and included an axe hammer which may be this item which measures 10ins (25.5cm) long, $2^3/4$ins (7cm) thick by $4^1/4$ins (11cm) wide. The hole for the shaft is $1^3/4$ ins (4.5cm) in diameter and is countersunk on both sides.

In *Prehistoric Cheshire* J.W. Varley records a Neolithic flint axe with pointed butt found at Stockton Heath some time before 1940 (which could be the same axe of grey flint previously mentioned) with a partly polished cutting edge measuring $4^1/8$ins (10.5cm) long by $1^1/2$ins (4cm) wide at the cutting edge and $5/8$ins (1.5cm) thick and given as found before 1949 at the Alexander Park end of Victoria Road, Stockton Heath, in the *Cheshire Sites and Monuments Record* (although no proof for this exact siting exists!). Moving on to other implements:

A small triangular flint scraper turned up at the entrance to Warrington Dock (opposite side of Manchester Ship Canal to Ellesmere Road where the Mersey connects), a location also known as 'Walton Lock'. This find is still on display in the museum (No. 20'32), as is another find - a flint core found at Arpley (No. 21'32). To clear up a confusion which has arisen: *Cheshire Sites and Monuments Record* describes a "Flint Flake, possibly a scraper, found in the Arpley Area - O.S.Record Card SJ68 NW79" and it is given as the one found near the 'crannog' site and recorded in *The Archaeology of Warrington's Past*. As can be clearly seen, these are two separate flint finds on display at the Museum which have become confused. More on the 'crannog' site later!

In 1933 a flint implement was found on the east side of Mill Lane close to Alexander Park, and is recorded in *The Archaeology of Warrington's Past.*

During trial excavations in 1981 Liverpool University Rescue Archaeology Unit also found a leaf-shaped arrow head and a flint flake in the area of Alexander Park, Stockton Heath, which probably indicates prehistoric activity centred on Lumb Brook.

As was the custom in ancient times, burial sites litter the sides of ancient 'ridgeways' and Celtic highways, and this area is no exception. Many burial mounds existed higher up above Stockton Heath in Appleton and are dealt with in Book 3 of this series, but quite a number appear to have followed the old roads through Stockton Heath and on to Wilderspool both before, during and after the Roman occupation.

During sand quarrying activities between 1867 and 1872 two Roman feeding bottles for infants were unearthed, contained in cremation burials, which were noted by Watkin W. Thompson in *Roman Cheshire*.

In 1895 a dug-out oak coffin lined with sheets of lead and containing a skeleton was removed from a depth of about 6 feet (2m) from the north bank of the Manchester Ship Canal, 120 yards (114m) east of the bridge at Stockton Heath. It would be interesting had this find survived as it sounds later than Roman and is possibly Norse/Celtic.

Close to this find, diggers also unearthed an 'Upchurch' burial urn containing a cremation 3feet (1m) below the surface. Noting the difference in burial depth between the urn and coffin, this site may represent a burial in a former mound.

It is recorded in A. Kendrick's guide book to the collection of Roman remains from Wilderspool that a deep vase of red pottery with a narrow neck, containing burnt human bones, was found on removing an artificial mound, upon which a windmill stood (site now destroyed by Manchester Ship Canal). This sounds like a Bronze Age burial mound rather than anything of Roman origin and it stood about 70 yards west of the Wilderspool excavations (of 1895-1905), placing it in old Stockton Heath before the building of the Manchester Ship Canal. A fragment of a burial urn from this barrow remains in Warrington museum and looks distinctly Bronze Age.

According to Varley & Jackson's 1940 publication, *Prehistoric Cheshire,* more fragments of Bronze Age burial urns were recorded as found on the Walton side of Wilderspool in 1893 (Ref: 'Shone' P 94) which would have been just before Thomas May began his concerted archaeological efforts on the Brewery site in 1895. These fragments of Bronze Age pottery recovered from Walton Inferior are included in a list and map as a "Middle Bronze Age burial".

During Thomas May's excavations of 1895 to 1905 four more burial urns containing cremations were found to the south of the Roman walled area he had uncovered, and appeared to have been buried either side of an ancient minor road in the area of Brackley Street and Algernon Street. This probably represents another burial mound site.

Fragments of several urns were found on the flood plain of the River Mersey during the 19th century in an area now occupied by the Manchester Ship Canal and factories (OS Record Card) which may help to explain later finds of non-cremated Iron Age burials in the area of Warrington Dock and the Mersey cutting to Bridge Foot.

Another burial urn has been recorded as being found near Wilderspool containing fragments of burnt bone, date unknown (County Treasures Record before 1976). The map reference places this burial at the present site of the gate to Priestley College Campus on Loushers Lane.

A Bronze Age burial urn was mentioned as found buried in sand near the old Twenty Steps Bridge close to the connection of the Runcorn & Latchford Canal (now the Linear Park) and the Manchester Ship Canal at Stockton Heath, by Thomas May, during an address to the Warrington Literary & Philosophical Society in 1894. A burial urn and bone fragments presently displayed in Warrington Museum (numbers RA 1279 and 1280) and recorded as found at "Wilderspool" may well be this find.

TWENTY STEPS BRIDGE AND LOCKS, STOCKTON HEATH ABOUT 1900

If this represented any form of burial mound it could have been damaged as long ago as the period of Roman occupation, as remains of the fortified outer wall of the Roman structure were found here when the Runcorn & Latchford Canal was constructed. Alternatively a continuation of burials could have taken place outside the new Roman settlement in the same way as burials at Southworth Hall in Croft continued on the same site. Roman burials in stone coffins and urn burials are recorded close to here in *The Archaeology Of Warrington's Past* at SJ 6120 8630. This places them under St Thomas' church, Stockton Heath, where Bill Griffiths remembers an unrecorded Roman child's burial being uncovered during 1980s exploratory excavations on the site of the former St Thomas' School (where the Health Centre now stands).

In Tim Strickland's book, *The Romans At Wilderspool,* he shows a photograph of half a Roman lead coffin recovered from the north bank of the Manchester Ship Canal during repairs in 1976, approximately 135 yards (150m) to the east of Wilderspool Causeway.

Several human skulls were found during the construction work on the New River Mersey Diversion across Arpley Meadows in 1893. One of these is recorded as being preserved, with the find spot shown on a plan, and described as *"human skull of Celtic type found 18th September 1893 in possession of Mr May"*. Warrington Museum acquired the bulk of Mr May's collection upon his death but this skull remains missing - although the remains of three pre-Iron Age skulls are displayed in the museum's ancient history cabinets, listed as found in the River Mersey in the area of the 'Arpley Crannog'.

All in all it would appear that a major Bronze Age burial ground surrounded the outer limits of the Roman site at Wilderspool which casts some doubt on the purely Roman origin of the walled and banked enclosure of the Roman site identified during archaeological activities. This burial ground probably also survived in use beyond the time of the Romans.

NOT THE ROMAN INVASION!
(OR: "WE WILL MARCH ANYWHERE IN THE WORLD BUT NOT OUT OF IT"!)

On the 5th August 55BC, Julius Caesar, the greatest Roman military general of all time, crossed the English Channel from Witsand near Calais in two divisions. 55 days later, this fine fighting force which had defeated the best armies Europe and Asia could throw at them, had moved no further than seven miles from their landing point. Defeated and very upset, Caesar retreated back to the Continent with the intention of making better preparations and trying again the next year.

On the 10th May 54BC he was back with five legions of Rome's best fighting men (possibly as many as 60,000) and a fleet of a thousand ships. Dion Cassius says that he intended to take this invasion into the interior of Britain but still found his forces inadequate to meet the opposition thrown at him by the Celtic/British leader Caswallon.

Caesar soldiered on for four months and penetrated only seventy miles in land from the Kent coast where Celtic forces had kept him pinned down, until, on the 10th September 54BC, he concluded a hasty and ignominious peace at St Albans and fled back to France under the cover of darkness. It was almost a hundred years before Roman eyes were to look towards invading Britain again. There is no doubt that Caesar's account of *"Blue painted British savages"* who

"live on milk and flesh and are clad in skins" written in *Caesar's Gallic War Volume II* is nothing more than a poor political cover-up for a very hurt military pride. The only blue painted Celtic Briton Caesar had ever seen was on the other end of a very big and victorious iron sword!

Before the renewed invasion of Britain in 43AD by Emperor Claudius, Caligula had assembled a fighting force at Boulogne but lost courage at the last moment declaring that: *"Nature itself had removed Britain beyond the power and jurisdiction of the gods of Rome"* and that *"to war beyond the bounds of nature is not courage, but impiety"*. He then went on to declare: *"Let us rather load ourselves with the bloodless spoils of the Atlantic ocean which the same beneficent goddess of nature pours on these sands so lavishly at our feet. Follow the example of your emperor - behold I wreathe for laurel this garland of green seaweed around my immortal brow, and for spoil I fill my helm with these smooth and brilliant shells. Decorated with these we will return to Rome....."*!

Britain's navy watched in absolute amazement as the best fighting force in the rest of the world collected sea shells from the shore line, 'packed up shop' and headed for home.

In later years the Roman army remembered the words of Emperor Caligula and mutinied rather than face the might of the British Celts saying: *"We will march anywhere in the world but not out of it"*!

Roman forces did eventually take the decision to march *"out of this world"* and into the Mersey Valley in about 70AD, although they may have been here as visiting invaders as early as 45AD and as traders at even earlier dates. Legend has it that they began building a bridge here in 27 AD.

In his book *Warrington A Heritage* published by the Beamont Press in 1947, Harry Boscow makes a very important observation which will figure largely in the next few Roman sections of this book. He states that: *"In all probability the actual course of the river* (Mersey) *would be difficult to define, as the land between the fifty foot contour line would be composed of peat marshes through which the river and streams wandered by diverse channels. Dense forests would cover the land up to the two hundred foot contour line, though woods on the more sandy type of soil would be less dense, and in these, pathways and small clearings could be made. Paths would lead down across the peat to the river-crossing, where sailors from Ireland and elsewhere could land from their dug-out canoes. This would be the part where the river came nearest to the higher ground with only a narrow stretch of marshland, and in all probability would be at Walton"* (and what is now Stockton Heath).

One thing is for certain, the River Mersey did not run along the course it does today at the time the Romans came to Warrington.

From here we may attempt a reconstruction of the land into which the early settlers came and from which the present day chapters of history are gradually emerging. By far the most important feature for all early settlers and invaders during the whole of the Prehistoric and Celtic period was the great and sacred River Mersey.

The RIVER MERSEY AND THE ESTUARY BELISAMA

Solving the mystery surrounding the original course, name and nature of the ancient River Mersey would answer some very fundamental questions which historians have been unable to answer for the hundreds of years that historic research has played a prominent role in Warrington, questions like:

1] Where was the Mersey ford crossing in ancient times and how did the area now at Latchford develop?

2] Where did the Romans site their crossings and build their first bridge and how did this relate to the position of the Roman port?

3] Out of the network of roads known to have existed in ancient times, which of them can be said to still exist and where did they originally go?

There is far more to the basic River Mersey than meets the eye. At source the river is fed by three smaller rivers; the Tame with its origins at Saddleworth in Yorkshire, the Etherow from Featherbed Moss beyond Ashton-Under-Lyne, and the Goyt flowing from Goyt Moss and Axe Edge near Buxton in Derbyshire.

It is true to say that the River Goyt is the most significant and direct river passage with the Etherow joining it first between Marple and Stockport and the Tame at Stockport. It then becomes the River Mersey and is joined by the Glaze Brook (now via the Manchester Ship Canal) and River Bollin at Warburton, the Sankey Brook at Warrington, the Ditton Brook and the River Weaver at Widnes. In the estuary the waters are also joined by the River Gowy.

Taking the River Goyt as the source and starting on Goyt Moss near Buxton (remembering that the reservoirs were not along its length in ancient times), the Goyt/Mersey waters pass through the towns and villages of Whaley Bridge, New Mills, Marple, Stockport, Didsbury, Stretford, Urmston, Flixton, Cadishead, Hollins Green, Warburton, Rixton, Woolston, Warrington, Great Sankey, Moore, Norton, Widnes and Runcorn, before heading out into the Irish Sea through the estuary past Ellesmere Port, Liverpool and Birkenhead. This may not always have been the case in ancient times.

TALES OF NAMES AND EARTHQUAKES

In the 1947 book *Companion Into Cheshire* produced by J.H. Ingram he makes the little known and slightly improbable observation that: *"An intriguing theory advocated by the late William Ashton of Stockport suggests that originally the Mersey entered the Irish Sea by way of the estuary of the Dee, and that what is now the Mersey estuary was in earlier times, a low boggy isthmus linking Lancashire with Wirral. The Shropshire Union Canal follows the line of the vanished channel of the Mersey and the old bed of the river is said to lie at no great depth beneath the present surface. Ptolemy's map of the second century* (Author's note: This should read 'mapping' as Ptolemy did not produce a 'map') *does not show the Mersey estuary, and an old couplet declares that*

> *"The squirrels ran from tree to tree,*
> *From Formby Point to Hilbree."*

A great cataclysm in the sixth century is believed to have resulted in the sea breaking through the isthmus where Liverpool and Wallasey now stand, thus diverting the Mersey into its present channel. This disaster is referred to in a poem attributed to the bard Taliesin (520-570AD) which is corroborated by the record of a great earthquake on September 6th, 543AD, included in the British Association list of earthquakes."

It is worth noting here that Ptolemy only recorded a travel journal of names and locations in 140AD, which were used to produce *Ptolemy's Map* of Britain, which appeared for the first time in print in Ptolemy's *Geographia,* in Bologne in 1477AD, over a thousand years after his survey.

There has also never been any historical confusion between the ancient identities of the River Mersey and the River Dee. The name DEE means the goddess. The Welsh called the river DW RDWY or divine water and the two springs at its source were called DWYAN meaning the High Divine One and DWYFACH meaning the lesser divinity. There also existed an alternative and possibly later name which may have been for daily use being AERFEN after the goddess of war, as the other name had become regarded as too divine to be commonly used.

The city of Chester resides on the Dee and often claims the attentions of historians whose eyes turn to the North. This settlement area only rises to prominence with the Romans as the 'Castra Legionis' or Legionary Fortress of the 20th (XX) Legion, who were also present in Warrington. Warrington may well have

been three thousand or more years old by this time, and have played a more prominent role in direct Romano-British affairs being a combined settlement of great age and an international port.

In later times the Welsh Celts made the Latin CASTRA for fort into CAER and LEGION into LLFON giving CAERLLEON which is the name associated with the many legends of King Arthur. Cheshire is the area whose name is derived from Chester. SHIRE is much later from the Saxon SCIR meaning the share or territory of a tribe hence the CESTRE-SCIRE of Domesday which became CHESHIRE.

It is not often realised that the Saxon Celts and Danes had already divided areas according to a feudal and agricultural system known as 'Hundreds' well before the arrival of the Normans, who simply modified the existing system for the production of Domesday between 1085AD and 1087AD. This was probably done at the time of the introduction of Danelaw after the Viking invasions of the tenth century (900-1000AD).

Of the many different deities worshipped all over the Roman world, a surprising number were associated with water; after all, the source of a great river or spring (particularly if the water is hot), is always likely to have a certain mystery about it. It was in places like these, in bogs and in the mature courses of rivers themselves, that many of the gods and goddesses were thought to exist and these frequently had to be placated with offerings. Most of the important rivers of Europe received dedications from primitive peoples and the Celts believed that the earth-goddess was most easily visible in major rivers such as the Mersey and the Dee responsible for the drainage of their lands.

Joan P. Alcock provides a good introduction to Celtic Water Cults in Roman Britain (particularly in our area) in *The Archaeological Journal* for 1965 where she comments that:

"Ptolemy refers to 'Belisama Estuarium' on the Lancashire coast, which Rhys (Sir John Rhys, 'Hibbert Lectures' 1880) thought could be either the Ribble or the Mersey. Belisama was the name of a goddess in Gaul who was assimilated with Minerva. It is possible that the river name refers to this goddess. She and her counterpart Belenus (the latter not present in Britain though present in Gaul) have a connection with the sun - the name means 'the shining one' - and this is another link between sun and water, similar to the one provided by Sulis."

"In a recent paper, Dr Ross has commented on the association between the sun and thermal water (A. Ross 'Chain Symbolism in Celtic Religion' - 'Speculum' 1959), the evidence for this being more apparent on the continent than in Britain. This was symbolised by the solar god appearing in the form of a bird or in association with one. A bronze figure of Sequana, goddess of the Seine, shows her standing in a duck-shaped boat, which holds a berry or votive cake in its mouth."

Ptolemy recording the Roman name of the Mersey estuary as the ESTUARY BELISAMA is the most important clue to the origins of the river's identity as it is a Romanised version of a known Celtic river name, best fitting the Mersey (for many reasons which are to follow). The Mersey would have been known by early Roman settlers as the BELISAMA and later as MINERVA-BELISAMA.

If Ptolemy was consistent with the Roman policy of the day he would simply convert the Celtic name of the river goddess worshipped in the local groves or nemeton ('clearings open to the sky') to the nearest Roman equivalent - which means that, up to approximately seventy years after the Romans first came to the Mersey valley, the Celtic name for the river BELISAMA had in fact been SEQUANA.

Considering the connections already noted with France going back into very ancient Prehistoric times, it is interesting that Sequana was the goddess who also ruled over the river Seine (which runs between Paris and Le Havre on the English Channel) - and no other Celtic river in all of Europe, apart from the Mersey! In its original form the name also contains a rare language trait of 'Q-Celtic' quite unique to Gaul, possibly indicating the original homeland region of the first Warrington Celts who followed the early Iron Age hunters. In a nutshell, they may have settled here from northern France (the same region as the later French Arthurian 'Grail Romances' and the Norman invaders).

TALES OF SHRINES, DOGS AND KNIGHTS

The French shrine of 'Sequana of the Seine' lies about 22 miles (35 kilometres) north west of Dijon and protects the hot spring source of the Seine. This delightful wooded valley was provided with an extensive temple complex in the Roman period (as was Warrington). It centred on a pool and spring in much the same way as Buxton at the head of the Goyt Valley centres on its hot spring which is next to Goyt Moss, the primary source for 'Sequana of the Mersey'.

Excavations of the French site had been undertaken sporadically by various Victorian antiquarians, culminating in the 1930s with the discovery of a magnificent statuette of Sequana draped in a gown and with hands outstretched, standing in a boat modelled in the form of a swan or duck holding a fruit in its beak (see illustration).

By 1953 the French site had become overgrown and it was decided to study the remains in more detail in conjunction with more permanent restoration work. Some buildings were already known including two temples, a colonnaded precinct and a ritual bathing pool enclosure, but in 1963 Professor Roland Martin, who was in charge of the work, decided to drain the pool and clear it as it was nothing more than an unsightly marshy area not much disturbed in previous times.

Work proceeded slowly until Friday 13th September 1963 when about a dozen wooden heads and wooden figurines were found, preserved in the water-logged layers. By the end of the operation no fewer than 190 votive offerings had been recovered. It soon became clear to the excavators that this was a ritual deposit and not a pool used for bathing.

It was suggested that these objects were moved into the Roman site during the first century AD at a time when the old Gaulish shrine was reconstructed as a formal building. This would also fit the picture existing in Ptolemy's day, in 140AD Britain, when Celtic shrines were still being taken over by the invading Romans, and towns like Buxton were being redeveloped. An earlier Celtic shrine is also known to have existed at Buxton ('Aquae Arnemetiae') later dedicated to Arnemetia who was worshipped in a local grove or nemeton. Evidently offerings from the shrine of 'Sequana of the Mersey' remained wherever this shrine once stood and were not moved into the Roman shrine in the way they were in France.

The collection of wooden offerings recovered is fascinating to us because, not only does it include oak heads ranging from full to half size, bodies from neck to thighs, limbs, organs and animals such as horses, but it also contains a bull (as found in peat at Croft, north east Warrington) and twenty seven complete human statues mostly depicted wearing full length and knee length hooded cloaks. Some hoods are up and some muffle the neck like the 'Gennius

Culcullatus' priest-figures of the Northumbrian kingdom of which Warrington was a part from the 3rd century onwards. It is possible that the Gennius Culcullatus fled the invading Romans in northern Europe during the last centuries BC and took the advice of Druids living on Anglesey, who undoubtably would have recommended the friendly port of Warrington, gateway to the mossland crescent, where they could land and head north to settle in the kingdom of Northumbria by the 2nd and 3rd centuries AD (100AD to 300AD) beyond the advancing Romans.

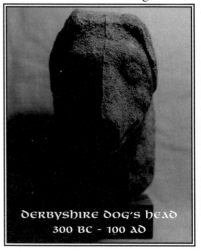

DERBYSHIRE DOG'S HEAD
300 BC - 100 AD

Several other human figures holding dogs were recovered from the Seine shrine, dog figures which are known to usually relate to thermal waters. Couple this with the fact that one of the few Celtic tribes in Britain known to venerate the dog existed in the Derbyshire area, it would appear that the River Goyt flowing from the thermal water region of Buxton would have been regarded as the principal source of the Mersey in Celtic times, and comparable to the River Seine.

TALES OF BOATS, MOUNDS AND SAINTS

In France the goddess Sequana's shrine lay at the river's source and, during festivals, her image was drawn along the river in a ship that looked like a swan or duck holding a berry in its beak. This image is most significant when related to the actual, physical shape of the River Mersey in ancient days and Prehistoric sacred traditions.

The bronze depiction of the 'swan boat' recovered from the source of the Seine resembles the earlier 'solar bark boat' representations found world-wide and may have originally inspired the naming of our river as 'Sequana' - a solar boat being the physical representation of the curve of the Mersey at Warrington in the BC/AD period and probably much more visible from Hill Cliffe, Appleton, at that time. It has already been noted in the article from the Archaeological Journal 1965 that Belisama or 'the shining one' also makes a link between the river waters and the sun.

Prehistoric settlers would have seen the great curve of the boat which carried their sun god across the heavens lit up along the valley by the golden rays of the actual sun which rises on the horizon towards the 'boats stern' at Urmston and sets at the 'prow' beyond Widnes. In their sun-boat symbolism the disc of the sun sits at its height where the Winwick temple mound or Town Hill in the Warrington town centre, resides in relation to the largest curve of the Mersey.

The first Bronze Age Celts simply gazed at the huge bend in the Mersey which led down to the river's 'head' (created by the narrowing at Runcorn and Widnes) and immediately the image of the curved boat

BRONZE AGE ROCK
CARVINGS OF SOLAR
BOATS

with a head at the prow and a narrowing tail would have sprung to mind. Their goddess who sailed in such a boat also related directly to the fertility of a river and the river name 'Sequana' was born in very ancient times and later copied by the Romans.

The later Norse settlers saw not a 'solar fertility boat' but a boat with a dragon's head, the 'great worm', and the shape of the ship which carried their souls away to Valhalla (but more of that, and the modern 'River of Life' sculpture in the books to follow).

Not all river shrines were developed to the extent of those found north west of Dijon on the Seine and at Buxton in Derbyshire. Another site in central France, at Chamaliers, not far from Clermont-Ferrand, yielded even more offerings than that at the Seine in a layer over 3 feet (1m) deep over an area of 60 feet (18m) - but showed no remains of structures, only two dried up vents where small springs had once emerged. This natural site was once just a sacred pool in a marshy valley in use between 55BC and 65AD, with offerings being either thrown in or set up round the sides to fall in at a later date.

Such a pool as this may have existed at the source of the Mersey, rising on the then wooded ridge of Goyt Moss and Wildboarclough beyond the Cat And Fiddle pub on the A537 to Buxton. Three to four thousand years ago this would have been a high hillside with a circular, oak wooded 'nemeton' grove (probably facing across the valley to the Crag high-point) from which a pool rose out of the ancient peat deposits and flowed away down the hillside to become the source of the Goyt and Mersey. A similar site may have existed at the salt springs in Dunham Woodhouses, covered later in this book.

In prehistoric times the river's 'sacred route' was marked all the way from North Wales by a chain of sacred man-made mounds almost as large as the famous Silbury Hill (in the Vale of Pewsey near Avebury). In the areas covered by this book the first of these mounds lies behind the ruins of Erwood Hall, just above the Goyt Reservoir and River Goyt, and has a small family

POOL ON AXE EDGE DERBYSHIRE
SOURCE OF THE MERSEY

cemetery from this century on top of it. The Macclesfield to Buxton Roman road called 'The Street' passes on the hill-crest just behind. The next is the hill behind Chadkirk Chapel or possibly the hill known as 'Werneth Low' marking the River Etherow at Marple.

Bowdon Castle, close to Dunham Massey Park, may have started life as an earlier mound or 'moot hill' marking the River Bollin, and Warrington Castle (behind the Parish Church of St Elphins and now destroyed) probably marked the Mersey or Sankey Brook. Both of these fortified mounds predate the later, true, castle building phases of history, fortifications probably being added to them at a later date.

Beyond the bounds of this book, mounds also exist overlooking the estuary beyond Frodsham, Helsby and on to the Wirral, probably including a pair near Treuddyn beyond Mold and ending with the giant mound known as

'The Gop' at Trelawnyd Prestatyn in North Wales.

The Romans constructed roads along the river, and the Celts created a sacred route of pilgrimage and marked it out using cats as the key (more under the section on Grappenhall). This pattern was continued by medieval builders and story tellers who used it as the path taken by Sir Gawain in *Gawain And The Green Knight* on his quest to save the 'fertility of the land'. But more of this later in the book.

Should any or all of this prove to be the case then a developed or undeveloped Celtic shrine to the goddess Sequana probably exists somewhere in the Buxton/Wildboarclough mossland region of the Peak District National Park still waiting to be discovered!

On a visit to Axe Edge I noted the existence of a small rock shelter next to which my attention was drawn to a large horizontal boulder. From close range nothing was greatly discernible but I photographed it and the greatly reduced size print is reproduced here clearly showing either a monumental horse head in full flight or that of a bristling wild boar. It is similar in style to an engraving of a horse head on a rib bone from Robin Hood's cave at Creswell Crags, Derbyshire, and the French Stone Age cave paintings of horses. It points directly towards Wildboarclough!

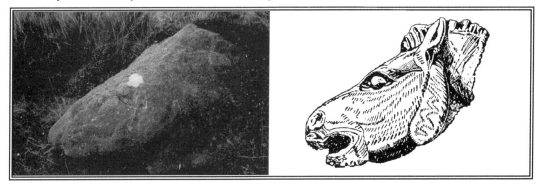

Where the Mersey enters Manchester in the form of the River Goyt is the town of Marple once in old Cheshire and called MEERPOOL. A short walk from the centre is the area known as CHADKIRK (CHAD'S-KIRK), after St Chad, a disciple of St Aidan, who was sent by St Columba to convert the heathens along the Mersey valley during the 7th century.

Southern Britain had officially become Christian under Constantine in the year 313AD, St Ninian evangelised the Picts in Scotland as early as 397AD, and St Patrick took Christianity to Ireland (legend has it from Warrington) in 432AD. All this, however, was little known to St Chad who significantly evangelised the Mersey Valley, Lancashire and Cheshire - but not on behalf of the Church of Rome! Significantly, as a disciple of St Aidan of Lindisfarne, he represented Celtic rather than Roman Christianity, and his brother, St. Cedd, also became a Celtic bishop to the East Saxons, founding many churches and monasteries. The British Celtic church adapted the liturgies and theologies of Middle Eastern, Egyptian, Byzantine, and Frankish Christianity, to create a very different form to that of the Roman Catholic variety.

Most of what we know about St Chad has been written by Bede in his *A History of the English Church and People,* written in Northumbria in 731AD, and, despite being of Roman persuasion, Bede had a very high regard for St Chad.

Chad was born in Anglo-Saxon Northumbria to Ceawlin and educated from about the age of twelve with his three brothers, Cedd, Cynebil and Caelin, at the monastery of Lindisfarne under St Aidan. All four eventually graduated as priests in the Celtic Church, St. Chad in Ireland in 653AD at the age of thirty.

Cedd and Chad both returned to England and became bishops and Chad succeeded his brother Cedd as Abbot of Lastingham Abbey in Yorkshire, going on to become Bishop of York. In 669AD

THE VIEW OF WILDBOARCLOUGH FROM THE "HORSE STONE" ON AXE EDGE

Archbishop Theodore of Canterbury ruled St Chad as an irregularly consecrated Bishop so he returned to Lastingham where Theodore made him Bishop to the Mercians, moving him to Lichfield. It is St Chad who helped convert King Penda of Mercia after Penda had killed his Christian rival King Oswald at Winwick (see Book 1).

St. Chad became famous for his diplomatic nature and always travelled on foot, giving a horse given to him by King Oswin of Northumbria to a beggar - until Archbishop Theodore insisted on him riding a horse. He also acted as interpreter between Celtic and Roman Saxon church leaders at the 'Council Of Whitby' convened by King Oswy of Northumbria in 664 AD to decide which form of Christianity would continue as the basis for the church. This time Roman Christianity, championed by St Wilfrid, won the day (see section on Grappenhall).

WHITBY ABBEY

The primitive British church celebrated Jesus's birth on March 28th until it was brought into line with Roman celebrations and changed to December 25th, originally the Roman Pagan festival of Fernalia to Pamona, Dionysos and Mithras. The date for Easter also had to be brought into line with the rest of the 'Roman Church' world. On March 29th, the day after Christmas, the Celts used to hunt for a wren 'the king of birds', capture it, place it in a box decked in ribbons and carry it round the village to bring joy, health, love and peace in the coming year. Of course this is now a lost tradition but some of the traditional stories surrounding St Chad have survived.

Near St Chad's house in Lichfield, there was a spring described by Leland in Tudor times as: *"... of pure water, where is seen a stone at the bottom of it, on which, some saye, S. Chad was wont to stand in the water and pray"* and in which St Chad baptised converts. It is now known as St Chad's well at Lichfield.

As you would expect from a Saint associated with water, Chadkirk also has an ancient sacred well, a short way further up the road from Chadkirk Chapel, just over the stone bridge by the farm to the left side of the road.

ST. CHAD'S WELL AT CHADKIRK

There is a legend which says that a hart (deer) disturbed St Chad while he was alone in his cell by the spring and, after drinking and departing, it was followed by Wulfhade son of King Wulfhere of Mercia in hot pursuit.

Wulfhade asked St Chad if he had seen the hart and Chad replied that it had been sent that way by God to lead Wulfhade to him to hear the Christian message. Wulfhade replied that he would be more likely to convert from Paganism if Chad's prayers could bring the hart back. St. Chad duly prayed and the hart ran out of the forest and stood before Wulfhade who fell at Chad's feet, converted and asked for baptism. Later Wulfhade brought his brother Rufine to Chad for baptism but their father the King had renounced Christianity at this time and slew them both in anger.

In remorse King Wulfhere himself later sought out Chad who he found in his cell which was filled with heavenly light. Seeing the King there St Chad rose hurriedly taking off his vestments and hanging them carelessly on a sunbeam which miraculously held them up (a miracle also attributed to the Celtic St Bridget). Seeing the King's remorse St Chad told him to destroy the heathen shrines and build monasteries which the King apparently did.

It cannot be established that either of the brothers, Wulfhade and Rufine, existed or that King Wulfhere lapsed from Christianity, but a great upsurge of Christianity in Mercia can be detected during St Chad's ministry. Heathen places were pulled down and monasteries were built with the King giving Chad fifty hides of land to build a monastery in Lincolnshire.

Sadly St Chad died of the plague (like his brothers Cynebil and Cedd before him) on March 2nd 672AD, after only two and a half years Mercian ministry during which time he had 'church planted' and converted virtually all of South Lancashire and Cheshire. At least thirty three ancient churches are dedicated to him and he could well be described as THE Celtic Saint of the Mersey. It was said that he knew the time of his death and Bede recorded that "...*the soul of his brother Cedd descended from heaven accompanied by angels, and carried away his soul to the heavenly kingdom*".

As with the relics of St Oswald of Winwick, the story of St Chad does not end with his physical death. A mentally deranged tramp who took shelter in the church where Chad was buried came out next day healed and, according to Bede, dust from inside his shrine could heal man and beast if mixed with water.

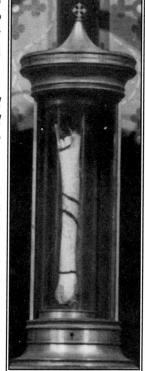

The fourteenth century Sacrist's Roll of Lichfield Cathedral lists: "*In the first place, the head of blessed Chad in a certain painted wooden case (the skull covered in gold leaf). Also an arm of blessed Chad. Also bones of the said Saint in a certain portable shrine. Also two silver shrines beyond the High Altar with the relics of divers saints. Also the great shrine of St Chad, ...*"

Tradition says that King Canute's second wife gave one of Chad's teeth to Winchester but the rest of the bones vanished during the reformation, possibly being buried behind the High Altar at Lichfield. Ironically four pieces of bone are now displayed in the Roman Catholic Cathedral in Birmingham attributed to St Chad and recent research has established that they are of seventh century date (600 to 700AD) but could make up three legs!

The church building at Chadkirk is first recorded in Domesday as CEDDE and local tradition says that a monastic cell was founded here by St Chad during his service to the church from 669 to 672AD.

The chapel itself was first recorded in the fourteenth century

(1300-1400AD) when there is a mention of a "Chaplain de Chaddkyrke" in 1347AD. Then it was owned by the Davenport family from 1381AD to 1548AD when it escaped the 'suppression of the chantries' as it was proven to be a private family chapel. It is from this period that the oldest surviving structures in the building date, being the black and white Tudor north and east walls of the chancel and the roof trusses.

After this date the building declined until William Webb recorded it in 1621AD with the words: *"At the foot of Werneth Low, towards the Merzey, lies an old dearn and deavly chapel, so people call desert places out of company and resort; called Chad Chapel, where seems to have been some Monkish cell"*. So bad was the decay that it may have been used as a cow shed during this period!

The chapel was then *"raised out of its ruins in 1747"* according to an old sign over the door. The bell is inscribed *"1750 God be with us all"* and the rest of the building dates from this quite recent point onwards. Sadly excavations in 1994 failed to locate any evidence of a Saxon chapel, but building and grave digging may have removed all early traces and, in plan, it does resemble other known Anglo Saxon churches.

The Celtic significance of St Chad existing at this middle point between the Goyt and Mersey should not be underestimated as he is the 'patron saint of medicinal wells and springs', and points the way to such 'sacred Celtic waters' up the Goyt valley, proving further that the Goyt was regarded as the source for the Mersey in ancient times. Besides this there is St Chad's Holy Well, as noted nearby, with the usual traditions of miraculous cures associated with such wells. His concentrated evangelisation of the Mersey and surrounding areas would have inevitably brought him into direct contact with the very ancient sites and legends associated with the area in the seventh century (600 AD to 700 AD). He would have used these associations with great sympathy in his dealings with the 'old religion' and their sites.

By medieval times, much of the early Celtic practices and faith had been forgotten - or at least assimilated. It takes many hundreds of years for a new set of beliefs to succeed earlier ones and a situation often exists where the shadowy forms of earlier traditions mingle with those of the new. Such was the important Celtic, Norman and Early Medieval transition of King Arthur and his knights of the round table.

CELTIC ALTAR INSIDE CHADKIRK CHAPEL

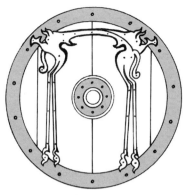

TALES OF GAWAIN, LANCELOT AND ARTHUR

"(Gawain) never came home without the Quest he had gone to seek. He was the best of walkers and the best of riders. He was Arthur's nephew, his sister's son, and his first companion."
'Culhwch and Olwen'.

It is interesting to note that the Mersey route to the Goyt Valley into Derbyshire and Staffordshire figures as important in the tales of King Arthur and his knights, especially the Middle-English Cheshire dialect tale *Gawain And The Green Knight* written by a Staffordshire monk in late medieval times (which actually relates to the 'Pagan' death and rebirth cycles of the land and the Celtic goddess as noted in her many forms).

It is highly likely that the original Gawain/Arthur stories first came to the Mersey Valley and Cheshire with Welsh, Irish and French settlers, and later, in more developed form, with the Normans.

It is also significant that Sir Thomas Malory (or Malorie), who wrote probably the most famous collection of Arthurian stories, *Morte D'Arthur,* and the monk who wrote *Gawain And The Green Knight* should both have very firm geographic ties to the North West (and during the same, later period in history Gawain, Lancelot and Arthur can also be found here).

Sir Thomas Malory, Knight and Lord of the Manor of Winwick, compiled his book from early Welsh, French and English sources between the 4th March 1469AD and 3rd March 1470AD while in prison at Lancaster for offences committed during the Wars of the Roses (1455AD to 1485AD). His book was printed by William Caxton in 1485AD but the discovery of the 'Winchester Manuscript' version indicates that both originate from a Malory original which either no longer survives or has yet to be discovered!

The Cheshire monk who constructed the *Gawain and the Green Knight* poem some time between about 1350AD and 1450AD is unknown, but evidently he set out to 'Christianize' his northern Pagan surroundings and brought together many recognisable local land marks, traditions and even aspects of his Patron in the composition which exists in its original late medieval form

In brief, it can be said that Lancashire has claim to

WINWICK CHURCH AS IT APPEARED IN 1900 WITH
GRAVESTONES AND TREES STILL STANDING

Lancelot in the legends of the *Mermaid of Martin Mere* and the *Conflict of Sir Lancelot and Sir Tarquine*. The first legend states that Lancelot's mother came to Lancashire to escape her enemies in France and, whilst attempting to save her husband's life, left baby Lancelot by a lake (now drained) between Formby and Southport called Martin Mere. Here the nymph Vivian adopted Lancelot and vanished into the lake taking him with her. When he appears at Arthur's court aged eighteen he is knighted 'Lancelot of the Lake'. At some point following this, Sir Lancelot makes his way to the ford in Medlock where he faces Arthur's enemy Sir Tarquine, beating him and capturing his castle at Manchester close by.

Current opinion also now places Arthur himself in North Wales and, therefore also bordering or in North Cheshire, which has been often connected with Wales in Celtic times. From evidence contained in place names it is thought that the Welsh once occupied Cheshire as far as the Mid Cheshire Ridge. Arthur's northern border may well have been Eddisbury and Kelsbarrow Hillforts and the hunting forests of Delamere.

From this we may deduce the possible legendary survival of territorial ownerships in our area, about a hundred years after the Roman withdrawal from Britain, in the Arthurian period about 510AD. It appears that King Arthur owns Wales as far as Delamere, Sir Gawain owns the Mersey Valley, Cheshire, Derbyshire and Staffordshire, and Sir Lancelot owns Lancashire including Manchester. The Wirral is recorded as a wilderness which may explain why later Viking invaders settled there. These very ancient Celtic divisions are surprisingly accurate to later known historic regional divisions, Gwynedd, Mercia and Northumbria, and place name locations.

Returning to Sir Gawain; he appears to be THE knight for the order of 'Knights Templar' or 'Poor Knights of The Temple of Solomon' founded at Jerusalem in about 1114AD. These were knights who had taken monastic vows and were connected to the orders of the Cistercians and Augustinians. Templar colours were white and black with red, and these colours are associated with Celtic goddesses by several commentators. The knights were avid seekers of biblical treasures, as was Sir Gawain (the Holy Grail, the shield of Judas Maccabeus, the spear which pierced the side of Christ on the cross, etc.) and they were accused of worshipping 'some kind of detached head' when the order was dissolved by King Philippe IV of France in 1307AD and by Papal decree in 1312-1314AD. Could this have been a 'Green Knight' type severed head? It is also unclear as to which order of knighthood 'Sir' Thomas Malory was admitted!

Gawain was ideal for this role since he had almost become the Holy Roman Emperor in his youth, following adoption into the Pope's own family (a position he declined to accept) and his 'God concept' included the 'divine goddess' as did the Gnostic/Celtic beliefs of Templar knights.

Gawain was dubbed a knight while still in the household of the Pope on 'St. John's Eve' otherwise known as Midsummer night or the Summer Solstice (June 24th), a festival kept by both Christians and Pagans. This St John (The Baptist) was also beheaded by Herod (Matthew 14 V 1-12) and the head presented on a 'dish' similar to those which appear in the later Grail romances.

Gawain and Kay (Gwalchmai and Kai) are among the foremost warriors of Arthur's court in the earliest surviving versions of the Arthur stories, with Gawain taking up more space in the adventures than any other knight including Percival and Lancelot. The specific Cheshire/Staffordshire tale of *Gawain and the Green Knight* goes something like this:

Arthur's court assembles for the Christmas feast when a loud thunder clap announces a monstrous green figure who rides through the door on a green horse weilding a mighty axe. This Celtic Christmas feast would have been on Jesus' original birthdate of March 28th, just after the Spring Equinox (the festival of Alban or Eilin) at the end of the month of 'Cutios' (the time of winds), our March/April.

Mocking the court, the Green Knight offers to play a 'Christmas game' with anyone who dares - he takes the blow of his own axe from any man present, then has the opportunity to return it.

Perhaps detecting that other-worldly forces are at work, no one comes forward to take up the challenge until Arthur himself rises, then Gawain (Welsh 'Gwalchmai' the 'Hawk Of May') accepts the challenge and strikes a single blow severing the Green Knight's head and saving Arthur and Guinevere from danger. Gawain, the 'Hawk Of May', is therefore shown to be the original champion of both the 'Flower Bride Of Spring' (Guinevere) as well as her husband Arthur.

This is also the case on the Porta della Pescheria of Modena Cathedral which shows Gawain (Galvagin) as her rescuer and is probably the earliest datable reference to him at between 1090AD and 1120AD, contemporary with the founding of the Knights Templar.

The giant then picks up his severed head which speaks telling Gawain that he expects to return the blow in one year's time at the Green Chapel. Setting his head back on his shoulders, the Green Knight then rides away having united his 'soul' to his body (the Celts believing that the soul resides in the head). Here the story becomes vitally geographic.

The year passes and Gawain sets out (from Wales) to keep his word, not knowing where he should go, and wanders (possibly via Anglesey) to the 'Wilderness of Wirrall' (Wirral) where he faces danger from trolls and the harsh weather. This part of the story takes place in the month of 'Ogronios' (the time of ice) in February/March, one year after the original Celtic Christmas.

Half dead from cold and fatigue he arrives at the castle of Sir Bercilak (somewhere in the Mersey Valley?), who offers him hospitality and introduces him to his beautiful wife who is accompanied by a hideous old woman, both obvious aspects of the triple Celtic goddess, the 'mother' and 'crone' aspects (only the 'maid' Guinevere is missing). As noted the triple goddess can be represented by the River Mersey.

Sir Bercilak declares that the Green Chapel is "a mere few hours ride away" (down the Mersey/Goyt Valley) and says he is going hunting (possibly the forests of Delamere or north Cheshire). Gawain prefers rest so Sir Bercilak proposes an exchange of winnings, he will give Sir Gawain any spoils from the days hunting in exchange for anything his guest has won during the same period. Sir Bercilak departs and his 'wife' does her best to seduce Gawain who only concedes a kiss which is all he has for Sir Bercilak on his return. This happens for the next two days during which Gawain concedes two, then three kisses before revealing to Lady Bercilak that he has little chance of surviving his quest. Lady Bercilak gives Gawain a green sash which protects the wearer from all harm and he does not include this in his days winnings on the return of Sir Bercilak.

Next morning Gawain sets off for the Green Chapel (Ludchurch on the Staffordshire Roaches?) and arrives to find the Green Knight sharpening his axe. As agreed Gawain kneels in the snow but his adversary twice faints until the angry Gawain bids him strike once and for all. This third blow only nicks Gawain's neck who jumps up declaring honour satisfied and calling the Green knight to defend himself.

The giant laughs and reveals that he is actually Sir Bercilak turned into the giant by "Morgane the goddess" who is the hideous 'old woman' back at the castle. The intention of Morgane (winter) was to frighten Guinevere (spring)

and test the strength of Arthur's knights. Morgane (Morrighan) is the dark and savage goddess of winter, Guinevere (The Flower Bride) once represented spring and the unfolding of life. Both goddesses are polarised in permanent opposition.

Sir Gawain has come through with honour in tact except for accepting the green sash for which he received the nick in his neck from the Green Knight's axe. He returns to Camelot and tells his story at which point all the knights decide to wear green sashes in honour of Sir Gawain's success.

In his extensive study *Gawain: Knight of the Goddess,* John Matthews lists three actual sites which have been identified as the end destination of Gawain - the 'Green Chapel'.

The first is the most unusual Bridestones Bronze Age chambered tomb in North Staffordshire suggested by Bertram Cosgrave in 1948; the second a cave at Wetton Mill, north east Staffordshire, known locally as 'Thurshole' (meaning FIEND'S HOUSE), identified in 1940 by Mable Day and R.E. Kaske; and the third, an open cavern feature on the Staffordshire Roaches known as Ludchurch or 'Lud's church' favoured by recent researchers R.W.V. Elliott and Doug Pickford.

In his books *Myths and Legends of East Cheshire and the Moorlands,* and *The Bridestones,* Staffordshire historian and researcher, Doug Pickford, comes down firmly in favour of Ludchurch. The 'simulacra' or 'natural sculpture' of a 'red rock knight's face' still faces that of a 'green, mossy man' either side of the rock crevice at the entrance to the gorge, which is undoubtably 'The Chapel in the Green' visualised by the Staffordshire Monk. Gawain wears a red surcoat over his armour and performs so well in tournaments that he becomes known as 'The Knight of the (red) Surcoat' (the Celtic/Danish/Saxon character depicted on this book cover).

The connection of divine figures to Bridestone, Thurshole and Ludchurch is immediately apparent, with BRIGIT (BRIDE) of the Saxons, THOR of the Norsemen, and LUD of the Celts, the latter being the most likely site given the evidence.

Sir Gawain is recorded as a 'Grail knight' along with Sir Lancelot and Sir Percival, but it depends which writer you read as to who attains the mystical 'Holy Grail'. The earliest successful knight recorded is Gawain, but he fades from prominence in later stories like the 'Didot Perceval' in which he fails to attain the Grail but witnesses an interesting vision in the light of our Mersey researches. As summarised by John Matthews the story goes:*"....passing onwards to other lands, he (Gawain) comes upon a fountain with a vessel of gold fastened to it by a chain of silver. A statue carved on one of the pillars speaks, foretelling that Gawain is not the one to be served by the vessel."*

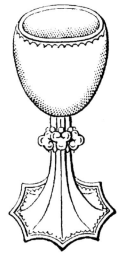

"He sees a priest approach, then three maidens in white come, one carrying bread on a dish of gold, one carrying wine in a vessel of ivory, the third bearing meat in a dish of silver. They leave their offerings at the fountain and depart. 'But as they went, it seemed to Sir Gawain that there was but one of them, and he wondered much at this miracle.'" Three aspects flow into the same river - but where was the fountain with the grail located and where is it now?

In the final battles between the knights of the divided round table, Gawain receives a mortal wound in combat against Lancelot in France. The wound opens on Gawain's return to fight Mordred with Arthur in Britain, and he dies from it. Engraved on his tomb are the words:

HERE LIE GARETH AND GAWAIN WHOM LANCELOT KILLED
THROUGH GAWAIN'S FOOLISHNESS

In some traditional writings it is Gawain that obtained sovereignty for King Arthur which explains Arthur's lament in the *Alliterative Morte Arthur*:

"*Then the valiant king looked and was sad at heart, groaned dreadfully, with tears of grief, knelt down by the dead body, and caught it up in his arms, lifted up his visor and kissed him quickly, looked on his eyelids that were tightly closed, his lips like lead, and his pale countenance.*"

"*Then the royal monarch cried aloud, 'Dear kinsman by blood, I am in sorry plight. For now my honour has departed and my struggle is ended. Here lies the expectation of my well-being, my success in battle. My courage and my valour stemmed wholly from him, my counsel, my succour that sustained my spirit. The king of knights in Christendom, thou wert worthy to be king, though I wore the crown. Mine good fortune, my good name on earth were gained through Sir Gawayne, and through his wisdom alone. Alas, now my sorrow increases. I am utterly destroyed in mine own land. Ah, treacherous, cruel Death, thou lingerest too long! Why dost thou hold back?*" (Translation by J.L.N. O'Loughlin).

As a postscript to Gawain's story, William of Malmesbury writes in his *De Gestis Regum Angelorum (Deeds of the Kings of the Angles* 1125AD) that: "*At the time (1066AD to 1087AD) in a province of Wales called Ros (Pembrokeshire) the tomb of Walwein (Gawain) was found who, by no means unworthy of Arthur, was a nephew by his sister. He reigned in that part of Britain still called Walweitha, a soldier greatly celebrated for valour, but driven from the kingdom by the brother and nephew of Hengist (about 450AD), of whom I spoke in Book I, he made them (the Saxons) pay severely for his exile.*" (Translated by L.B. Hall in *The Knightly Tales of Sir Gawain* 1976).

Four hundred years later William Caxton noted in the introduction to his 1485AD edition of *Morte D'Arthur*: "*Item in the castle of Dover ye may see Gawaine's skull, and Cradok's mantle: ....*"

Sir Gawain's age is given at the time of his final conflict against Lancelot as 76 so he was 76 or 77 at the time of his death.

It is an interesting observation that WALWEITHA must break down to WALWEI-THA, the region or THA of Walwein. Using this break down as a model there is a marked resemblance to the name of Warrington in use during the same time period WALINTUNE (Domesday 1086AD). WAL-IEG-TUN could equate to WAL-(W)EI-THA, TUN probably equating to THA in meaning.

This presents intriguing possibilities in the light of our present explorations into the Mersey Valley, but they will probably remain forever conjectural. Are we now still living in the lands of Sir Gawain?

In *Gawain and the Green Knight* we have, enshrined by a Cheshire monk, the entire yearly fertility cycle of the Mersey and its geography, placed in a framework of Celtic legend and yet made palatable for a Christian medieval audience, most of whom would not appreciate the full significance of what they were hearing. It is unmistakably a later continuation from the early Celtic religious patterns and beliefs of North West England and the River Mersey.

> "PEACE MAKES A GOOD MAN PERFORM GOOD WORKS;
> FOR ALL MEN ARE BETTER AND THE LAND IS MERRIER."
> GAWAIN IN 'LAYAMON'.

Turning our attention to the primary reason often given for the existence of Warrington - the ford - we find important information again in the stories of King Arthur which will lead us into Latchford (just north east of Stockton Heath).

LATCHFORD

"HE RIDES ALL NIGHT, SUMMER AND WINTER, IN NOTHING BUT A WHITE SHIRT ....
HIS HORSE IS ERMINE WHITE, HIS SHIELD WHITE, HIS BANNER WHITE ON A RED
LANCE; AND HE HAUNTS THE FORD OF THE BLACK THORN."

GASOZIN IN 'DIU CRONE' (THE CROWN)

Why has the original ford at Latchford never been located and why isn't it clearly marked by the presence of a great deal of ancient settlement? Why, indeed, did the Romans appear to avoid it altogether and build their own bridges instead? The answer to these questions clearly lie with the local Britons and Celts.

In the various tales of King Arthur several significant conflicts take place at the site of a ford. In 'Diu Crone' Arthur faces the knight Gasozin but determines to fight him there at the ford in a years time; in 'De Ortu Waluuanii' Arthur faces Gawain at a ford and is soundly beaten; Lancelot faces Sir Tarquine at Medlock ford; and in 'The Didot Percival', Percival fights the knight Urban and defeats him at a ford. All four conflicts are initiated by a 'Flower Bride of Spring', either unnamed or identified as Guinevere, and the conflict is between the champions of Summer (Arthur/Lancelot/Percival) and of Winter (Gasozin/Gawain/Tarquine/Urban) for the maiden of spring.

Hidden in this type of story lies the sacred nature of the Celtic ford, a place where no development would ever be permitted to take place, a gateway to 'other-worldly' places and seasonal conflicts for which any representation would be insufficient. In short, a most holy place.

I have observed that the use of the word 'black' often links to the supposed location of a ford along the Mersey. In the introductory example from 'Diu Crone' (The Crown) we have a Celtic 'ford of the Black Thorn', at Latchford we have the 'Black Bear' bridge and 'Black Bear'

BLACK BEAR BRIDGE

THE BLACK BEAR PUB

pub on the supposed ford site, and at Wilderspool we had the 'Black Lion' bridge before the Causeway was constructed over it. I have no doubt that more examples have existed along the Mersey at various times.

If an earthquake did indeed change the entire pattern of the Mersey estuary in 543AD, then this further lends support to the theory of a changed river course at Warrington and takes us back to our three original questions:

ANCIENT MERSEY CROSSING NUMBER 1

1) Where was the Mersey ford crossing in ancient times and how did the area now at Latchford develop?

In terms of Stone and Bronze Age finds in Latchford, there are not as many as might be expected, considering the supposed importance of the ford in ancient times. I am yet to find any records of Stone Age finds from the immediate 'ford' area!

A bronze axe without side loops was found on Ackers Common in the vicinity of Common Lane, Latchford, by a Mr J. Chorley, some time before he donated it to Warrington Museum in 1858. This axe is interesting in that it has a 'trident ribbing' design along its 6 ins (15cm) length associated with axes manufactured in Wales, and has a 3 ins (7.5cm) crescent blade. This axe is recorded at least eleven times in various archaeological publications under variations of the above account, although fortunately the museum is still exhibiting it, the find being known as 'RA 8'.

Before the building of the Manchester Ship Canal, the Ackers area was linked directly to Latchford by Ackers Lane, which joined Loushers Lane at the corner by the Baptist Chapel, and was first recorded as 'Le Akkirs' in a land survey of 1465AD produced for Peter Legh. ACKERS appears to come from the Old English AECER meaning a 'plot of cultivated land', but the word can also mean 'wild undeveloped land' and 'a plot of land cleared for use'. Evidently the land

 had developed under the plough over a long period of time and boasted a medieval water mill driven by Lumb Brook and still standing in the 1880s, the remains still faintly visible in 1970.

A Bronze Age palstave axe was found just over Knutsford Road Swing Bridge, Latchford, in 1860, and is mentioned in the *Archaeology Of Warrington's Past*, without any further details being given.

Even less is known about another bronze axe except that

it was also a 'loopless palstave' found some time before 1977, and first recorded in the *Longley Notes* produced by D. Longley. After being recorded in three different places it has now been lost!

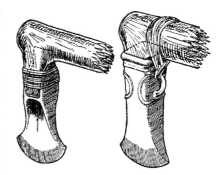

On March 29th 1953, Mr Garrod, engineer for the Manchester Ship Canal Company, found a bronze spear head dating from the Middle Bronze Age (about 1300BC) on the north bank of the river Mersey during reinforcing work at Howley Weir. It is thought to have originated in Ireland and is broken near the shaft end which has side loops, and would originally have been 6¼ ins (15.5cm) long when it was found complete. However only 3¼ ins (9.5cm) remains because the point was broken off and lost by workmen

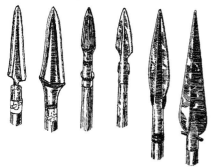

who used the 3300 year old object to play darts with! These four finds are the only pre-Roman discoveries recorded from the area where the ford was supposed to be.

A Roman coin of Constantine from 306-307AD, struck at Treveronum (?), was found at the top end of Park Avenue, Latchford, by the old course of the river, but only counts as an interesting stray find, possibly connected to Constantine's presence in northern England before his departure to become the first Christian Emperor of Rome.

The name of LATCHFORD is derived from the Old English LAECC or LACU meaning 'a stream or watercourse' combined with the possibly Norse word FORD meaning 'crossing' making LAECC-FORD or LACH-FORD the 'crossing over a stream'. It is worth noting here that, although this name does derive from 'a ford', there were a great many streams crossing this area in ancient times in addition to the River Mersey. The name does not prove the existence of a river crossing as such and does not appear in Domesday, and is presumed to have been treated as part of Grappenhall or Thelwall and surrounding areas, which only had about 40 occupants in 1087AD. (400 years later, in 1465AD, this had only increased to about 190).

A version of the place name first appears in a deed from the reign of Richard I (The Lionheart) dated 1189-1199AD granting toll rights to the Norman Baron Hugh De Boydell. This deed is interesting in that it does not specify the actual site of the crossing but gives the Baron the right to charge tolls on all crossings down stream as far as Runcorn. It reads:

HOWLEY WEIR

Randle De Blunderville, 6th Earl of Chester, grants Hugh De Boydell: *"....the way in Latchford, with the passage of the water of the Mersey, between Runcorn and Thelwall and that no cart (wagon) of two horses shall pass the said way and passage except by the allowance of the said Hugh and his heirs".*

It is known that the Boydell family, of south Warrington (see section on Grappenhall), pursued their toll duty because the abbot and monks of Stanlowe were made exempt from paying the tolls in about 1250AD, and the Warrington Friars in 1308AD. However, in about 1285AD, the Boteler family of north Warrington constructed their own bridge from our present town centre to Wilderspool creating the first of the long-standing north/south divides of the town based on waterways, and this may have led to the final abandonment of any original ford site at Latchford.

howLey weir

It becomes evident from the study of very old maps of the Latchford area that it has gradually expanded further and further to the south east of Warrington's 'Bridge Foot' since the time this alternative crossing was created. As recently as the 1930s the 'Township of Latchford' began on the opposite bank of the Mersey to Bridge Foot, and stretched as a long 'ribbon

The EARL Of DERBY's BRIDGE (1495AD) AND WARRINGTON AS DEPICTED ABOUT 1550AD

development' along Knutsford Road, past the weir, through the original supposed crossing area, until the new boundary of the Manchester Ship Canal defined the border with Grappenhall. Now, Latchford could also be said to have expanded to include the whole area of Victoria Park and the housing estates of Westy either side of Kingsway South, 20th century developments more than doubling its original size.

A hundred and fifty years ago Westy was an expanse of farmers' fields and Kingsway South and Victoria Park did not exist. Two hundred and fifty years ago John Banks of Winwick produced a land survey for Matthew Lyon of Appleton Hall, which is the oldest map so far located, showing the ford site, and dated 1746.

Apart from the peculiar name of the area - 'Hell Hole', and the origin of the 'Old Warps' being the 'Hole Warps', three important observations can be made from this survey:

1) Despite the importance of recording such features, no ford or roads leading to a ford or any riverside access points are recorded on the map at this point on the Mersey - even though field gates are!

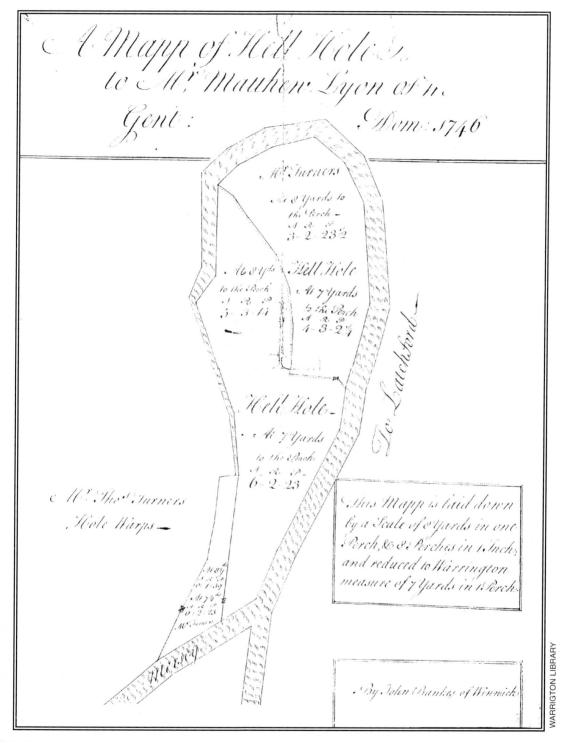

A Mapp of Hell Hole &. to Mr Mathew Lyon of n. Gent: Ao Dom: 1746

Mr Turners

At 8 Yards to the Perch —
A. R. P.
3 - 2 - 23½

At 8 yds to the Perch A. R. P. 3 - 3 - 11

Hell Hole

At 7 Yards to the Perch
A. R. P.
4 - 3 - 2¼

Hell Hole —

At 7 Yards to the Perch
A. R. P. —
6 - 2 - 23

To Latchford —

Mr Thos Turners
Hole Warps —

This Mapp is laid down by a Scale of 8 Yards in one Perch, & 8 Perches in 1 Inch; and reduced to Warrington measure of 7 Yards in 1 Perch.

Mersey

By John Bankes of Winnick

2) The Howley Weir, which has been supposed to have been built by 1721AD, is not shown here at 1746AD raising the observation that, while a connection channel was perhaps constructed before 1736AD to aid navigation, no weir was added until after 1746AD. The Mersey and Irwell Navigation Company, who were attempting to make the Mersey navigable, were only Incorporated by Act of Parliament in the early part of the reign of George III, about 1760AD to

1770AD. It was not long before plans to make the Mersey permanently navigable had been abandoned in favour of canals so the weir probably dates from the 1780s.

3) Most significant of all is the fact that the ancient name 'Hell Hole' originates from this area - being just that, an impassable bog - even before river improvements caused the shrinkage to a stream shown to the left hand side of the river curve.

The local antiquaries of the nineteenth century (1800 to 1900) originated and supported the theory of the Mersey ford at Latchford which eventually resulted in the site being labelled 'Ancient Ford' on the 1805 to 1873 OS map revisions. Dare I suggest that the evidence which once pointed to the theoretical location of a ford may also be used to indicate the existence of a known Roman bridge at Howley instead! A lot can change in two thousand years but no sign of any river crossing remained in 1746 AD.

This does not, however, rule out the possibility that one or more fords did exist at other locations along the river at Warrington, but it may serve to turn our eyes away from this 'accepted theory' for the town's development to look again at other reasons, geographic, civil or religious, for the original choice of town site.

I believe that the original Celtic ford was located close to Black Bear Bridge but further south west on a much older dried up curve of the prehistoric Mersey; probably finally destroyed by the building of the Roman station's docks at Stockton Heath, then obliterated by the Runcorn to Latchford Canal completed in 1805 (also known locally as the Black Bear, Old Quay or 'O.K.' Canal).

TALES OF FORDS, ROADS AND BRIDGES

The main Latchford highways hailing from ancient times were Knutsford Road (pre 1189AD but connecting to Bridge Foot probably after the bridge was built there around 1285AD), Thelwall Lane (pre 1328AD) and Grammar School Road crossing the Canal and becoming Hill Top Road (known in medieval times as Grappenhall Road before 1328AD).

It is interesting to note here that an enquiry into rights of highway through Warrington held in March 1354 made Knutsford Road a 'King's Highway' with public right-of-free-passage but declared the Roman A49 Wilderspool Causeway/London Road to be a private road from which the Lords of Appleton and Latchford were welcome to exact tolls! (We now regard the A49 as the major road). The priority route, for entry into the town, had moved back from the Roman road 'King Street', in Appleton, to the Prehistoric/Celtic roads of Latchford, probably due to the collapse and non-repair of the Roman bridge at Stockton Heath (brought about by changes in river course).

The medieval Knutsford Road appears to have an ancient termination point to the east of Black Bear Bridge where the first OS map, compiled from 1805 to 1873, approximately sites the 'Ancient Ford'. In 1843 human remains and sword blades were found next to Wash Lane, and more human remains at Frederick Street, which may be evidence for a conflict at an important road or ford site more to the south west during the Civil War of 1642-48AD. Cromwellian cannon and musket balls have also turned up in this area in reasonable quantities over the years.

It certainly looks likely that this site was a major highway point for the general population of the area during the medieval and Civil War periods, but as to the existence of an earlier crossing point here, no evidence has yet been found.

Partly through a new theory for the very ancient course of the Mersey (which I will outline later) and partly through other available evidence, I am of the opinion that the Mersey was probably shallow enough in this area to cross at low tide but flowed in a different configuration than previously thought. Evidence does exist, however, for at least two probable Roman bridges.

ANCIENT MERSEY CROSSING NUMBER 2

2) Where did the Romans site their crossing and build their first bridge and how did this relate to the position of the Roman port?

The best evidence for the first arrival of the Romans at the Mersey in Latchford comes from a brief and suprising archaeological outing supervised by a Mr G.A. Dunlop and Colonel B. Fairclough in 1930. Between the years 1928 and 1932 they set out to establish, beyond doubt, the route of the Roman north/south highways through Warrington, but the unpublished report of their efforts to locate the road in the area of the Parish Church, Howley, north of the Mersey, is undoubtably of most interest in establishing its meeting point with the river and, therefore, the location of the Roman bridge. I shall reproduce the brief unpublished report in full with the original site plans:

```
ROMAN ROAD WARRINGTON - WINWICK. JANUARY 25th 1930.
     Present Mr G.A. Dunlop and Colonel B. Fairclough.
```

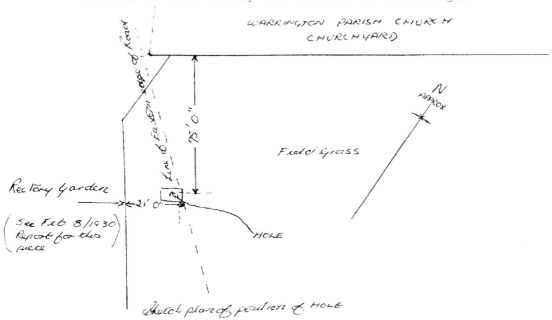

The Rev.Canon Willis, Rector of Warrington, kindly gave us permission to seek for the ROMAN ROAD in his garden. Eventually the probe gave sandstone and on developing the clue, a hole was dug as per sketch plan and gave the following section.

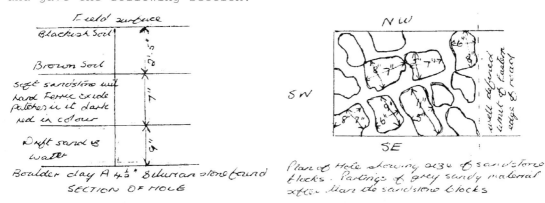

The sandstone blocks were measured as per plan of hole. It was too dark to develop the exact west edge of the sandstone road in the rectory grounds.

No organic layer was found on top of the sandstone, but occasional pieces of gravel were found embedded in the partings. A series of holes were probed north and south of the eastern edge of the road exposed in the hole, to get the line of the eastern edge of the road, and on taking a sight, the line was clearly seen to run in a certain direction, and on "setting" the 6" map, it was found that the line ran straight for the eastern boundary of the road found January 19th 1930, just to the west of the Warrington Grammar School playground.

ROMAN ROAD WARRINGTON - WINWICK. FEBRUARY 8th 1930.
Present Mr G.A. Dunlop and Colonel B. Fairclough.

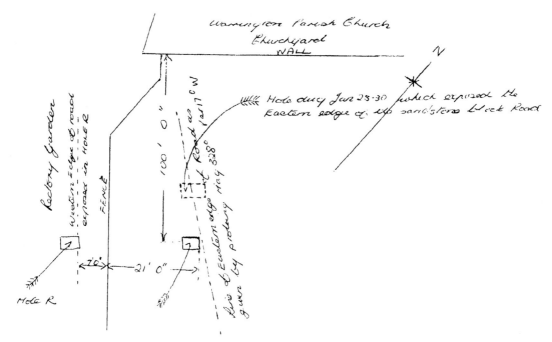

In the field just south of the Warrington Parish Church a hole, 'S' was dug 100ft. (31.5m) south of the churchyard southern wall and 21ft. (6.6m) eastwards from the Rectory eastern fence. Very soft sandstone was found, so soft that it could have easily been overlooked as being unimportant. Some spots in it were harder than others and much redder in colour. The general shade of colour was as if prolonged or constant wetting had bleached most of the binding and colouring matter out of it and it had become pale red.

The top of the sandstone layer was not very clearly defined as it bordered on the sandy red soil, a good many gravely pebbles were found. The parting at the underside on top of the underlying grey alluvial sand was very marked.

Another hole, 'R' was dug in the rectory garden. In it was exposed the western edge of the sandstone layer, 7ft (2.2m) west of the fence, and in line with hole 'S'. so we had sandstone over a width of 28ft. (8.8m) and more eastwards, about a foot (30cm), as felt by probe. The line of probed eastern edge had a magnetic bearing of 328 degrees (about Var.17 degrees west).

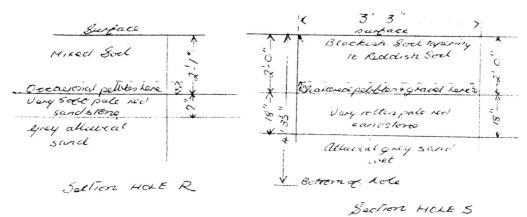

We were unable to trace any shape of a single stone in the sandstone layer which is suprising as it runs continuously North. In a hole 25ft. (7.9 m) further north, dug on January 25th and 30th, we were able to record the shape and sizes of the stones comprising the paving.

The section in which the report notes; *"Very soft sandstone was found, so soft that it could have easily been overlooked as being unimportant ..... as if prolonged or constant wetting had bleached most of the binding and colouring matter out of it ....."* is a very important clue when looking for the Roman river crossing. It clearly indicates the effect of the introduction of the weir in raising the up-stream Mersey waters and the surrounding water table. If any remains of the Roman bridge foundations exist they will be well below both ground and river levels today, and too far below the water table to be easily excavated.

The final results of the 'Dunlop/Fairclough Survey' were reported to the public in a newspaper article of February 1932 in which Mr Dunlop states that:

Whitaker, and Gibson after him stated that the road passed between the Mote Hill (Warrington Castle) and the (Parish) church, but it has taken the shorter route. Where it crosses the Mersey is still a mystery. There is a tradition (present in 1932) that the Roman road passed the dye-house on the banks of the Mersey, and it is probable that it crossed the river near the parsonage house at Latchford.

The dye-house was located in the Mill complex (which is now the 'Mississippi Show Boat' and 'Secrets Night Club'). The 'parsonage house', however, is now unknown; it may be the Old Warps nursing home. Both buildings must sit on the site of the Roman bridge and road over the Mersey.

Further support is given to this location by William Beamont who sums up in his 1889 *History of Latchford* by affirming that there has never been considered to be any more than two possible sites for the Latchford crossing. The first, the approach road to the Old Warps nursing home, and the

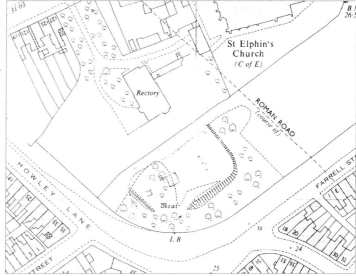

other at the end of Brook Place, nearly opposite to Wash Lane (ie. Black Bear Bridge). The first is the Roman bridge, the second close to the Celtic ford.

The Howley location for a Roman bridge would help to explain why the oldest Celtic parts of the town centre began with the castle at Mote Hill, north

of the Mersey and next to the Roman road, before expanding west down Church Street towards the present town centre. A prehistoric sacred site of some kind, situated on Town Hill, may also have prevented domestic development in that area during our first millenia, and a Celtic sacred site or 'moot hill' on Mote Hill may have encouraged it there.

ROMAN TIMBER BRIDGE

Having established communication links in the area around the original ford (and possibly a military camp somewhere on the road to the North), the Romans turned their attention to developing the town and economy of the region, and chose a firm, circular area of river deposits situated inside the circle of a bend in the river, to the west of the ford, to build their port.

THE RIVER BEND IN HOWLEY WHERE THE ROMAN BRIDGE FORMERLY STOOD BELOW THE MISSISIPI SHOWBOAT (SHOWN IN CENTRE OF PICTURE)

On both sites there was commercial and domestic development which linked them between Latchford and Wilderspool, and the Wilderspool port became the centre of export and import activity on the river.

Pipe laying and excavations on the possible course of the Roman link road, in the area of Loushers Lane, in 1930-1933, by B. Fairclough, brought a hypocausted building and working floors to light. Excavations of 1973 by Warrington Local History Society, and 1974-1976 under J. Hinchcliffe, revealed signs of the unpaved link road, timber buildings and working floors, some possibly pre Roman in origin. One of the more exceptional finds was the small top of a Corinthian style column carved from hard sandstone which may have adorned an, as yet, unlocated temple.

NOT THE ROMAN FORT!

It is my considered opinion (and that of many others) that no 'fort' ever existed on the Wilderspool site. Having examined over two hundred years of finds and archaeological data, I firmly believe that the features, always associated with the Roman 'fort', point more directly to a vast, defended, commercial trading centre and river PORT of international importance, supporting a large urban manufacturing centre (almost certainly pre-Roman in origin).

This is a view increasingly being taken by the archaeological community of today but first originated by George A. Carter, Deputy Municipal Librarian, in the 1947 landmark local history book *Warrington 100 Years A Borough,* where he states: *"It has never been claimed that the Roman station discovered at Wilderspool was a city, or indeed, that it was anything more than a Romano-British 'civitas', or walled town, occupied by a civil population engaged in industry, which also served as a 'mansio' or resting place on the Roman military highways passing through the town."*

THE WILDERSPOOL ROMAN SITE IS BELOW THE BREWERY BUILDINGS SHOWN MIDDLE LEFT AND THE REST OF THE ROMAN SITE LIES BELOW THE CHURCH AND HOUSES IN THE FOREGROUND

I concede the presence of soldiers to protect the facility against hostile tribal and pirate attacks, but a wall is no protection from an enemy unless there are people on top of it to take advantage of the braking effect it has on enemy progress. Romans fortified towns in coastal and estuary areas in the fourth century (300AD to 400AD) to protect the people who lived inside from those wishing to take their property and valuables.

The evidence here at Warrington, points almost exclusively to commercial use over the four hundred years of Roman occupation and the military presence undoubtably became 'mixed' as time went on, with Celtic warriors also defending the port. As far as can be ascertained, Roman administration was also generally adjusted to Celtic tribal structure as time progressed, not the other way round. Examples of the multi-racial nature of the town can be shown from the timber foundations of Celtic round houses with Celtic bronze and iron finds (especially broaches) found INSIDE the 'fortifications' of Wilderspool previously always assumed to be military.

Other finds from the site on show in Warrington Museum include: 9 locks and keys, 12 lead weights, 8 iron farming implements, a large iron axe head, 3 'mattocks' or legionary spades, 3 knives, a folding rule, 2 pickheads, a horse shoe and spur, at least 34 other assorted iron objects and much pottery, including the famous clay theatrical mask.

The earliest Roman coin found on the site is probably the Republican denarius identified in 1966 as dating from about 190BC, but excavations in the 1970s only located coins from 41AD onwards. Coins found on the site mainly date from the time of Vespasian 69-79AD, up to the reign of the Christian Emperor Constantine 306-337AD, with the majority between 69AD and 138AD, in the reigns of Flavian and Trajan. A sharp drop in coin dates occurs after 222AD and hoards of hidden coins found on the outskirts of Manchester date from just after this time at around 280AD. This probably provides a good indication of the time at which the Roman strongholds in the Mersey Valley began to revert to British occupation. Coins of Constantine may have been brought to the area by later Christians.

All the names so far found on pottery wares are thought to be Celtic and not Roman (ie. British names written in Latin). Examples include: NANIIIACO (or ANIACO for Nanieco), DECANIO, DECMITIUS, MIMICIUS (?), ICOTASI, OVIDUS (or OVIDIUS), AUSTINUS MANV (or AVSTINVS, AVSTI, AVSTIN), DOCCIUS (DOCI or DOCCI), BRICO (BRCO or BRICOS) and BRVCI. The potter ICOTASI or 'Icotasgus' worked in the Midlands so this pottery had found its way north up Watling Street along with quite a large quantity of pottery from Dorset. Other imported wares are found coming into the port from factories in Lezoux in the Puy Du Dome district of France, Heilegenberg near Strasburg and Arezzo in Tuscany which are all Gaulish/Celtic areas. Other stamps found include C.C.M. and DIS/LDB plus several trade marks. All the pottery produced on the Wilderspool site dates to a short period between about 100AD and 165AD when the port was evidently at its commercial height.

In addition to potters, the town also boasted glass furnaces (quite a unique archaeological find in the UK), jewellers, bronze founders and enamellers (who could obtain their materials from Parys Mountain, Anglesey and the Great Orme, Llandudno), lead workers and a thriving salt trade from Northwich and Mid Cheshire.

Food products of every kind were available, including fish, game, farming and livestock products. A military service industry also undoubtably existed, which later resulted in legends of a colony of medieval armourers descended from most ancient roots, centred on Halton Castle and Warrington. Maybe Caliburn or Excalibur were forged here in the old Roman ore smelting furnaces? It was said that the mysteries of forging and tempering steel were still in the local veins at the beginning of the industrial revolution and led to the unrivalled skills of the Warrington

THE IMPOSING FACADE OF THE VICTORIAN BREWERY WHICH SITS DIRECTLY
ON TOP OF THE ROMAN SITE

wire-making industry. The glass-making industry also continued in pre-industrialised Warrington as the well known 1772 oil painting by D. Donbavand shows with Bank Quay Glassworks clearly shown on the extreme left.

WARRINGTON GLASSWORKS AND TOWN HALL FROM THE PAINTING BY D. DONBAVAND, 1772, IN WARRINGTON MUSEUM

The Roman Wilderspool development established Warrington as the most important non-military Romano-British trading centre in the north of England. It allowed natives and visitors to trade. As well as being the most northern safe major port on the west coast, it could also trade with Wales, Scotland, the Isle of Man and Ireland where recent excavations outside Dublin have uncovered a forty acre Roman military camp and settlement which undoubtably would have had direct sea links with Warrington. It also represented the border crossing between the major Roman provinces of 'Flavia' (Britannia Inferior) to the north and 'Maxima' (Britannia Superior) to the south, good reason for the Romans to invest in bridges here.

All this having been said, I have included a suggested map reconstructing the town as it might have looked, and I will now select the more interesting points raised by the mass of available evidence, rather than attempt to cover a long description of Roman activity which can better be found in Tim Strickland's excellent 1995 book, *The Romans At Wilderspool* (as well as almost every other Warrington history book ever written!) It is fairly obvious to any local history student that the Romans have been 'flavour of the month' at Warrington for over two hundred years with little or no attention paid to the other civilisations represented here.

On the basis of the evidence of Prehistoric, Bronze Age and Iron Age activity which has survived in the area surrounding the Wilderspool Roman site, I would like to introduce the theory that a banked enclosure of some kind may have existed on the site before the Romans arrived.

The site commends itself as an ideal position for a Druidic enclosure of worship and burial on the Mersey and would be precisely the type of site the invading Romans would want to suppress. It was Roman military policy to subdue any Druidic activity which they encountered, as the Druids were the custodians of the Celtic religious, political and social institutions of Britain. In this respect the Romans often took over Druidic religious sites in order to permanently subdue the local population and impose their own structures. It is thought that Druids used open sanctuaries inside sacred enclosures similar to the Greek 'temenos', literally a cut of land consecrated to the god or goddess containing the altar and sometimes being square in shape. The Romans had the same idea expressed as a 'fanum' or 'templum' and theirs was located at Stockton Heath, just outside the south eastern corner of the banked enclosure of the Roman port.

In one corner are at least four shafts identified as wells and there are several other wells on the site. These may have been pits for earlier Celtic offerings and they were never fully excavated. Dr Baguley (who was on the 1960s and 1970s digs) remembers a large chunk of expensive blue lapis stone, possibly an offering, coming from the upper layer of one well shaft but thinks that even this find was not recorded. In addition a circular sandstone well structure over 6 ft (1.9m) in diameter was found, 7 ft (2m) under the present Francis Road, by Dr Kendrick in April 1869, and it was set up in the Town Hall gardens with several Roman steps from Wilderspool.

The abundance of well shafts, the rectangular nature of the original port site at Wilderspool, the fact that this area is completely surrounded on three sides by Bronze Age and later burials, the addition of the later Roman temple and its site directly on the river course, all lend the 'sacred enclosure' theory further support. This having been said, a complicated reappraisal of evidence would be required to conclusively establish it and the majority of the well shafts now sit under Morrison's Superstore! The enclosure may only represent the point at which the larger port developed (eastwards) and may have been removed from Druidic control as early as 20-30AD.

ANCIENT MERSEY CROSSING NUMBER 3

Back to the original question 2). again, and the location of the third crossing over the Mersey. Where did the Romans site their crossing and build their first bridge, and how did this relate to the position of the Roman port?

As an additional question: If Wilderspool was a 'port' and not a 'fort', how did the river run then and where did the Romans build the docks for their ships?

If all the Roman finds are studied in detail and plotted on a map they leave a noticeable 'corridor' of absence running roughly along the north side of Stetchworth Road and West Avenue, Stockton Heath, under the village centre and then along the south side of the old Runcorn to Latchford Canal; this was the Black Bear Canal (now a linear park) meeting the Mersey at Black Bear Bridge and the sight of the supposed original ford.

If the river bends shown on the 1746 survey and 1805 OS map are all later developments, this would explain why the actual location of the ancient ford has always eluded historians and archaeologists, since it may have been further south west of Black Bear Bridge and swept away by the building of the canal between 1783 and 1805.

If it could be conclusively shown that the ancient course of the Mersey had changed from a completely circular bend, as suggested above, to the 'squashed' shape encountered in maps before the building of the Manchester Ship Canal, then the ford location would almost certainly have been further south-west than shown in 1805. With this in mind I share a personal experience from the baking hot summer of 1976.

IN SEARCH OF SAND - LOOKING FOR THE LOST RIVER BED

In 1976 I supervised a small dig, assisted by four volunteers, in the rear garden of a house at the top of Egerton Street, to try to establish the existence of the old Mersey river course in this area.

At a depth of 3 feet (1m) the black top soil gave way to a layer of mid-brown earth for another foot (0.3m), then becoming light coloured sand, which continued in three main primary layers for another 10 feet (3m) until a distinct river bed comprised of water-rounded pebbles and cobble stones mixed with clay deposits was reached.

This was tested for another 12 ins (0.3m) depth by which time the cobbles ended and clean clay was found to continue. These clay deposits were too hard to proceed any further down and it was concluded that they constituted the underlying boulder clay deposits.

The pit was then widened to 6 foot 6 ins (2m) and the deposits found to be the same in all directions. A further 'test tunnel' through the river sand followed the 'river bed' eastwards for a distance of 13 feet or so (4m) and it continued unbroken. As expected, no finds of a human nature were discovered. The ancient course of the river had been established at a maximum depth of 14-15 feet (4.5m) under later river sand deposits. A bottle was filled with samples of the layers and I include a photograph here.

The change in river course after the Roman period is most probably represented by the dark brown flood plain or organic silt type deposits dividing the upper top soils from the lower river sands at a depth of about 3 to 4 feet (1m). This was probably laid down over a period of time from deposits left along an ancient tidal river bank or flood plain before top soil developed and the ground level was raised further by the building of the Manchester Ship Canal. Most Roman remains in Stockton Heath have been found, in times past, on the dividing line between the sands and darker top soils.

Surface

Dark top soil

Roman level

River sands

River boulders and clay deposits

Underlying clay deposits

THE TEMPLE OF MINERVA-BELISAMA – GATEWAY TO ROMAN WARRINGTON

In his book *Warrington A Heritage*, H. Boscow reports the following:

"Outside the fortifications, on the east side of Roman Road, Stockton Heath, was unearthed the head of a bronze figure of Minerva. As walls and platforms and a stone bust of the same goddess were subsequently discovered, also an altar-stone just outside the southern corner of the fortifications, it was thought that here had been erected a temple."

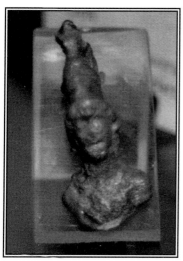

"It is known that Minerva, the symbol of wisdom, was the patroness of all the arts and crafts, and was worshipped especially by craftsmen, so what is more likely than the artisans of Veratinum should erect a shrine to her honour and worship her amidst their workshops here."

What is equally as likely is that she was directly linked to the goddess 'Belisama'. After discussing the gods of Persia, India and Greece, Jaan Puhvel in his 1987 book *Comparative Mythology* examines the Roman view of deities and their attempts to transfer the Celtic god-characters into their own Roman ones. In a passage valuable to our discussions he states that the Romano-Celtic goddess: *'MINERVA, with the epithet (addition of) BELISAMA, 'Brightest', is the cover term for a great goddess. Powerful female types stand out in Celtic mythical lore at both the divine and the saga levels .... MINERVA had a temple with 'eternal flame' in third century Britain and is*

TINY BRONZE BUST OF MINERVA FROM WILDERSPOOL

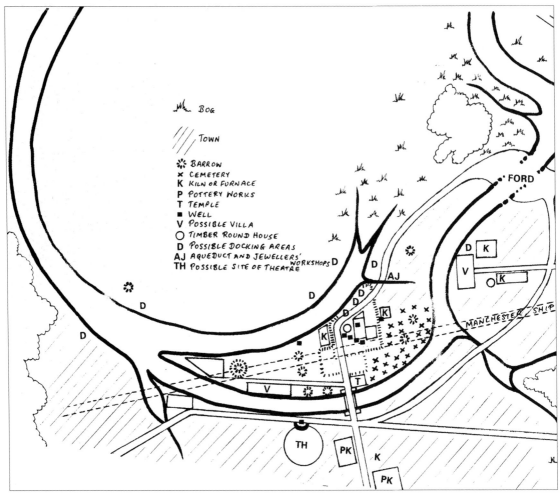

ROMAN WILDERSPOOL AS IT MAY HAVE LOOKED ABOUT 150AD

A RECONSTRUCTION OF THE POSSIBLE ROMAN BRIDGE AT STOCKTON HEATH ABOUT 280AD.

identifiable with the British Celtic theonym BRIGANTIA, formerly identical with the Sanskrit feminine adjective BRHATI, 'great, lofty' and with the Irish BRIGIT, the later saint with her feast day of Imbolc (1st February) and her monastery with perpetual fire at Kildare. (Unlike the usual overlay, ... (this) Celtic deity was simply Christianised, name and all.)'"

Jaan's passage is interesting because the Celtic tribe of the BRIGANTES held the lands of BRIGANTIA to the north east and east of the Mersey in Yorkshire and Derbyshire at the river source. Jaan goes on in the same paragraph to say:

"Triplicity or triunity is in evidence among the Celtic mythical females: BRIGIT herself had two synonymous 'sisters', there was the triad of Irish MACHAS, Gaul had the triple MATRES or MATRAE or MATRONAE. Just as the Greek three-by-three Muses did not perturb Homer's Muse, the Matronae did not preclude a single great Matrona, embodied in a river (MATRONAE = MARNE), ... Matrona was the mother of the 'Divine Son', MAPONOS, matching MODRON and her son MABON in Welsh saga ...."

Could it be added that 'three rivers' having Celtic names (Goyt, Etherow and Tame) merge to complete the 'single great Matrona' of the Mersey with a notable similarity of result? Have we discovered a new possibility for the origins of the river name: MATRES/MATREA = MARNE/MUSE = MERSE/MERSEY? This may be a better alternative to the always obscure interpretation of 'MERSE' meaning simply 'a border'.

It is yet another of Warrington's spiritual mystifications that a Cheshire County Council school (Stockton Heath Junior School), opened on the 2nd of May 1910, should now sit at the very precincts of the Roman Temple of Minerva. It was under Minerva's special care that schools

were placed two thousand years ago, with Roman school children having their holidays during her festivals!

Roman Road also still exists off Ellesmere Road, Stockton Heath, to this day, and vanishes under the foundations of Stockton Heath Junior School, which I believe sits over the ancient course of the River Mersey, so far identified, and, therefore, indicates the location of the Roman bridge which brought the original A49 road into the Roman port complex.

THE CENTRAL BUILDING OF STOCKTON HEATH JUNIOR SCHOOL UNDER WHICH SITS THE TEMPLE OF MINERVA AND POSSIBLY A ROMAN BRIDGE

This main entrance into which travellers were entering would also have been the logical place to put the primary shrine of the town, hence the positioning of the road-side temple of Minerva-Belisama at the south gate, just over the river bridge.

ROMAN ROAD AS IT IS TODAY
LOOKING TOWARDS THE SCHOOL

The absence of recorded bridge finds during the building of the school may be explained by a local legend described by Bob Fretwell. He edited a small booklet entitled *Warrington's All "Write"*, produced by North Cheshire College Reprographics Unit, Padgate, for the Warrington Writers Group in 1991, from which it is taken:

"(The Twentieth Legion) was commanded by Tribune Aulus Plautius. Now Aulus was considered a hero and a true servant of Rome, and he was, ... until one day he was ordered to collect, from Chester, a gift to be delivered to Caesar. This gift was a breast plate, made from Welsh gold, covered with pearls collected from the oyster beds of the east coast. This was said to be the finest example of British workmanship they had found in their eighty odd years of occupation. (The year was 27AD*)." (*Author's note: This assumes that the Romans probably had settlers here directly following Julius Caesar's failed invasions of 55/54 BC and some Roman finds may support this).

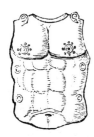

"Now Aulus had always been an honest man, but when he saw this magnificent gift he forgot his scruples and decided to steal it, hoping to settle down and spend the results of his ill-gotten gains. He buried the plate deep underground under the corner stone of the bascule. (This was the first proper bridge over the Mersey). He intended to take the empty container to Rome, where he intended to show great surprise at its mysterious disappearance. It did not work out that way. A centurion, responsible for guarding the gift, could not resist taking a peek .... So poor old Aulus, who might have got away with this audacious crime in the civilised atmosphere of Rome, was executed at Colchester."

"The plate was never found, for the unruly Warringtonians had dismantled the bridge for its valuable dressed stones by the time the Romans had returned to look for the hiding place. So if you can find the place where the first bascule was constructed ...." (there lies the golden breast plate). He gives one further clue in his account:

"The double X refers to the Roman numerals XX (representing the Twentieth Legion), which according to scanty records and legend, were carved into the rectangular cap stone under which was hidden the stolen gift. This was covered over with several feet of mud, and has caused the stolen item to remain hidden for close on 2000 years. This information came from the accounts of Claudius, the friend of Aulus, who led the search for the missing gift after the execution of Aulus ...."

Bob is of the opinion that this hiding place was the bridge suggested by the road through Howley into Latchford, but it is more probably the Stockton Heath bridge which terminates the oldest major road in the area (the A49 'King Street') and would be more likely to be a stone construction serving the port and urban area, to which the breast plate would have been brought. Sadly the source of this fascinating tale is not given in the booklet and I have been unable to contact the author who is no longer at the College.

It has long been a mystery to archaeologists why the Romans appeared to break all military construction rules by building their main complex undefended on the south side of the Mersey. The answer is simple - they didn't! The river has sufficiently changed course to appear north of their settlement today, but they may have unintentionally contributed to this.

It is possible, given Roman engineering skills, that a cutting was undertaken to create a docking channel to the north west side of the port which later developed into the main river course by connecting over marsh lands, following today's Wilderspool Causeway (possibly after the earthquake of 543AD which would have created freak tidal effects on the Mersey). The original course of the river through Stockton Heath was then neglected during the Dark Ages and eventually dried up, becoming invisible for the next 1500 years or so (see map). This is happening to the old Walton Lock in the present lifetime of local residents.

EUROPEAN ROMANO-CELTIC BREAST PLATE FROM ABOUT 300BC TO 100AD

THE OLD MERSEY RIVER COURSE AT WALTON LOOKING WEST (L.) AND EAST (R.)

The plan of the Roman station shown on page 11 of *Warrington 100 Years A Borough*, clearly shows the fortified area of the settlement, excavated by Thomas May in 1895-1905, as following the former line of the old River Mersey behind Greenall's Brewery site (which is now filled in to provide a park and extra car parking). This is where the ships would have landed their valuable cargos directly from the river into the most secure part of the Roman station, and this stretch of the river may have started life as an artificial cutting solely for this purpose.

KISSING FISH AND CHRISTIANITY

Herbert James Westbrook makes the following note in his 1929 book *Stockton Heath and Immediate District*: *"The Sandhole (between the bottom of Egerton Street and Roman Road) was also a happy hunting-ground for pieces of Roman pottery and Roman coins. Several such were gathered by me in schoolboy days (around the 1880s)."*

This account is typical of the situation regarding Roman finds during the Victorian era and before, and it was probably in this area of Stockton Heath that a small bronze item described as "the handle of a casket" came to light near to the surface at this time.

For the last hundred years or so the significance of this find (number 230'13) has been lost on most historians, but the two 'kissing fish' which comprise the small bronze handle are a universally recognised symbol for early Christianity which can be found from the Mediterranean regions to all the European lands of the Celts.

ROMAN CASKET HANDLE   BOWL ESCUTCHEON   ROMAN BUCKLE   'ALPHA' FISH
STOCKTON HEATH   FAVERSHAM KENT   COLCHESTER   OROSIUS M.S.

'Kissing fish' or 'dolphins' are featured as the handle mount or 'escutcheon' of a bowl found in Faversham, Kent, facing each other in the same way as the Warrington handle but either side of a central Christian cross. The same fishes and dolphins are also known to appear on early Christian memorial slabs and individually on the famous 'Pictish stones' of Scotland, the Picts being evangelised by St Ninian after 397AD.

There is evidence for Christianity at Manchester as early as 175AD, but the port of Warrington was already well established by this time and undoubtably represents the avenue through which the first Christians came to the Mersey Valley, probably with early sailing ships, the same method by which the Apostles spread the Gospel message from Israel right round the Mediterranean and beyond. Potentially the bronze 'kissing fish' could date back to the time of the founding of the port between 50 and 70AD (although ships were undoubtably docking here in earlier times) which, incredibly, would still be in the life-time of Jesus's disciples, the last of which, the Apostle John, only died at Ephasus about 98AD. The 'kissing fish' come from the side of the Wilderspool settlement area associated with cemeteries and the temple structure, in which early Christians would certainly have added their contribution to daily spiritual life and where the 'casket' from which the handle came may have been used.

BROACH (ANTRIM)   ESCUTCHEON (FAVERSHAM)   SAXON BROACH (FAVERSHAM)   BROACH (N.IRELAND)

ROMANO-BRITISH TRAVELS AROUND WARRINGTON

And so to our third and final question raised at the very start of this section

3) Out of the network of roads known to have existed in ancient times, which of them can be said to still exist and where did they originally go?

It is good to remember that the Roman period in Warrington spans over four hundred years and it would be quite naive to think that the local population would rely on only one bridge over the Mersey for all of that time. It is evident from the research for this book, that the local Celtic inhabitants probably began by relying on a pedestrian tidal ford, stepping stones or a primitive stone slab clapper bridge.

It was probably situated somewhere in the Black Bear Bridge area of Latchford, but there may have also been more later wooden structures at Walton, Stockton Heath, Latchford, Thelwall or Warburton. The Mersey was fordable on horse back up stream from Latchford and the later Celts definitely used canoes to cross from sites all along the river banks from 800AD up to the bridges of the late Norman/early Medieval period.

The Romans added another dimension to river crossing by constructing military and civil bridges, the initial military bridge (made at least in part of timber) crossed behind the Old Warps into Victoria Park, but the more permanent civil bridge probably linked the industrial port complex at Wilderspool with the very ancient Bronze Age A49 London Road into Stockton Heath. This was probably a stone structure, built once the settlement became Romanised, and to serve the main Roman highway 'King Street' (now the A49).

It would be good at this point to summarise the road situation established as existing during the Roman occupation of Warrington following Caesar's original visit to these shores in 55BC and up to the removal of the Roman military prescence in 410AD.

THE MAIN ROADS OF STOCKTON HEATH AND APPLETON

KING STREET (SOUTH): The main north/south highway which pre-dates the Roman occupation by possibly as much as 2000+ years (see Appleton section in Book 3), was undoubtably constructed over an existing Bronze Age/Celtic highway. This road is now approximately the A49 which enters our region through Stretton and crosses Appleton, leaving the A49 at the golf course on London Road to plunge over Hill Cliffe, down through Stockton Heath, over the site of the Roman town bridge under the School and into the Wilderspool settlement south gate.

It is not known for certain why this is called 'King Street' but this was the main salt highway from Northwich (Salinae) to the port of Warrington and appears on all maps of every kind going back to Tudor times.

In 1800 this Roman road was found running through a field in Stockton Heath called 'Street Lunt Back' where West Avenue is now and heading towards Hill Cliffe. In 1831 Mr Beamont and Mr Robson found the same road in the adjacent 'Town Field', and Mr Lyon of Appleton Hall laid bare a section in 'Dogs Kennel Field' in 1849, opposite the present side gate to Bridgewater High School on London Road. At 'Dog's Field', Stretton, the road was found to be 18 feet (5.5m) wide, a measurement comparable to the main roads located in Delamere and the rest of Cheshire.

Following the activities of Mr Beamont an inscription was commissioned on the sandstone wall slabs at the side of London Road towards the south end of the present golf course perimeter stating that the Roman road lay over the hedge some 40 yards (12.5m) into the field.

The golf course wall south of the club house is deliberately only two courses of sandstone high as it sits directly on the curb stones of the Roman road which are clearly visible in places jutting out from below the wall.

THE CASTLE ROAD (TO HATTON): So far a stretch of cobbled road, raised field features, ancient boundaries and a massive sandstone marker have been found as distinctive traces of this road which passes the suspected site of the Anglo-Saxon castle in Appleton (hence my chosen name).

Now situated in a private garden, the massive marker appears to have been rebated on one corner to take a gate post, which was fastened by an iron bar set in lead, and the 'square' of the post aligns with the 'castle' features. On the corner facing south, in the direction of King Street, appear marks which may be a message written in Ogam script and the whole block, weighing several tons, gives the impression of great age. Axe marks on the sides of the stone appear Roman. Elderly local residents can remember the block always being there well before the area was developed for housing.

THE KING/WATLING SOUTH WEST LINK: It is also thought that a link existed between the Appleton section of King Street and Watling Street west of Northwich. The actual intersection has been located and excavated behind Eddisbury Hill Fort beyond Delamere Forest (This intersection will be explored in more detail in Book 3 of this series). The Appleton intersection may have converged at the same point as the Castle Road or close to Stretton Church and the North Cheshire Ridge Road.

THE NORTH CHESHIRE RIDGE ROAD: Was located over several years by the late E.M. Hughes of Lymm who died in 1984. He began at Newhouse Farm in Hatton and found that the road approximately follows the B5356 through Hatton, Stretton and Appleton Thorn to the moated Bradley Hall, before joining the A50 close to Redbank Bridge.

Excavated at 22 sites down its length, the road was found to be between 44 and 57 feet wide (14 to 18m) with a cobbled surface and having drainage ditches on either side, which is a unique feature for this part of Cheshire. It also had retaining curbs made from larger stones and was in use right up to early Medieval times. My own feelings are that this road is Celtic in origin hence the unique ditches and continued use by local inhabitants. Many sections have now been destroyed by recent house-building activities.

THE MAIN ROADS OF GRAPPENHALL AND HIGH LEGH

THE FORD/WATLING SOUTH EAST LINK: Would have been the continuation from the Roman river crossing behind the Old Warps at Victoria Park, Howley, which has now become the A50 Knutsford Road through Latchford, Grappenhall and High Legh (where it is joined by the North Cheshire Ridge Road), and crosses Watling Street at Mere before heading for Knutsford.

THREE SMALL FORD ROADS: At least three (as previously listed) would have carried mainly local travellers (except for the A50 Knutsford Road) towards the ford from the south and the Roman port at Stockton Heath, along a route roughly parallel to Loushers Lane (see the section on Wilderspool).

THE MOAT ROAD: May have developed in Celtic times as an additional track through Stretton and High Legh, linking the moated sites together in a line from the castle at Appleton to the village of Rostherne and beyond. This is a route which deviates considerably from the North Cheshire Ridge Road and appears to follow the next ridge south into Cheshire, before joining the Ridge Road at High Legh.

Some Stone Age finds, enclosures and Bronze Age ditches, have been discovered along this route, which may hint at the Romans avoiding an established local road in favour of the North Cheshire Ridge in the same way as they did with the A49 through Winwick.

THE MAIN ROADS OF DARESBURY AND NORTON

CHESTER ROAD: It is supposed that this once followed the course of the present A56 Chester Road from North Wales and Chester, past Helsby and Frodsham, through Preston Brook, Daresbury and Walton, apparently entering the Wilderspool settlement by either the north gate or an undiscovered link to the south. Should any additional roads appear in the western areas of Warrington during research for books 3 and 4 they will be listed in detail in book 4.

THE SEQUANA ROAD: So named in this volume because it was an ancient east-west link situated south of the Mersey, along which sacred sites obviously developed over a long period of time. This poorly defined road linked sacred sites at the head of the 'serpent river', Runcorn Hill, with Halton Hill, Norton Priory, the Temple of Minerva and earlier settlement at Stockton Heath, the tumuli burial ground at Grappenhall and the ford and the villages of Thelwall, Lymm and Warburton - where it may well have carried on to Urmston or 'Worms Town' (the 'tail' of the 'river serpent' in legend) and on along the river to the Goyt Valley (see section The Mersey Celtic Pilgrim Route Revealed).

This may have been the road taken by Sir Gawain to face the Green Knight covered in the earlier chapters of this book.

The main Roads of Glazebrook and Winwick

THE WOLF VALLEY SALT HIGHWAY: As outlined in Celtic Warrington Book 1, a major north/south highway existed, along the Glazebrook and Woolden Valley B5212 from Hollins Green to Culcheth, which would have been a continuation of the B5160 south of the Mersey linking Warburton with Watling Street at Bowdon.

This route would have carried traders in salt and other products, avoiding the centre of Warrington and the travelling complications associated with a busy international port. The traders would take their goods to the major centres which were at ancient Culcheth, Legh and beyond.

MANCHESTER ROAD: The present A57, heading east, was the Roman highway linking the possible original Trajanic Roman fort (98AD to 117AD), in the Howley area of Warrington, with the fort at Salford in Manchester (where the road has been excavated). It is thought that this Warrington fort stood on the crossroads of Manchester Road and the Ford Road from the bridge which runs into the A49 King Street North, in the area of the present St Elphins Parish Church at Howley and aerial photography has revealed the road in fields at Rixton.

It was Manchester Road, in the form of Church Street (and later Buttermarket Street) which was chosen to become the original Warrington town centre main street after the departure of the Romans.

From Warrington this road also headed west later becoming.

The main Roads of Sankey and North Warrington

LIVERPOOL ROAD: It is highly probable that the A57 Liverpool Road to Prescot-on-the-Hill is of great age, as is the Widnes Road.

WIDNES ROAD: The A562 Widnes Road, which becomes the A561 to Speke, are both probably ancient routes utilised by the Romans and dating back into prehistory. The Warrington junction of these two roads was known as the 'White Cross' probably after a white painted Celtic cross which stood here in ancient times on a triangle of land shown on the plan attached to the 1465AD 'Legh M.S.', the oldest known map of Warrington.

KING STREET (NORTH): This links the Howley river crossing, the possible fort at Church Street, Warrington and Winwick, to north Lancashire, and ultimately the Roman activities at Hadrian's Wall in Scotland. In Book 1 of this series it was noted, however, that the Roman highway veers away to the west towards Vulcan Village at Winwick, while the Celtic ridgeway continues north along the high ground towards Golborne and may have continued south to Town Hill, the present day town centre. An east/west highway crosses here at Winwick also.

DRUID AVENUE: This was the ancient avenue approach to the mound at Winwick and links the lost Celtic monastic site and Druidic mosslands in the east beyond Culcheth with the north/south highways at Winwick, forming a ley line detailed in the first book.

It will be noted that most of the highways listed are only developments on much older road patterns existing at the time of the Bronze and Iron Age Celts, and that later Celts continued to use many of these routes even in preference to Roman roads.

The Celts were internationally famed for their excellent wheeled vehicles, which leads to the obvious conclusion that they possessed reasonably good quality roads of some kind, well before the Romans came into their lands. For example, I feel that the North Cheshire Ridgeway may turn out to be of Celtic rather than Roman construction along with the A49 King Street. Areas of Europe unconquered by the Romans still possess ancient roads made by highly skilled road builders such as those found in Ireland.

British bardic tradition tells of certain Celtic roads that were the direct responsibility of the King to maintain. These were the 'Four Royal Roads Of Britain'.

Legend has it that these were built by the Celtic King Dunwal Molmutius and his son Belinus as sacred routes for "all nations and foreigners" and it is not too far-fetched to suggest that the major, national 'north road' west of the Pennines, running from Stone Henge and Avebury in the south to Carlisle and Edinburgh in the north, would have followed the basic path of the A49 'King Street' and through the ford at Warrington. Interestingly, this route also links most of the traditional Arthurian sites identified over the years, from Tintagel in Cornwall, through a left turn at Avebury, through Viriconium, to 'Arthur's Seat' in Edinburgh. Truly a 'King's Street'!

Returning to the saga of the Roman road systems of Warrington; one highway is noticeable by its absence but deserving of further examination - Wilderspool Causeway.

THE ROMAN KING STREET LOOKING SOUTH TO STRETTON (L.) AND NORTH TO STOCKTON HEATH (R.) AS IT APPEARS TODAY

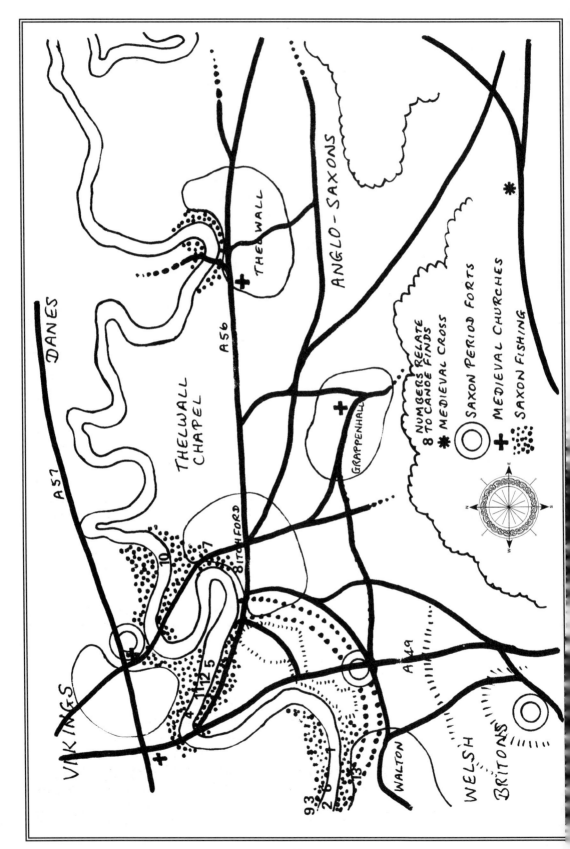

WILDERSPOOL

NOT THE ROMAN CAUSEWAY!

Although there is no dispute that the Roman site on Wilderspool was a major centre of Romano-British activity, the common mistake is made that the entire Wilderspool Causeway is of Roman origin.

In his 1929 book, *Stockton Heath And Immediate District,* H.J. Westbrook's father recalls a time before the causeway even existed, as recently as about 1870. The causeway was only constructed, from the traffic lights at the Loushers Lane/Gainsborough Road junction to the old St James vicarage at Bridge Foot, in the late Victorian era. Mr Westbrook writes:

"Crossing Black Lion Bridge one enters upon Wilderspool Causeway proper, for it is a misnomer, in my opinion, to apply the name Causeway to any other length of the road except that between the said bridge and the house formerly belonging to Mr John Brown, situate between the Malt-kiln and St James' Vicarage.

I distinctly remember my father telling me of the times before the Causeway was made when pedestrians to and from Warrington were at flood times taken over the flooded road-way in carts. There were then, and even in my time, many more trees growing at that spot than now ...Proceeding from Black Lion Bridge towards Warrington there were then as now open fields until one reached the Foundry (just before what is now Bridge Foot).

The fields (on the right) ..have been, since the time now being referred to, raised more to the road level. At the time alluded to they were considerably below road level, and the fence not being of the best, it was not unusual for a pedestrian on a dark night to step off the footway and plunge into the fields. Loushers Lane, at least not the present one, did not then exist."

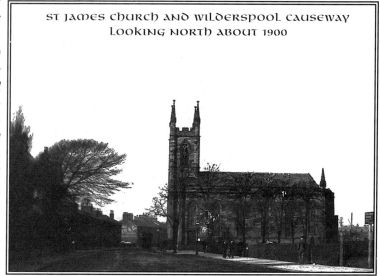

ST JAMES CHURCH AND WILDERSPOOL CAUSEWAY LOOKING NORTH ABOUT 1900

"Evidence is still furnished of the original Causeway (in 1929) by the fences over the roadway bridges (arches), which permitted the flood waters to flow back from the east to the west, and thence into the river (which was where the long park is now situated). Stout iron posts, with iron tube cross-bars, may still be seen at intervals along the Causeway, starting immediately after Black Lion Bridge (Loushers Lane traffic lights) - and extending to the garden of the said house (next to St James' vicarage)."

"Wilderspool Causeway was widened to 60 feet in or about the year 1898, when the old Pleasure Boat House Inn was taken down, and the present Causeway Hotel substituted for it."

It is said that the former St James' vicarage is haunted by the ghost of Marian Dutton (or Duggins), a maid who was pregnant by a canal worker in the 1890s, and the ghost of her boyfriend, the handyman Roland Jacket, who strangled her when he discovered the pregnancy. Eighteen months later a body was recovered from the Mersey at the back of the vicarage. The male ghost is often seen as a 'hanged man'. Did Roland get his own back on the canal worker or did the worker get to Roland first? Did Roland really murder Marian or was it the canal worker?

SOUNDINGS OF RIVER MERSEY, CHESTER ROAD. J. LONGDEN, BOROUGH SURVEYOR & A. JACKSON, RIVER SURVEYOR IN BOAT

During road repairs by the traffic lights at the junction with Gainsborough Road in the early 1990s, the arch of Black Lion Bridge was revealed, residing a few feet below the present road and silted up to the top of the arch, as it evidently was in 1929.

RECONSTRUCTION OF BLACK LION BRIDGE UNDER PRESENT ROAD

The whole Causeway is, in fact, an early Victorian structure built over a medieval trackway which was probably not a main highway (if a highway at all) in Roman/Celtic times.

The present site for the bridge at the bottom of Bridge Street (which leads on to Wilderspool Causeway) is a medieval development, brought about by the construction of the first toll bridge there by the Le Boteler family, in about 1285AD, and the later improved bridge of 1364AD. This was followed by the Earl of Derby's bridge in 1495AD, when the toll was abolished and the present causeway was developed into the main town, north-south, highway is is today.

So there you have it - there was no Roman causeway under Wilderspool, it is nothing more than a local legend based on the use of the word 'causeway'. A track or a road here would serve no useful purpose unless it led to a bridge, ford or boat crossing and no evidence of any of these exists, during the first millennium, when the northern part of the town centred on Church Street and Latchford, not its present site.

One very ancient road did exist however, running east from the area of the Saracen's Head pub and having its beginning at China Lane which is the short stretch of cobbled road to the right side of the pub. This would have become Loushers Lane (which only took on its present form in 1899) at a point just to the east of the former canal bridge where it once served the Roman settlement, and then on along old Wash Lane (now Common Lane) before following the new route of Wash Lane northwards towards the ford at Latchford.

In 1877 before the building of the Manchester Ship Canal, two footpaths branched off this road and turned south towards Stockton Heath. One path terminating at Ackers Pits, the other becoming Mill lane, although these would not necessarily have been the routes taken prior to the building of the Runcorn to Latchford (Black Bear) Canal completed in 1805.

Although it was long thought that the name WILDERSPOOL was fairly modern in origin it eventually turned up in a charter from the reign of Henry III (1216AD to 1272AD) as WILDRESPUL, possibly from the Old English WILD DEOR meaning a 'wild beast or deer' and PUL meaning 'pool, pond, pool in a river, creek or stream'. This makes Wilderspool the 'pool of the wild beast or deer'. Another version equally of note makes WILDRES (WILDER) the Saxon who owned the PUL making it WILDER'S POOL.

Moving on to another familiar name.

WARRINGTON - THAT FRUSTRATING NAME!

It is worthy of note here that no major settlement is recorded at Liverpool ('Lifrugpool' or 'Leverepul') until the time of the Market Charter granted by King John around 1216AD and the Borough Charter of King Henry III of 1229AD. (Domesday records, only briefly, 'Allerton', 'Speke', 'Woolton', 'Huyton' and 'Sefton' settlements).

LIVERPOOL CHARTER AND
SEAL OF 1216 AD

Manchester remained just a Roman fort and religious site up to Domesday times when it was credited briefly in passing with "a church"!

The struggles against Danes, Norsemen and the Mercian enemies of Wessex carried on by the successors of King Alfred, which reached climax at the battle of Brunanburgh in 937AD, forced the movement of the Northumbrian boundary north from the Mersey to the River Ribble.

This meant that the land between the Ribble and the Mersey became a royal domain separate from Mercia which it remained until after the Norman conquest - which explains why the northern parts of our area are given as a sort of appendix to the more detailed Domesday accounts of Cheshire. By this time (and despite being included in this 'appendix') Warrington had been a major 'city-port' and centre for industry for over a 1000 years and could boast a detailed entry in Domesday numbering some ten lines.

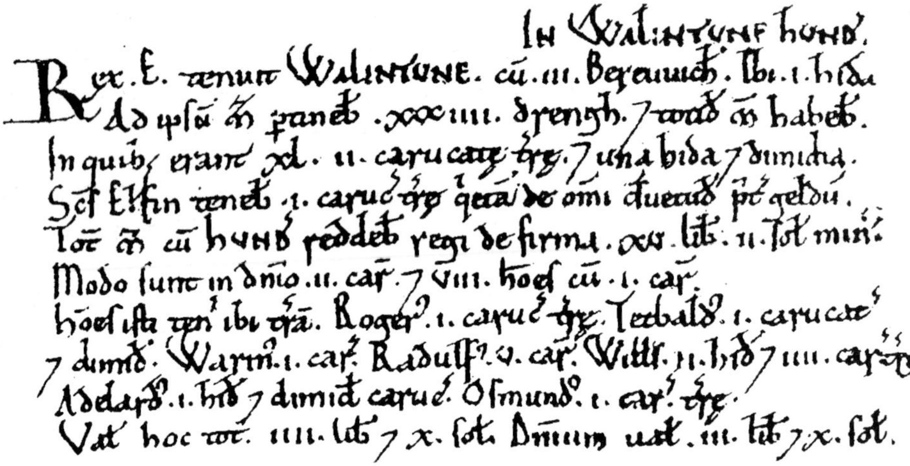

[handwritten medieval Latin Domesday entry]

The Domesday entry in translation from the contracted Latin reads:

"*IN WALINTUNE HUNDRED King Edward* (901-924AD) *held Walintune with three berewicks* (smaller manors thought to be Little Sankey, Orford and Howley). *There is 1 hide* (the total town covered about 720 acres at that time). *To that manor used to belong 34 drengs* (Saxon land owners), *and they had as many (34) manors, in which there were 42 carucates of land and one hide and a half* (about 5049 acres of land). *Saint Elfin* (the church as it is now) *held 1 carucate of land* (about 120 acres) *quit from every due except the geld* (a tax to buy off Danish invaders levied in 991AD). *The whole manor with the hundred used to pay in farm (de firma) to the king 15 pounds, less 2 shillings. Now there are in desmesne 2 ploughs and 8 men with 1 plough. These men hold land there. Roger 1 carucate of land* (120 acres), *Tetbald 1 and a half carucate* (180 acres), *Warin 1 carucate* (120 acres), *Radulf 5 carucates* (600 acres), *Willrn* (William) *2 hides and 4 carucates of land* (1920 acres), *Adelard 1 hide and half a carucate* (780 acres), *Osmond 1 carucate of land* (120 acres). *This whole* (desmesne) *is worth 4 pounds and 10 shillings. The desmesne* (of the chief manor) *is worth 3 pounds and 10 shillings.*"

The Warrington 'hundred' was comprised of a small section of South Lancashire north of the Mersey, covering the parishes of Warrington, Prescot and Legh and the township of Culcheth which was then large enough to have held Anglo-Saxon synods between 700 and 900AD. Warrington came under the lands of Roger of Poictou, after Domesday, when William the Conqueror granted him the lands between the Ribble and the Mersey. Roger then sub-granted the Manor and Hundred of Warrington, along with the three berewicks (hamlets) of Little Sankey, Orford and Howley, to Pagnus de Villars, who probably died about 1156AD leaving seven children, the eldest Matthew de Villars becoming the second Baron of Warrington.

It is becoming evident that civilisation before the Romans had already 'staked its claim' on the area now known as Warrington - but where does this enigmatic and frustrating town name originate? Considering the evidence developed in this volume, I will attempt the unthinkable, to finally bring out the true origins of the name by examining the evidence and presenting considered conclusions. During my research I have encountered all of the following variations and definitions of the name.

1] WARRINGTON - It is worth stating at the outset that this name was firmly established by Robert Morden's and John Speed's maps of Tudor Lancashire and Cheshire, produced before 1610AD, and is probably over four hundred years old in its present form. We at least begin our investigations with this genuine and reliable name dating back to about 1520AD.

2] WARIN'S TUN - A Saxon landowner named WARIN is listed in the 1086AD Domesday survey as owning about 120 acres of land somewhere in the Warrington hundred but the location is not specified and may not have corresponded with the present town at all.

3] WEARRA'S TUN - Everyone identifies the characteristic TON ending as TUN meaning 'an area of land' later becoming 'a town', but this most popular of ideas adds that the WARRING is derived from the personal name for the town's founder WAER or WEARRA, a similar but less well supported idea to number 2].

4] WAERING TUN - This suggestion is derived from the Old English word WAER or WAERING meaning a 'weir or dam', of which quite a few may have existed all through the town's history. The name WERINGTON appears in the Assize rolls for 1246AD (records of feudal court cases). Despite fragments of timber structures associated with the River Mersey log boat finds, firm evidence for a weir or dam older than the one built at Howley after 1770AD has not so far been found. This may be partly due to Thomas Patten who cleared all the fish weirs up to Bank Quay at his own expense in 1698AD in order to make the Mersey navigable.

5] WERINTON - And the closely related WERENTON appear in the Assize rolls for 1246 AD to 1247AD and 1259AD along with WERINGTON. Variations appear again in the later charters of William le Boteler in 1310AD as WERINTON, and 1390AD as WERYNGTON. These are obviously medieval scribal variations of a primitive form of the present day name WARRINGTON but do serve to push its pedigree back another three hundred years to about 1240AD.

6] WOERING TUN - In this case is supposed to be derived from the Saxon WOERING meaning a RAMPART associated with a castle - like the one which existed on Mote Hill, formerly behind St Elfin's Church in Howley, before its final removal in the 1930s, or possibly that which surrounded the Roman port at Stockton Heath.

7] WERYT TON - A GWERYT, WERYT or WERID is a 'ford or river crossing', which may have led to the early name WERIDTON. In support of this theory the town map produced in the Legh Manuscript of 1465AD names Warrington as WERYNGTON. This was the theory favoured by William Beamont in his book *The Annals of the Lords of Warrington* where he quotes an earlier writer thus: *"We incline to the opinion of the learned editor of "Penwortham Priory", that the British word WERID, 'a ford', is at the root of the first two syllables of the present name of Warrington, and that the word meaning 'ford town', originating with the Britons, has only assumed its present form in the process of transfusion through the Saxon tongue."*

The 'weir or dam' and the 'ford or river crossing' are probably simply nice linguistic ideas created to fit one aspect of the local historic picture. As yet no firm evidence of any kind has been found to support this or the other claims of WARIN, WEARRA, WAERING or WOERING, and the town was already over a thousand years old by the Saxon period from which these possible names are taken.

The oldest confirmed names here so far are WERINTON (or similar) from 1246AD, and WERYNGTON dated as late as 1390AD. Now moving on to much older suggested names for the town:

8] CONDATE - Victorian antiquaries were quite preoccupied in the search for a name for the obviously large Roman station being progressively uncovered at Wilderspool. In this they turned to an itinerary or 'road book' which belonged to 'Antonius' between 138AD and 144AD when the station would have been fully operational. This itinerary gives names for towns and stations on the main military highways with the distances between them, distances which were used to deduce that Wilderspool corresponded to CONDATE.

In 1886 Mr W. Thompson Watkin laid this idea fairly convincingly to rest by establishing that CONDATE was not WARRINGTON but actually a place called KINDERTON (NORTHWICH), although these two possible place designations divided antiquaries at the time until another 'more famous' alternative emerged:

9] VERATINUM (1) - This was a stray name which appeared written next to the Roman name DEVA (DEVA VICTRIX) for Chester in the *Ravenna Cosmography,* the work of an unknown 7th century geographer called Ravenna, and meaning 'ford town' in latin. This is the source for the name VERATINUM used by archaeologists for at least a hundred years and yet may just indicate that Chester also once had a ford!

10] VERATINUM (2) - One local historian suggests that this popular name for Roman Warrington came about because of the similarity between the pronunciation of words like WERYT (pronounced 'VERIT') and the Roman Latin word VERAT meaning 'truth'. If this is the case then it is unprecedented in the Roman Empire that the name should remain unchanged from the local tongue to become VERATINUM, as no other town has ever been colonised by the Romans without the original native name being completely changed as a mark of conquest. It is said that VERATINUM then led to WARRINGTON in the same way as MANCUNIUM became MANCHESTER.

No actual Roman evidence has ever been found to ascribe any name to Warrington. Thus the words of Tim Strickland in his 1995 publication *The Romans At Wilderspool* are still true that: *"....its accuracy is hotly debated by scholars".* The Roman settlement's name thus remains shrouded in mist.

Returning to reality:

11] WALINTUNE - This is, in fact, the actual name for the town which appears in the Domesday Book of 1086AD and herein lies the only present source of the original, unromantic, truth about the name. I believe this name to have developed from three key Old English words:

- **WALH, WEALD or WAL(L)** meaning 'Welshman, Briton, foreigner, serf or slave'; all of which resided here over the previous 3000+ years before the Domesday survey. The place remaining as WALTON also originates as WALETUN from 'the Welshman's or serf's farm'; plural WALAS, the Old English for foreigners, serfs and inferior races, which was applied to the Welsh by the Romans and Saxons.

- **IEG or EG** meaning 'Island, peninsula, dry area in a fen, well-watered land'; upon which the Romans had settled and built a port here on the Mersey and:

- **TUNE or TUN** meaning 'enclosure, enclosed dwelling, farmstead, hamlet, village, estate and manor'; which had developed in the run up to the Domesday survey of 1086AD, out of the remains of Roman and other later occupations.

All these words describe perfectly the town that was and is Warrington, known to the Anglo-Saxons, Danes, Ancient Britons and Celts in ages past as WALH-IEG-TUN. However this still leaves us without a Roman or Welsh name.

SOME NEW ALTERNATIVES

12] WALWEITHA - Was recorded by William of Malmesbury in his *Deeds of the Kings of the Angles* (1125AD) as the area known to have been reigned over by Sir Gawain (Walwein) before he was driven from it by the brother and nephew of Hengist in about 450AD to 500AD. Was this also the name used for Warrington by the Welsh?

Hengist and Horsa the Jutes (Saxons) landed in Britain at the request of Vortigern in 449AD and drove back the Picts and Scots. Then Hengist founded the Kingdom of Kent (457AD). This period of conflict took place throughout the North West, concluding with Arthur attacking the Saxons at Wigan, and finally defeating them entirely at Badon in about 515AD to 520AD.

The area of WALWEITHA was probably still known to the Normans in 1066AD and it is in Domesday 1086AD that we find the remarkably similar WALINTUNE as noted in the section on Gawain and the Green Knight.

13] INSULA PEREGRIUM - If the Romans used the same elements found in the Domesday name minus the later Saxon designation of TUN then, based on the words 'peninsula' (INSULAR) and 'foreigner' (PEREGRINUS), the name in common use may have been INSULA PEREGRIUM.

14] BELISANTIUM - If the Roman name was based on the Roman river name BELISAMA then it would have been known as BELISANTIUM, under the patronage of the primary water goddess Minerva-Belisama, and the name would have meant BRIGHT-TOWN.

This is my personal favourite as a Roman name and probably has as much chance of being right as any of the other Roman names so far suggested over the years!

So in summary, the only actually known names of Warrington confirmed with dates are: WALINTUNE (Norman - 1086AD), WERINTON (Medieval - 1246AD) and WERYNGTON (Medieval - 1390AD), both possibly derived from Anglo-Saxon, and WARRINGTON (Tudor - 1520) all of which demonstrate a fairly clear development sequence over a thousand year period.

Just to conclude this section on important ancient Celtic place names, *The White Book Of Rhydderch* gives the old names for Britain as follows: *"The first name that this Island bore, before it was taken or settled - Myrddin's (Merlin's) Precinct. And after it was taken and settled, the Island of Honey. And after it was conquered by Prydein, son of Aedd the Great, it was called the Island of Prydein (Britain)."* The name BRITAIN used by Latin writers like Julius Caesar may just be a poor rendering of the old Celtic PRITANI or PRETANI. The representation of the lady figure 'Britannia' first appeared on Romano-British coins of Emperor Hadrian (117AD to 138AD) holding a spear (which was later changed to a trident by Elizabeth I to show Britain's growing sea power). She only left British coinage in the 1970s with the introduction of decimalisation.

RETURN TO STOCKTON HEATH VILLAGE

To the south of the present town of Warrington and Wilderspool is situated the modern day settlement of Stockton Heath - locally thought to derive its name from the STOCKS-ON-THE-HEATH.

The area was indeed a sandy 'heath' covered in gorse and broom bushes, owing its existence to the clearances of the former Roman workshops and settlement, and divided only by two main cart roads for much of its early existence. Once the Roman A49 fell into disrepair, roads to the east and the ford assumed greater significance.

SARAH GRIFFITHS

THE HILAL RESTAURANT (TOP PHOTO) SHOWING HENRY ISHERWOOD'S COTTAGE TO THE
FAR RIGHT, NOW A VACANT SITE, AND SHOWN IN CLOSE UP ABOVE
VICTORIA SQUARE SHOWING OLD MULBERRY TREE INN (BOTTOM PHOTO) SITED OVER
POSSIBLE SAXON BURGH, SHOWN ABOUT 1875

The village name does not appear on any map produced before 1739AD when it appeared on *Moll's Map of Cheshire* as STOKEN and under the same name on *Bowen's Map* of 1777AD. The name then vanishes until the OS mapping of 1805 to 1873.

In 1871 the Rev Wm. Hayes M.A., Vicar of Stockton Heath, interviewed the then four oldest living residents regarding memories of the undeveloped village. These residents were two sisters, Ellen Sudlow aged 90 and Mary Shaw aged 89 (maiden name 'Yates') and Mr William Johnson aged 78, with his wife Ellen aged 82. (The two sisters even remembered their grandfather talking of his meetings with the Duke of Bridgewater while he worked on the construction of the Bridgewater Canal, begun by Act of Royal Assent on the 23rd March 1759). Rev. Hayes gives an account of part of his interview (recorded in *Stockton Heath and Immediate District* by H.J. Westbrook) as follows:

"The little girls, Mary and Ellen Yates, often heard their mother and grandfather speak of the time, still fresh in their remembrance, when it (Stockton Heath village) *was all an open space, mostly covered with furze and broom, and extending from Lower Walton village to Lumbrook, and from Hill Cliffe to Wilderspool."* (This land was only enclosed by Act of Parliament in the reign of King George III, 1760-1820).

"On the Common, as it was then and for years after called, there were at this time very few tenements (houses) *of any kind, but it was crossed in all directions, as commons generally are, with numerous pathways. There were, however, only two recognised cart tracks."*

"One which still remains, round by the turf pits (Hill Cliffe Road).... *to Lawrinson's Brow and along the Red Lane into Stockton Heath Toll Bar Row.... across the Northwich Road* (upper London Road), *then unpaved, into what was and still is called the "Black" or "Sandy Lane".... branching off on the one hand to Lumbrook* (Grappenhall Road) *and on the other to the Mill* (Parkgate Road/Mill Lane).

C. 1855

The other recognised cart track was that which still goes in from Stockton Heath Street at the end of the Red Lion (West Avenue), *and at that time it went straight to Lower Walton, but is now blocked up at about half the way...."* (by a stile at the parish boundary ditch which ran along Walton Heath Road).

The 'Northwich Road', mentioned in Rev. Hayes' account, was the only other road to figure in the life of the village and dated back to the Roman 'King Street', the A49 north-south road into Cheshire.

So here we have the HEATH part of the name, but where were the stocks? Rev. Hayes' account also includes their location: *"There was then no Red Lion or Black Lion. The old Mulberry Tree (formerly the 'Grapes' or 'White Bear Alehouse')*

TWO VIEWS OF THE NOW DEMOLISHED MILL, MILL LANE, LOOKING S.W.

C. 1885

SARAH GRIFFITHS

opened as the 'Mulberry Tree' by Greenall's director Mr J.H.Clarke on the 19th March 1907 was the only hostel. Opposite were 'The Stocks' (only taken away in my own time) ...."

The stocks would have stood in Victoria Square before 1870 near the old Bridewell (the present police station site) and a saw pit and grind stone then used by the proprietors of the local village smithy. Their present whereabouts is not known, if indeed they have survived at all, and while the name of the village now popularly in use may derive from the old STOCKS-ON-THE-HEATH, its true origins are a great deal older and of more considerable importance to the local Celtic historian.

If the name is rendered the ancient way as HEATH OF STOCK-TON then its origins can be detected more easily in STOCK-TUN.

In *Words and Places* by Isaac Taylor (former Canon of York) it is stated that the suffix TON now in use is especially characteristic of an Old English township, the name TON or TUN meaning a 'farmstead' (enclosure, enclosed dwelling, hamlet, village) commonly being preceded by a term which describes the situation or character of the place.

The prefix STOCK is said to derive from Swedish or Icelandic origins meaning 'a log' (or tree-stump) making STOCKTON literally the 'Farmstead by the Logs'. This is interesting in the light of the absence of trees on 'the heath' originally derived from the Mersey flood plain which has only given up clay and sand deposits with no woodland remains from any period! In *Names And Places*, Gordon J. Copley makes a suggested name which is far more likely when he renders it STOCC-TUN - 'Farm or Enclosure Made of Tree Stumps', possibly indicating the existence of a man-made wooden 'Burgh' type fortification somewhere on the flat heath lands.

The idea of an Icelandic name appearing in the Warrington area during the latter half of the Celtic period is not as far-fetched as it may sound. In *Pre-Conquest Cheshire, pp.383-1066*, J.D. Bu'Lock observes: *"The situation of North-west Mercia (Cheshire) was becoming more critical through the increasing settlement of Irish-Sea Scandinavians (Vikings) there. This was the immigration which left such clear traces in the place names of Cumberland, West Lancashire and Wirral, but which achieved hardly any specific reference in the historical sources, perhaps because the settlements were effected gradually and without serious armed conflict; nevertheless the existence of this settlement, and the threat it always posed, are keys to our understanding of tenth century history (900-1000AD)...."*

"The immigrants were a mixed lot, mainly of Norse (Viking) origin but coming now from the settlements in Ireland and the Isles and consequently bringing a substantial proportion of Irish followers with them; as with the contemporary immigrants into Iceland, their outlook was more individualistic and egalitarian than in the Danish armies, and their community correspondingly more turbulent and less coherently organised. They developed a form of government through the assembly, the 'thing', which is an ancestral to parliamentary democracy (directly so IN ICELAND* at least) and an economy based on farming, trade and piracy. The main sea-trade of Chester port was with Ireland, but the Viking traders MOVED FREELY FROM ICELAND* to Russia, ... The greater part of this sea trade was conducted by Vikings, and particularly by the Norse-Irish. Eastward trade was by land (through Warrington?) to the Anglo-Scandinavian centres of York and the Midland boroughs, and by river to the Welsh border towns."

As you can see from the emphasis I have added *, and the social and economic pattern of the Mersey Norse/Viking settlers, they would certainly fit the bill as developers and settlers of a wooden stockade at Stockton Heath during the tenth century.

One other alternative translation for STOC with a single C makes the word mean a 'cattle or dairy farm' in Old English, but, given the evidence, this translation is unlikely. Records in antiquity show evidence of STOCKTON with the family name De Stockton recorded from the end of the thirteenth century (about 1280AD) to the end of the fifteenth century (about 1480AD). In 1288AD, Geppe de Stockton was fined at Chester, and in 1465AD Robert Stokton owned land in the area recorded in the Legh Manuscript.

Other similar examples of the Old English TUN usage in local place names include: STRETTON, the STREET-TUN meaning the 'farm by the street', the street being the Roman 'King Street', Northwich Road (now the A49 London Road), or the Roman North Cheshire Ridgeway (B5356); HATTON similar to Stockton Heath as HEATH-TUN, the 'farm on the heath'; BOLLINGTON as BOLLIN-TUN, simply the 'farm by the (River) Bollin'.

If the name STOCC-TUN has Swedish or Icelandic origins in the visitation to the area of the Danes, Norse and Vikings, then one of the greatest long-running local mysteries could be solved - the location of the long-missing 'Thel's Burr'.

NOT 'ThEL-WALL' BUT 'STOCC-TUN'

Despite extensive searches in the area now known as Thelwall, no trace has ever been found of the 'famous' fortifications originally recorded as being built there by the Anglo-Saxon king, Edward the Elder, and his sister, Ethelfleda, between 915AD and 923AD.

Edward, King of England, and his sister, conducted a series of campaigns after the death of their father Alfred the Great, which resulted in the re-capture of lands held by the Danes after the introduction of 'Danelaw' in the Treaty of Chippenham 878AD. 'Danelaw' was a payment made to the Danes to prevent them from taking any more land by force (and is recorded as still being paid by St Elphins church in the Domesday survey of 1086AD). Parts of Warrington were gradually re-captured and fortified over a ten year period with Ethelfleda building forts at Warburton and Runcorn in 915AD and Edward building 'Thelwall' as recorded in the Anglo-Saxon Chronicle for 923AD.

But at this time the area known as 'Thelwall' stretched as far as Walton which would place the modern village of Stockton Heath in Thelwall and on the boarder with the Welsh settlers at Lower Walton.

This can be clearly shown, as all maps produced from earliest times up to just before the Victorian OS mapping show only 'Thelwall' or 'Thelwall Chapel' for the entire south side of Warrington up to Grappenhall and 'Nether Walton' adjacent to the west. In his *History of England*, George Trevelyan says: *"Alfred had set the example.... and his son and daughter spread the net of fortified English 'burghs' up the Severn Valley and across the Midlands. They repaired the stone walls of ruined Roman cities, or piled up new earthworks round tactical points unguarded before."*

Both of this type of fortification are recorded at Stockton Heath, the Roman fort and an earthwork used as a fort during the Civil War in the battle of Stockton Heath (April 1643AD) and now under the Mulberry Tree pub. Combine this with the Danes own naming of the STOCC-TUN and it looks like this is the most likely location for King Edward's missing 'burr' fortification of 923AD.

AN ATTEMPT TO REGRESS STOCKTON HEATH AND SURROUNDINGS

Evidence in the Stockton Heath area appears to indicate a distinct occupation pattern over a long period of time. A long-term Welsh Celtic/Ancient Briton settlement remained at Walton from the Stone Age and Bronze Age right up to Medieval times and represented the western 'gateway' to the town. It was probably these settlers who removed any trees to form the original heath.

The Old English WEALH or WALH (plural WALA) is taken to mean 'a foreigner' or 'Briton' (the Welsh after Roman times), and the name WALTON (WALH-TUN) to mean 'town of the Britons', a place where Britons continued to live for many ages. It may be made up from the word WEALD meaning 'Bank, Ditch or Wood' but this is less likely, given the evidence.

Between 55BC and 41AD representatives of Rome arrived in Warrington and took over the site at Wilderspool used by local inhabitants as a burial ground and enclosure. They left the Bronze Age burial grounds but developed the enclosure into a temple and a town to the east. As the Druids were falling from favour this development phase was assisted by the local Cornovii tribe who had disputed ownership of the valley with the Brigantes to the north over a long period of time. The Brigantes, followers of the goddess 'Brigit', probably took sides with the Druids who concentrated their efforts in the Mossland Crescent further to the east.

The Roman army arrived in about 70AD and settled at Wilderspool, Latchford and Stockton Heath, a respectable distance up-stream from the local Welsh/Britons, and constructed bridges of their own to avoid conflict at the sacred Celtic ford. This created a southern gateway to the town at Stockton Heath. The mixed Romano-British port of Warrington then existed for two hundred years under Roman control until some catastrophe occurred between 220AD and 290AD which caused commercial activities to come to an end and Roman coinage to be buried.

In 286AD the Roman admiral Carausius withdrew his allegiance to Rome and declared himself 'Sovereign of Britain' indicating the first major slip in Rome's control of these islands. He was murdered by his minister Allectus in 294AD who was in turn killed in 296AD and Emperor Constantius brought Britain back into the Roman alliance. Upon his death in 306AD his famous son Constantine was made Emperor.

The Romans declared Britain militarily independent in 410AD and it appears that the lands of the Mersey Valley were divided into four distinct areas. The Brigantes retained control of the north east. North west lands in Lancashire were separated (in legend) as 'Lancelot's Shire' under the Setantii tribe. The Wirral, Mersey Valley and parts of Cheshire and Staffordshire became Sir Gawain's and the Cornovii tribe. Most significantly, King Arthur controlled the lands of the Welsh/Britons or Deceangli which reached Walton and bordered the Mid Cheshire Ridge. The year would be about 515AD.

In 586AD the Anglo-Saxon invaders had taken control and Crida had founded Mercia (Cheshire). In 617AD, Bernicia and Deira united under King Edwin to form Northumbria, and the two great powers began the struggle for the Mersey Valley. For the next two hundred years south Warrington remained under Celtic control until Viking ships came sailing up the wide Mersey estuary in about 800AD bringing yet another race of invading settlers. Following various trials lasting a hundred years, a border fortification was sited by King Edward at Stockton Heath in 923AD.

By Medieval times the land containing Stockton Heath and Wilderspool belonged largely to Adam de Dutton (of Warburton) whose son Geoffrey de Dutton distinguished himself on the Third Crusade with King Richard the Lionheart, earning himself the emblem of the 'Saracen's Head' - the name of the pub now opposite the brewery on Wilderspool Causeway. Here written history begins with Adam owning much of the local area south of Warrington including Wilderspool, Stockton Heath, Warburton, Appleton and Appleton Thorn.

So to summarise, the present format of the area has changed greatly since the first settlers came in Prehistoric times. Forest clearance and building of settlements has destroyed the original identity of the land and road routes have moved accordingly to accommodate both. The Manchester Ship Canal and the earlier Runcorn to Latchford Canal both changed the area on which the Romans built their town. The line of the River Mersey has changed naturally since Prehistoric times and by the various new cuttings made which gradually drained the area of Wilderspool, formerly a marsh and collection of pools in Celtic times.

Considering how the Romans would have used the fresh water from the Cress brook and Lumb Brook at Stockton Heath, setting the precedent for fresh water supply and water power, it is tempting to identify either the former mill pond close by Alexander Park or the enigmatic Ackers Pit as the remains of the original Celtic 'Wilder's Pool'.

STOCKTON HEATH LAKE, THE FORMER MILL POND

The introduction of the Howley Weir and other river works after 1770AD further changed the form of the river, cutting off the ford and dramatically raising the water level up stream. More recently, many of the original river loops or 'eyes' east of Warrington have been removed by diversion and the building of the Manchester Ship Canal. During the turmoil of change, it is the ever-present River Mersey that has remained a constant shaping feature and it is to the river that we return again for our next episode in the chronology of former Warrington inhabitants.

THE GREAT MYSTERY OF THE 'STONE AGE' CANOES

For a period over a hundred years the residents of Warrington have been led to believe, by various archaeologists and authorities, that we are the inheritors of a legacy of canoes which date back over ten thousand years or more to the late Stone Age.

Modern dating techniques have now proved beyond doubt that this is simply not the case but news of this embarrassing discovery has never been fully released. Due to damage from climate, the surviving canoe fragments have also been placed into permanent storage to prevent further decay, the consequence of which is that museum visitors may never see these important finds, or, worse still, may not be made aware of their continued existence. This is the reason for my slightly more detailed approach in this section. This may be the last glimpse of these ancient treasures that the public will ever get.

All the canoes are in fact from the Celtic period and date from the arrival of Viking (Danish and Norse) settlers in the Mersey Valley just after 800AD and continue right into early Medieval times, until about 1200AD after the Norman invasion. The canoes may represent a distinct cultural period of four hundred years during which fishing and river travel became a primary economic factor in the region. Furthermore, not many people know that evidence for a staggering 14 canoes has been found so far to date.

Dug-out canoes were made in large numbers and seem to have been widely used in the rivers and meres of Cheshire. They would have provided the main means of communication between settlements separated by water, or built in the form of crannogs (on stilts in water or marsh land). Archaeologists have found the remains of many of these canoes, varying in length from six feet to over sixty feet (2m-20m) made from a single tree trunk, usually oak, and roughly shaped at either end. One of the Warrington canoes is unusual, being made from an elm tree. The inside would either be burnt or chipped out with an axe and the canoe bottom is left thicker than the sides to add to the stability and make it easier to right if it is capsized. So let's take a closer look at the canoes of Warrington. (See map on page 16 for positions of canoe finds)

1] The first was found in 1893 at the junction of the River Mersey with the Manchester Ship Canal at Walton Locks opposite Ellesmere Road. On a plan reporting this find, drawn by the museum photographer Mr C. Madeley in 1894, there is a note about 25 feet (7.9 m) east of the boat find which states *"Rough piles with brushwood behind seen at low water"*. This first boat has been carbon-dated to about 1190AD.

2] & 3] Two more were found at the new River Mersey diversion junction with the Old Mersey at Morley Common and Walton Lock in the same year (1894) accompanied by a bear and/or ox (urus) skull. The large complete canoe came from the cutting operations and was found upside down at a depth of over 18ft (5.7m) in sandy-silt accompanied by a grooved anchor stone, the other was then dredged up from a similar depth in the river. This complete canoe, measuring 12ft 4ins (3.9m) long x 2ft 10ins (85cm) wide x 15ins (43cm) deep, was examined in detail by Mr S. McGrail in 1978 and found to be made of oak. He classified it as a first rate personnel and bulky load carrier of canoe form, propelled by pole or paddle at good speeds. It gave a carbon-date of about 1020AD and it was this magnificent canoe that was on display in Warrington Museum until the 1980s when it was removed for storage.

4] The fourth canoe to come to light was found in 1908 just a little further upstream of the new Sainsbury's Homebase retail development, beyond Bridge Foot in an area then known as Mersey Way. It measured 10ft 3ins (3.2m) long x 2ft 8ins (80cm) wide x 1ft 7ins (48cm) deep. Mr. McGrail also examined this canoe in 1974 which remained only as a collection of fragments (some now lost) and found it to be oak. It carbon-dated to about 875AD.

Next came two canoes found in the 1920s.

5] This turned up on the 18th October 1922 on the same part of the Mersey as 4] but closer to Victoria Park. This boat is 11ft 6ins (3.6m) long 2ft 11 ins (88cm) wide and 20ins (80cm) deep and was found covered in 20 feet (6.3m) of river sand, mud and earth. Mr. G.A. Dunlop observed that it was found in association with two rows of Alder stakes forming a forerunner of the later medieval fish-yards or traps. This canoe was carbon-dated to about 1072AD by McGrail.

6] Was turned up by a dredger on the 22nd June 1929 back at the Morley Common/Walton Lock site on the River Mersey, only a few yards to the east of canoe number [2] (and possibly close to [3]). It is 11ft (3.4m) long x 2ft 4ins (70cm) wide x 22ins (85cm) deep and made of oak, carbon-dated by McGrail to about 958AD.

7] The stern end of canoe number seven turned up on the 23rd October 1930 while the foundations were being dug for the Westy Lane housing estate in Latchford, and gave some indication of how far the original course of the River Mersey once cut into the Latchford area (where the ancient ford may have been). The canoe was recovered from a depth of 2ft 6ins (75cm) in the remains of a completely silted up creek which once ran into the river Mersey through the former marsh land. This redundant creek had then become part of the ground over which the old road surface of Poacher's Lane had been laid.

8] *The Archaeology Of Warrington's Past,* by Shelagh Grealey, records a different OS map reference for canoe [7] at SJ 625875 where the Manor Industrial Estate is now situated, off Lower Wash Lane. This raises the possibility of two canoe finds in this area (or separated parts of the same canoe). McGrail examined two fragments from a canoe presumed to be the Latchford boat [7] or [8] and pronounced them as probably of late Saxon date comparable with the other carbon-dated canoes from Warrington.

9] The ninth canoe was dredged from the River Mersey west of the central pier of Walton Arches railway bridge on the 4th February 1931 back at the Morley Common site where canoes [2] [3] and [6] were found. It is likely that this canoe had been moved to this spot from the location of the other canoes by the previous two weeks dredging operations. It measured 13ft 6ins (4.3m) long by 2ft (60cm) wide but only survives as two warped fragments with three holes at one end, two containing wooden 'tree-nails' or pegs. G.A. Dunlop reported it once having a discernible 'beak' at the bow end and tool marks which have disappeared. It has been carbon-dated to about 1090AD.

10] A large fragment of a canoe was dredged from the River Mersey in the area of Westy Barn, to the left of Kingsway Bridge as you approach from the Latchford side, on the 8th April 1933, about 15ft (4.7m) out from the bank. This 'fragment' measured 9ft (2.8m) long x 2ft 4ins (70cm) wide x 5ins (13cm) deep and had a ridge running along its length about 4ins (10cm) thick and two vertical holes through the bottom of the boat. Only the bottom and sides of the canoe were recovered as the ends had been broken off square, probably by the dredger. Much of this canoe is now missing and surviving fragments are badly warped and have developed fungal decay although enough remains to identify it as late Saxon.

11] & 12] In McGrail's survey of Warrington canoes he records two that were found during the construction of a new power station at Warrington on the 18th December 1941 at OS map reference SJ 611877 which places them on the present site of the industrial estate at the Howley Weir end of Wharf Street. This is the same stretch of the Mersey where canoes [4] [5] [7] [8] and [10] have been found making a total of seven from this stretch of the river. One of these logboat canoes is recorded at 14ft (4.4m) long and the other as 12ft (3.8m) long, both identified by McGrail in 1974 as late Saxon although their remains are now entirely lost!

13] The thirteenth fragment is recorded in *The Archaeology of Warrington's Past, Gazetteer of Sites,* as being brought up by a Manchester Ship Canal dredger, and no location or date of the find are presently available. It may be reasonable to assume, however, that it originated in the region of the Walton Locks like canoes number [1] [2] [3] [6] and [9]

14] The spoon-shaped prow of a dug out canoe came to light on the Gateworth Sewerage Works site near Sankey Bridges on 25th February 1971. This measured about 4ft 6ins (135cm) long x 26ins (66cm) wide x 17ins (43cm) with a half-circle cross section, a raised rib cut across the floor and a protruding 'beak' on the prow cut through with a horizontal hole for tying the boat up. McGrail carbon-dated this boat to about 1000AD making it late Saxon or Anglo-Scandinavian (Viking) and, unusually, it is made from elm.

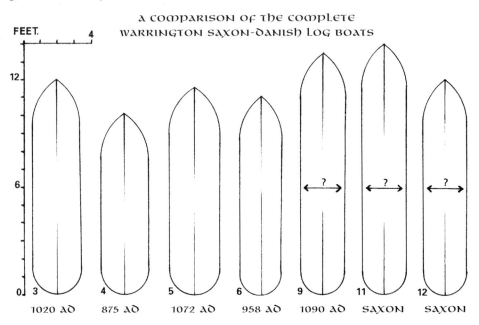

A COMPARISON OF THE COMPLETE WARRINGTON SAXON-DANISH LOG BOATS

No more canoe finds are recorded after 1971, although the above selection more than proves the point. It becomes fairly obvious from the carbon-dates and general observations recorded of the canoes found at Warrington that all are probably 'Anglo-Scandinavian' (Viking, Danish and Norse) from the late Saxon, Norman and early Medieval periods NOT the 'Stone Age' as has been assumed for the last hundred years. The entire collection of logboat canoes are Celtic and developed after the Danes reached Warrington.

This leads to the obvious conclusion that the majority of structures found with them must also date from the same period between 800AD and 1200AD just after the Norman influence reached the Mersey Valley and became established. Sadly most of this evidence will have been destroyed by navigational activities along the Mersey in the 17th and 18th centuries (1600 AD to 1800 AD).

Four canoes have been found on the old Mersey Banks within easy reach of the pile dwelling at Howley and four on the Mersey Banks at Ellesmere Road, Stockton Heath. So what about the two "Stone Age pile dwellings" or "lake villages" around which the canoes appear to cluster, the one at Howley and the other at Walton?

THE LONG HISTORY OF 'BRONZE AGE' CRANNOGS

For a considerable period of time many races, including the Celts, have produced collections of buildings suspended over water on stilts known together as 'crannogs' or 'pile dwellings'. These were artificial islands in the middle of lakes or marsh-land areas constructed from layers of different materials like peat, brushwood, logs, stones, straw, rushes and even animal remains.

These man made islands were then fortified with timber stockades, piers, trackways and living structures.

Crannogs are a common feature of the Irish Celtic culture, with over 200 sites identified in Ireland to date, but the Welsh and English Celts also followed in the earlier Bronze Age and Iron Age traditions of 'floating settlements'. Not all crannog structures are ancient as the extraordinary account given in Frank Murphy's book, *The Bog Irish,* demonstrates (Penguin 1988). This tells of an Englishman's visit to an Irish tribal dwelling in 1698AD where construction techniques matched prehistoric Celtic ones from 500BC! Canoe finds are common at crannog sites as they would have been the main means of communication between the crannog and the shore, as well as being used for all the commercial and industrial purposes related to water at that time, fishing, river transport and delivery of goods, passenger services, reed and rush gathering. Two potential crannog sites have been identified at Warrington over the last two hundred years.

CRANNOG NUMBER ONE

In October 1931, builders working on the new Howley sewer system 6 feet (2m) inside the gate of Peaks the Builders' yard at the end of Dutton Street, Howley, found a timber structure buried 9-10 feet (3.5 m) below the ground, dug out the timbers and gave them to a Mr Arthur Mounfield who owned a neighbouring business.

This site location now approximately equates to the Old Paper Works, Sports Ground and Canoe Club about 15 feet (4.5m) in on the North bank of the Mersey at the end of Howley Lane.

KINGSWAY BRIDGE VIEWED FROM THE APPROXIMATE LOCATION OF THE 'CRANNOG'

These timbers eventually found their way to Warrington Museum into the hands of Mr G.A. Dunlop, the curator, who identified them as the remains of an Iron Age crannog structure similar to those he had seen at Lochlee in Ayrshire, Meare in Somerset and Glastonbury, and dated them to the 'La Tene' period at about 100BC.

In a long article on local archaeological finds in 'The Examiner', the Warrington newspaper, on Saturday February 27th 1932, there appeared a summary of an address given by Mr Dunlop to The Warrington Society at a meeting in the Old Academy that Thursday (25th), which included the Howley crannog. In the article Mr Dunlop is quoted as saying that:

"One of the most important historical discoveries ever made in the borough of Warrington was the finding of the remains of a crannog or lake dwelling ...in Howley...

To my regret I only received information about this interesting find after the trench had been refilled, so no opportunity was given for taking measurements, descriptive notes or photographic records. When I saw the shaped and mortised pieces of oak I immediately recognised their crannog character, the worked timber from crannogs all over the British Isles are very similar in workmanship.

It is hardly necessary to remind you that the situation at Howley was well suited for a crannog, being as it was on the very edge of low-lying marshland liable to frequent floods. The round posts were on the North side of the trench in an upright position, the flat pieces of oak were lying flat, and the worked and other shaped pieces were sticking in the sand at various angles. Mr. Mounfield informs me that the timber was all found within a width of about 10 feet, the direction running approximately north and south."

In terms of any associated finds the account continues:

"The only object discovered with any connection with the crannog was a single tine of a stag's horn. Great numbers of similar fragments have been found in connection with lake dwellings in Britain. Whether it was ever used as a human implement is doubtful. It has the appearance of a rejected waste product. It is partly sawn, and then broken off. On the other hand, the polished condition and the marks on one face suggest it may have been used for currying leather, .."

Two other finds were discovered on this same site at the time, a medieval repoussee copper pendant in the shape of a fleur-de-lis, which is still on display in Warrington Museum, and a fragment of Elizabethan slipware pottery decorated in two colours of slip glaze. Nineteen mortised and worked pieces of timber and nineteen other unworked pieces from this crannog are also still stored at Warrington Museum.

As late as the 18th century the banks of the Mersey at this point were in use as a timber fishing wharf before the introduction of the Howley weir after 1770AD.

THE RIVER BANK IN 1783 SHOWING THE SITE OF THE 'CRANNOG'. NOTE THE THREE CHURCHES, OLD ST JAMES, LATCHFORD (L.), HOLY TRINITY (M.) AND ST ELPHIN'S PARISH CHURCH (R.)

The scanty evidence appears to indicate that the Viking period occupants of the nearby Mote Hill castle (formerly behind the Parish Church) simply developed a quay side at Howley to serve their town (along Church Street), a site which persisted in use to one degree or another over the next thousand years. This is further supported by the possible remains of medieval fish traps in the proximity of boats found further down-stream towards modern Warrington.

The fleur-de-lis pendant probably dates, not from the Elizabethan period, but from a time almost contemporary with the carbon-dates of the later Howley log boats (ie. after the Norman Invasion) and up to 1200AD, but the oak boats may have remained in use for well over a hundred years from the date of manufacture taking the site well into Medieval times.

We should not be too critical of Mr Dunlop's date of 'La Tene' 100 BC probably being a thousand years too early, as crannogs cover a period well over three thousand years and this is a fair mid-point date, all be it almost certainly wrong with hindsight. This site is a fishing wharf and not a crannog.

CRANNOG NUMBER TWO

When the Manchester Ship Canal was being constructed through Stockton Heath and Walton in the early 1890s, it became necessary to create a lock between the 'new cut' of the canal and the course of the old River Mersey. This took place at Walton with the creation of Walton Lock, and the Warrington Dock opposite Ellesmere Road, which used to curve behind Greenall's Wilderspool Brewery utilising the original course of the Victorian River Mersey. This lock is in a very poor state today.

It is interesting to note here that there are three all-concrete Manchester Ship Canal barges buried under the Greenall Brewery car park which now covers the old Mersey course (a few hundred yards south west of the traffic lights at the junction of Wilderspool Causeway and Loushers Lane). Five more of these, plus one in timber, lie abandoned and still visible today on the old Mersey course at Statham, Lymm, which is still fed by the Manchester Ship Canal.

UNUSUAL ABANDONED CONCRETE BARGES IN STATHAM (AND SHOWN FOLLOWING PAGE)

At the site of the Walton Lock two canoes and a crannog or 'pile dwelling' were unearthed by canal construction workers who notified the local archaeologist and historian Thomas May.

Unfortunately I cannot trace any original account of the discovery from the hand of Mr May, however another local historian and writer, H. Boscow, in his book *Warrington A Heritage* gives a credible account of what followed:

"During the excavations, innumerable piles were discovered in an irregular fashion for two hundred yards (190m). They were about six inches (15cm) thick and nine feet (2.8m) long, and were in two irregular lines, thirty feet (9.5m) apart. Between them were rows of stakes three inches (9 cm) thick and five feet (1.6 m) long, crossed in herring bone fashion. At the eastern end Mr May, who investigated, found oyster shells and bones ten feet (3.1 m) from the surface, and sticks and sedges in horizontal layers."

The other associated finds are described:

"The larger of the two canoes was found in the sandy silt close to the western end of the lock. The canoe itself was found upside down, over eighteen feet (5.7m) below the surface, and twenty yards (18.9m) from the northern bank of the river. An anchor stone, eighteen inches (45cm) square by nine inches (23cm) thick, with a groove round it for a rope, was also found. Charcoal and signs of a hearth were observed. The second canoe was dredged from a depth of eighteen feet (5.7m). All this evidence suggests a Pile Village dwelling once existed at this spot."

In his own account of this crannog site, photographer Mr C. Medeley gives the date of the finds as 28th March 1894 which may not be accurate as the first ship, the private yacht 'Norseman' belonging to Sam Platt, a Canal Company director, had already sailed up the "completed" Manchester Ship Canal on January 1st that year! Cheshire Sites and Monuments Record quotes Mr Medeley stating that:

"The logboat was 18ft (5.7 m) deep with the lower ends of the piles, with sand washed clay and silt over it, more than 20yds (18.9 m) from the north bank of the river. In the sand a little higher and a few yards west of the canoe, a perfect skull of the great wild Ox or Urus was found. Associated finds of a few water-worn fragments of Roman tile were also found at the same level as the boat, as well as an anchor stone, and, a few yards south of the canoe, charcoal and other signs of a hearth were noticed."

I have little doubt from the recorded evidence and location, that this site represents a true 'crannog' type dwelling, probably first created by ancient settlers in the area, possibly the Welsh Celtic Britons after which Walton is named. Human and animal remains, the hearth, burial mounds in the area, timber structures and the canoes all point to long term occupation and the use of the river in the local economy.

Some time around 1974, one of the owners of the allotments now on part of this site, on the spur of land to the west of Chester Road between the old Mersey and the new cut, found a fawn-coloured tapered bone net-making peg (or stone), about 6 ins (15cm) long, in the top soil. It is not clear if this was used here or brought in with the dredgings from the Mersey used as top soil, but it adds to the picture of an ancient fishing settlement in this area. Sadly the peg was broken and lost over the following years. The Roman tile-fragments may have 'travelled down stream' from the Roman port at Stockton Heath and represent a stray find. If this site was first created during the Roman occupation it was probably superceded in commercial importance by the later riverside developments at Howley.

If the structures examined by Thomas May date from the same period as the canoes, then the oldest date for the timber finds remaining in Victorian times would be after 825AD and the latest before 1245AD (allowing plus or minus 50 years on the dating) and we are back to the invasions of the Danes, Scandinavians, Norsemen and Vikings who would have conquered and taken over the site. It is their customs that provide the substance of our next investigation.

HODENING AND SOULING

There is little doubt that Viking ships came sailing up the Mersey, initially bringing terror and death. The first appearance of these invaders, higher up on the east coast of the Kingdom of Northumbria, is recorded in 787AD thus:

"First came three ships of Northmen out of Haerethaland (Denmark), and then the reve (sheriff) rode out to the place and would have driven them to the King's town because he knew not who they were, and they slew him." Abrupt, but there you are!

News of this event would have filtered down to Warrington quite quickly at the time and the town would have gradually made ready for yet another invasion. Initially this may have been intended as a bloody conquest but the archaeological evidence only shows how easily the Vikings settled down to become farmers and traders in the Mersey valley.

It has often been suggested that the suffix FORD in a name is derived from the Norse FIJORD (a river valley) so that the names Latchford, Orford, etc indicate most probably that the Vikings (Danes, Norse, Scandinavians etc) were there. They would have joined the existing population at Walton in the west as they came up the Mersey, and then occupied additional sites in Howley, Rixton and Warburton later in their invasions over land from Northumbria and the Pennines in the east. This process reached a peak about 910AD, with most of the Mersey Valley under Danelaw.

With a greater part of Northumbria overrun the Danes presented a big threat to the Mercians (Cheshire), so King Alfred and his children, King Edward the Elder (of Wessex) and his sister Queen Ethelfleda (of Mercia), combined to contain the menace by building a row of fortifications at Runcorn, Stockton Heath (Thelwall Chapel), Warburton and Manchester.

This secured the lands south of the Mersey for the next hundred years, but ultimately all became irrelevant when the Danish King Canute took the throne, making England united again but under the Danes, in 1020AD. These sea raiders, however, on acquiring land, settled down and became good husbandmen, eventually evolving a system of farming (that of open fields and common land) which became the basis of English country life beyond Domesday, right up to the industrial revolution (with its origins in the 18th century, 1700 AD to 1800 AD). The Danes remained virtually in complete control of England until the Normans came in 1066AD and it is during the Danish/Viking period that the next local tradition has its origins.

In ancient Scandinavian mythology the horse was a frequent sacrificial offering, at times of war, to the great god Odin. In *Notes and Queries,* seventh series, volume 11 (January to June 1891) the following, edited account, from about 1845 occurs:

"It was always the custom on Christmas Eve with the male farm servants from our parish, to go round in the evening from house to house with the hodening horse, which consisted of the imitation of a horse's head made of wood (or a horse skull), fixed on a stick about the length of a broom handle; the lower jaw of the head was made to open with hinges, a hole was made through the roof of the mouth, then another through the forehead coming out by the throat; through this was passed a cord attached to the lower jaw, which when pulled by the cord at the throat caused it to close and open; on the lower jaw, large-headed hobnails were driven in to form the teeth.

The strongest of the lads was selected for the horse; he stooped, supporting himself with the stick carrying the head; then he was covered with a horse cloth, decked with bridle and reins and mounted by one of his companions. As soon as house doors were opened 'the horse' would pull his strings incessantly and often shine a candle through the eye holes. How horrible it was to one who opened the door to see such a thing close to his eyes."

A similar custom was known to have existed during Celtic times, as the 7th century *Penitential* of Archbishop Theodore records penances for those: *"....who on the kalends of January clothe themselves with the skins of cattle and carry heads of animals"*. He also condemns the practice as "daemoniacum" (demonic) but this would not have prevented Pagan invaders from indulging in similar practices abandoned or kept hidden by the 'Christianised' Celts.

The festival of sacrifices to Odin at which the horse was the victim is the favoured source of the term HODENING, probably then known as ODENING, although the custom was also kept on All Soul's Day or Halloween at Northwich during the early 1900s, by children who knocked on doors and sang snatches of songs accompanied by a man dressed as a white horse.

This leads us nicely to the tradition which still prevailed in the village of Stockton Heath recorded by Herbert James Westbrook in his 1929 book *Stockton Heath and Immediate District*. While this book is largely a geographic survey of properties and ownership, Mr Westbrook does include information regarding the Stockton Heath 'Soulers' who included 'the horse' and appeared in his day at All Soul's Eve and for some time afterwards.

The text of the play which the 'Soulers' or 'Soul-cakers' performed was not written down in complete form, but rather 'larned' from one rural generation to the next, and only extracts are recorded in the book. The characters included 'Enter In', a bold and courageous youth who began with:

> I open the door and enter in,
> Whether we lose or whether we win,
> Whether we rise, stand or fall,
> We'll do our duty to please you all.

Apparently 'Enter In' could also be named 'Father Christmas' depending on the time of year of the play and was accompanied in Stockton Heath by the 'Hodening Horse'. This opening character and his 'horse' companion probably represent the oldest tradition.

Next to enter were 'Slasher', 'The Turkish Knight', 'St George' and 'The Doctor'. The play would then commence with 'St George' being challenged to armed combat by 'Slasher' and

'The Turkish Knight', who proclaim their deeds of valour. In the fight 'Slasher' falls and dies, followed by 'The Turkish Knight', who is wounded, revived by the doctor to fight again, and then is killed by 'St. George' (British knighthood). These characters are thought to have obvious Crusader origins in conflicts in Europe ('Slasher') and the Middle East ('The Turkish Knight').

Loud calls then follow for a doctor who can "raise dead men from the ground" and 'The Doctor' steps forth, declares his skill and concludes with the words:

> *This little bottle of alicampane*
> *Will raise dead men to walk the earth again.*

'Alicampane' or 'Elecampane' (Latin 'Inula Campana') was a medicine extract or tonic produced from a tall wild plant which was commonly cultivated over the centuries. It is also thought that 'The Doctor' is the last character in history to be added to the play as 'The Quack Doctor' of early Victorian times. The 'dead' characters duly rise and conclude with a song which repeats the last line:

> *We hope you will prove kind with your apples and strong beer,*
> *For we'll come no more a-souling until another year.*

And then indulge in the eating of 'soul-cakes' and the drinking of wine and strong beer. Younger followers were just given items of food.

Dr. J.C. Bridge writes on 'Some Cheshire Customs, Proverbs and Folk-Lore' in the book *Memorials of Old Cheshire*:

"The day after All Saints' Day is All Souls' Day. This was established as a festival of the Church about the tenth century and in the Middle Ages it was customary for persons dressed in black to traverse the street, ringing a bell at every corner and calling on all to join in prayer for the Souls in Purgatory, and to contribute towards the paying of Masses for them.

After the Reformation the demand for money was transformed into demands for liquid and solid refreshment by the 'Soulers'. Such is the origin of our 'Souling', and it seems probable, therefore, that 'Soulcakes' were not, at first, meant for consumption by the 'Soulers' themselves.

At Northwich, Tarporley, (Stockton Heath, Lymm, Daresbury, Leek) and other places, the Soulers are accompanied by one bearing an

MEIEVAL COURT MUMMERS (HARLEIAN M.S.)

imitation head of a horse, which snaps its jaws in an alarming manner. Thus 'Souling' has got grafted on to the Pagan custom of 'Hodening'. At Over, the 'Soulers' blacken their faces. This is a survival of the wearing of black already mentioned.

Souling seems to have been confined to, or at all events to have only survived, in the counties of Cheshire and Shropshire, though why this should be so it is difficult to say. It is also met with in the adjacent counties of Staffordshire and Lancashire, but only because it seems to have drifted over the borders."

Dr Bridge adds; *"the constant demand for apples and ale was to make a 'wassail bowl of lambswool' or hot spiced ale, with toast and roasted apples in it."*

And so it was that the 'otherworldly' Celtic 'cauldron of life' also continued to travel from house to house, giving life to the living and the dead, in peace time and at victory in war, pleasing both to the church and the people old and young, Pagan and Christian. The British 'St George' had overcome the threats of 'Slasher' and the 'Turks' in the Crusades. The land which had 'died' in winter would also 'rise' again, healed by THE 'Great Doctor' and His ancient 'Alicampane' tonic. Gawain had once again found his Holy Grail!

TUDOR CHRISTMAS FESTIVITIES FEATURING ST GEORGE, SLASHER, THE CHESHIRE CHAMPION (GIANT), FOUR FOOLS AND A TRADITIONAL 'HAIRY SOULER' AT HADDON HALL, DERBYSHIRE

It is also worthy of note that there is a direct and obvious link between 'Souling' and 'Mumming' which will be dealt with in more detail in the section in Book 3 of this series covering Daresbury.

TALES OF DRUIDS, HILLS AND GRYPHONS

The old London Bridge Inn clubroom, Stockton Heath, was used for a good many years by the local Ancient Order of Druids, from the turn of the twentieth century. Knowing the history of Stockton Heath and Appleton the choice of location, below an ancient hill and amongst Bronze Age burial mounds and sites, is understandable in an age when the green fields of Hill Cliffe, Appleton and Stretton remained largely undeveloped. Only very recently in this century have we lost this entire area under bricks and mortar.

William Hole's 1607 AD Map of Cheshire

shows four hills in the North Cheshire Ridge, starting next to Mere and terminating at Highcliff Hill. Robert Morden's map later the same century has developed this into six hills with a windmill on a small seventh between Bradley and Stretton Chapel.

WILLIAM HOLES MAP 1607

APPLETON HALL AND HILL CLIFFE ABOUT 1785

WARRINGTON LIBRARY

Highcliff Hill (Hill Cliffe) is shown with a large and small peak in both instances, a situation still remaining in the days of the Lyon Family of Appleton Hall who had paintings of the hall produced showing a high, sandstone peak and a lower hill in front with the estate flag pole on top. I believe that this smaller hill has now been quarried away as it once stood where the quarry is now on Quarry Lane.

The high sandstone peak is Hill Cliffe before the full development of the tree plantations now covering it and a second hill often shown to the south is on the golf course at Appleton with the Lyon family monument and reservoir now on top. The remaining hills string out to the last forested hill which must be the remains of the forest in the grounds of Mere Hall beyond High Legh.

THE SAME VIEW OF HILL CLIFFE FROM A DISTANCE

At the turn of the century the Chief Druid and leader of the organisation for all England was a man named Mr Allen from Warrington. A leading character in local affairs, he died in about 1920 shortly after his son Edwin had started an art shop on Buttermarket Street. The third Mr Allen still runs 'Edwin Allen's Art Shop' at the same location and still has his Grandfather's Druidic medal for service.

From the days of Edwin Allen comes the final mystery of Stockton Heath in the form of a mysterious double-sided cast-iron plate measuring about 10 ins (25cm) across and about 0.5in (1.5cm) thick, dug up in a garden at the top of Egerton Street during the 1960s. It features the image of a rampant heraldic Gryphon and writing which says "T. Green & Son Ltd - Leeds & London", and there is a small motto above the Gryphon's head which is unreadable but comprised 3 letters, 5 letters and 4 letters. It may have been hung from two anchor points which have broken off from the top sides as it is readable the right way round from both sides.

What was its use and where did it come from?

THREE VIEWS OF LUMB BROOK, THE SECOND JUNCTION ON THE A56 GRAPENHALL ROAD OUT OF VICTORIA SQUARE, STOCKTON HEATH. TOP 1879, MIDDLE 1969, BOTTOM 1999

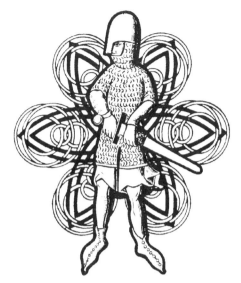

GRAPPENHALL

THELWALL

LYMM AND STATHAM

THE OLD POST OFFICE

SARAH GRIFFITHS

GRAPPENHALL IN THE 1880S

SARAH GRIFFITHS

GRAPPENHALL IN THE 1880S

SARAH GRIFFITHS

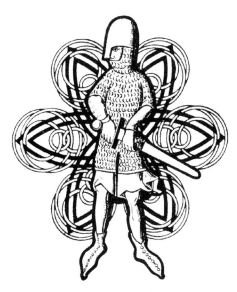

GRAPPENHALL

Now comes the time to depart from the comfort of Victoria Square, Stockton Heath, and set off on our journey into the south east quarter of Celtic Warrington. Take the A56 Grappenhall Road east out of Victoria Square and it will become apparent after about a mile that the road follows the course of the Bridgewater Canal to the right. Once the canal becomes visible it will not be long before the first small and narrow hump back bridge comes into view. This is 'Stanny Lunt Bridge' mentioned in the Colonel's Note Book which follows, and the Bronze Age burial mound complex was once here on the left.

Take Church Lane over Stanny Lunt Bridge and turn left into Grappenhall Village on the sharp right bend. The road will quickly give way to a Victorian cobbled street with St Wilfrid's church just ahead. There is space to park and explore from here.

Although there is little doubt that Grappenhall has very ancient origins, I have only been able to find two stray implements in the Grappenhall area dating from the Stone Age. This may indicate that the woodland here was only cleared from the Bronze Age onwards.

The first find is noted in the 'County Treasures Record' simply as a 'flint implement' and was presumably just a small flint tool found in 1932 on the east side of Clarence Road.

The second find was reported to myself by Dr Rodney Baguley of Cambridge (who is a keen local historian and archaeologist) who found a stone hammer-head some years ago holding open a farmer's gate in the extreme eastern part of Grappenhall bordering on Thelwall. This was given to Warrington Museum but is not presently on display.

The bulk of early finds in Grappenhall are from the Bronze Age or later and, included in this list, is the very early Bronze Age axe often recorded as "*....found under a log near the Dog and Dart Inn, Grappenhall*" probably in the 1850s. It is 5.25ins (13cm) long with an expanded cutting edge, narrow shaft and (when it was donated to Warrington Museum by Dr Robson in September 1860) it was found to be badly pittied and corroded. W.J. Varley considered it to be of Irish origin in his 1940 publication *Prehistoric Cheshire,* as is thought to be the case with all Bronze Age Implements of this kind so far found in our part of the Mersey Valley. It has been dated to about 1800BC+.

In the first published record of the find, *Prehistoric Man in Cheshire,* by W. Shone, in 1911, it is recorded as being found "beneath a bog" raising the possibility that it was a religious deposit or votive offering, a view further supported by the poor state of preservation. In *The Archaeology of Warrington's Past*, the location of the find is given south east of the traffic lights, at the junction of the A56 Chester Road and A50 Knutsford Road by Grappenhall Bridge No 1. This is the more likely find spot considering the pub referred to at this junction in 1860 was in fact called The Dog and Duck (the Dog and Dart standing now not being built at this time). This illustrates perfectly the often dubious nature of Victorian find recording and the degradation of information passed down to us over the years.

TALES FROM THE COLONEL'S NOTE BOOK

Heavy rain cascaded down the windows of Alan Leigh's office tucked away at the back of the Victorian bulk that is Warrington Museum (the first public museum in Britain). At my request

he had supplied me with a hip-height pile of paper work to wade through and I had only four hours to do it in.

Through clouded pages of white foolscap and official reports I found a tiny red canvas-effect pocket diary dated 1932 to 1933 with entries from the 18th November 1933 up to the 12th February 1935 lightly pencilled in. This was the actual note book carried in the top pocket of Colonel Brereton Fairclough as he

WARRINGTON MUSEUM C 1885

surveyed the discovery of strange burial mounds at Grappenhall by Mr Massey, assisted by Mr Leslie Armstrong and Mr Dunlop, the then curator of Warrington Museum (and others).

SARAH GRIFFITHS

REFERENCE LIBRARY, WARRINGTON MUSEUM C 1908

As I delicately turned the yellowed pages it was as if Howard Carter were telling me of the opening of Tutankhamun's tomb for the first time in his own words. Pale pencil sketches of the sites littered the pages from which I attempted to redraw and reappraise the evidence.

I copied all the entries, thanked Alan for his time (the last he was to spend with me before his retirement) and fought my way back home through the rain that day, a happy man.

I will present this lost discovery in the form in which it has been recorded - as a diary.

The burial ground at Grappenhall came to light from 1930 to 1934 during building work on the development of Euclid Avenue in close proximity to Stanney Lunt Bridge where stoney fields had been recorded over many centuries, hence the name STANNEY LUNT meaning STONY LAND. This name also appears in the area of this book at the burial grounds in

Grappenhall, a field comprising part of Wilderspool's Roman settlement, a burial field in Appleton and at two fields, formerly part of the 1765AD Barley Castle farmlands, called near and further STONEY FIELD.

To the best of my knowledge, the findings from archaeological activities at the Grappenhall Bronze Age cemetery and the associated reports and diagrams have never been made fully available, so it is my intention to present as complete a report here as I can using as much original material as possible. Sixty five years is a long time to wait for a report so crucial to ancient local history, so I feel entirely justified in 'leaking' the whole truth in unedited form.

Although the author of the notes compiled at the time does not give his name, internal evidence suggests it was compiled by Mr Dunlop and Mr Fairclough from his note book and I feel positive that they would approve of its final publication. Time then to travel back sixty eight years to 1931 and join them on their archaeological dig.

BRONZE AGE BURIAL MOUND AT GRAPPENHALL - 1931
(COMPILED FROM THE NOTE BOOK OF COLONEL B. FAIRCLOUGH)

On the 15th February, 1931, Mr J.J.Massey of CRANFORD, CHESTER ROAD, GRAPPENHALL whose house is about 200 yards East of STANNEY LUNT Bridge and North of the Bridgewater Canal reported to Mr Dunlop that sandstone blocks had been found in the field immediately North of his house (belonging to Wheelers' Farm) and that some were being removed. It was obvious that this required investigation.

Mr Massey showed us the place the next day 16th February, and Mr Dunlop picked up several pieces of a burial urn which were of the Bronze Age.

The site was probed and excavations began where the sandstone blocks had been disturbed and some removed. It soon became obvious that there had been a fire and that burnt bones were being encountered, also an occasional small piece of dark pottery was being uncovered.

Mr Leslie Armstrong was informed and he accompanied us the next day to the site and had no difficulty in recognising it as a Bronze Age cairn Burial. He carefully excavated from where we left off and found more bones and pieces of pottery and finally uncovered a flat stone about roughly 1ft 6ins square at 18ins below ground level with about 1.5ins of calcined bone on the top of it. A very careful examination of the ground failed to disclose anything else except a few more small pieces of pottery and bone remains.

In the meantime the probe showed that a large area was paved with sand stone blocks. The edge was found in a number of places and five trenches were dug to cut the outside diameter of the paving and long enough to show virgin ground outside that, the probe failed to disclose anything hard further out.

Trench No.1 dug at the extreme west 3ft deep exposed rough hewn sandstone blocks 26ft from the flat stone uncovered by Mr Armstrong the sandstone rose gradually as it approached towards the centre of the mound till it was 9ins below ground. Sizes of stones 12ins, 9ins and 11ins across, reddish sandy earth was used as filling between the stone, the whole being on whitish virgin sand, with reddish sand still lower. This trench ultimately was carried to the centre exposing the surface of the paving and photographed.(Photo now lost).

The remaining four trenches disclosed slightly different construction from No.1 but they agreed within themselves, highest stone surface 4.5ins below ground to 10ins below, lowest stone surface 1ft 9ins to 2ft 1ins below ground, the area between the lowest stone which was further from the centre than the highest stone, had rubble paving in white sand. There were not any signs of tool marks on any of the stones which were very irregular in shape.

Mr Massey reported also that he had come across sandstone blocks about 1ft 6ins below ground in his garden to the East of his house, he showed us a hole he had dug exposing some which measured across as follows 13ins, 12ins, 15ins, 12ins, 16ins, 12ins, 11ins, 12ins, 10ins and were irregularly placed. He stated he had removed a lot in making his garden. The formation seemed to extend eastwards inside the next garden. He was under the impression that a similar paved area existed here as is reported in the field to the North of his house.

13th FEBRUARY 1931: Mr. Dunlop and Col. Fairclough examine sandstone blocks 10ins to 16ins (25cm to 40cm) across. Mr Massey had removed these previously. Evidence of cairn.

15th FEBRUARY 1931: Mr Massey, "Cranford" reports sandstone blocks in field behind his house (Mr Wheeler Farm). Mr Dunlop and Col. Fairclough investigate, Mr Dunlop picks up fragments of a burial urn.

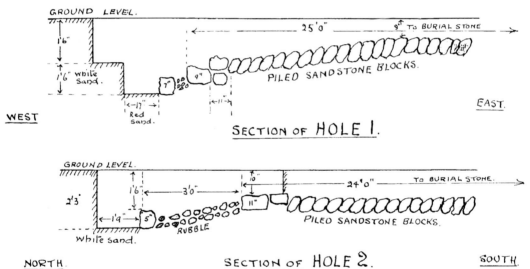

16th FEBRUARY 1931: The above gentlemen return, with tools and begin to dig. Charcoal and burnt bones found. Mr Massey reported finding a quantity of charcoal and burnt bones. Also a 'saddle' quern. Found in association with the above were the fragments of an urn of the beaker type.

17th FEBRUARY 1931: Mr L. Armstrong is informed and identifies site as Bronze Age (cairn). Trenches were dug to ascertain dimensions of cairn. Mound found to be circular. five trenches 3 foot wide, were dug at different points, to expose the edge, running towards the centre. Trench No.1 opened on west edge 3 feet deep, exposed rough hewn sandstone blocks. These extended continuously 26 feet from the centre (burial stone, see below). The blocks rose gradually towards the centre, until they were 9 ins below the level of the surface. The virgin sub-stratum was of white sand and the filling in between the blocks, red sandy soil

Stones - irregular in size and shape, and showed no signs of tool marks. Roughly about 9, 11 and 12 ins across. Stones in all trenches piled with a definate leaning towards the centre. Operation continued at highest point by Mr Armstrong and he discovered several more pieces of urn, and a layer of bones, on top of a flat stone about 18 ins square at 10 ins below the present level.

Work abandoned owing to the ground being required for farming purpose. Drawing and measurements Col B.Fairclough.

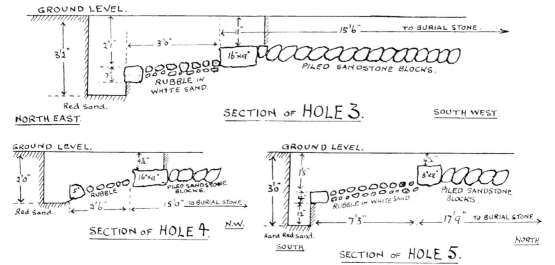

Author's Note: In his diary B. Fairclough records the finding of two layers of thick charcoal with *"many split pebble scrapers in the black bands"*. At this point the original diary accounts develop into small quantities of published results including a Newspaper article in the *Warrington Examiner* on Saturday 27th February 1932, which repeats most of the above, adding only that the first barrow dug was visible above ground as a 'slight mound'.

At this point an intriguing possibility comes to mind from Anne Ross who observes in her 1967 book *Pagan Celtic Britain* that the French/Gaulish god Taranis, the 'thunderer', was offered victims burned to death in wooden vessels. Was this just such a site? It is sad that it has been destroyed as Bronze Age cremation platforms are virtually unrecorded and yet cremations have obviously taken place.

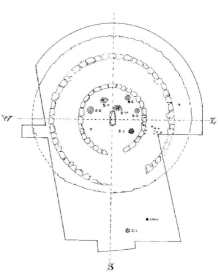

MAIN CAIRN MOUND EXCAVATED FEB 1931, FROM ABOVE AND IN CROSS SECTION

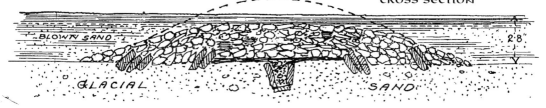

REPORT ON FINDING OF A CLAY VASE OF A SOFT BURNT NATURE AT
GRAPPENHALL, CHESHIRE.
PRESENT MR G.A. DUNLOP, MR HOWARD, BUILDER OF "LINDI" KNUTSFORD ROAD,
GRAPPENHALL AND COL.B. FAIRCLOUGH, MARCH 3RD 1932.

Acting on "information received" Mr Dunlop and Col B. Fairclough interviewed Mr Howard on March 3rd 1932 with regard to a reported find of a clay vase. Mr Howard took us to the rear of a house on the south side of the Grappenhall, Chester Road, about 300 yards east of Stanney Lunt Bridge, Grappenhall and said his men some time ago when excavating for sand, found a clay vase, lightly baked, brown in colour and similar in shape to this sketch:

About 8ins in diameter and about the same deep, it had been broken by the spade. There was no sandstone about, only sand, and he did not hear of any bones or anything else being found. He took the pieces to his yard and not considering them to be of any great interest no care was taken of them and he is unable to find them now, but promised to try and find them again. The vase was found about 3ft down. Plan of site of find as below marked 'X':

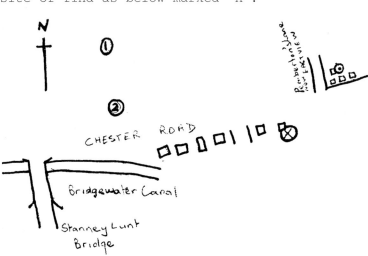

Mr Howard also stated that while excavating for the foundations for the pair of the most southerly cottages on the east side of PEMBERTON'S LANE now called EAST VIEW which runs north from the above CHESTER ROAD, GRAPPENHALL, he found a vast amount of loose sandstone blocks about 20ins long and less. They were about 8ins to a foot below ground level.

He does not remember seeing any bones or pottery in connection with the sandstone blocks, as it was about 5 years ago (1927 or 1929) since he built the cottages. Site marked 'O' in sketch above. The sandstone blocks only seemed to be over one area of about one cottage.

The above finds should be considered carefully to see if they have any relationship to the two Bronze Age burials recently found in the approximate positions marked '1' and '2' on the above sketch.

23rd FEBRUARY 1933
Mr Swinder informed me that very soon a sewer would be cut through Mr Massey's garden and also a road through the garden adjoining (to the east).

4th MARCH 1933: Went with Mr Armstrong, Col. Fairclough and T. Dale and commenced to dig to the east (3ft) of the point where the urn etc. had been discovered in the garden. On this day we discovered three urns; the first was broken into fragments (probably by a spade) but the others were removed from the sand almost intact. One was inverted. This had two pieces out of the rim and the circumstances of its removal indicate that it was in the same condition when it was buried. In association with the two unbroken urns were bones and flints. Two of the flints were found inside one urn when it was emptied later.

In addition to the above urn burials there were indications of a number, one or two, of burials without urns, also a small quantity of charcoal. Measurements were taken by Col. Fairclough and Mr Armstrong took photographs, both of an urn in site and of a section showing urnless burial. (Photo's now lost).

6th MARCH 1933 An area of approx. 20 square yards was combed out during the following week, but no more urns were found. NOTE: The urn numbered 3 showed, on being emptied, a greenish line in the colour of the bones. Mr Armstrong interprets this as indicating the presence of bronze (a pin) in the urn at the time of burial.

Archaeological records sum up as follows: *As Euclid Avenue was being cut in 1933, Armstrong returned with a Mr F. Dale and Mr D Ridyard of Warrington Museum and conducted a rescue excavation on another 'cairn' which appeared devoid of urns. From outside of it they recovered fragments of a food vessel and a stone mortar and pestle for pounding grain known as a 'saddle quern'. It was decided to excavate a larger part of the area outside the cairn and two large urns came to light about a foot below the surface, each containing human remains and surrounded by numerous other burials not contained in urns, of which five were noted.*

"NOTES ON A FIND OF BRONZE AGE URN BURIAL FIELD
AT GRAPPENHALL, CHESHIRE,
TO THE NORTH OF THE STOCKTON HEATH - THELWALL ROAD, TO THE NORTH EAST
OF THE STANNEY LUNT BRIDGE OVER THE BRIDGEWATER CANAL,
BETWEEN THE HOUSES 'CRANFORD' AND 'KANTARAH'. MARCH 3RD 1933.

The enterprise of Mr Massey of "Cranford", Grappenhall, in reporting in 1931 to Mr Dunlop, Curator of the Warrington Museum, of the unusual presence of sandstone blocks below ground on a bed of white sand in a field to the North of his house, led to an investigation.

An urn burial was found under a layer of sandstone blocks, circular, about 40feet diameter, 18ins thick and 9 to 11 inches below field level, the urn being badly broken into small pieces.

A further discovery of sandstone blocks in his own garden resulted in finding another urn (broken), under a saddle stone quern under the hedge between Cranford and Kantarah. A new road is being cut between the two houses and the maker, Mr. Howard, builder, of Grappenhall, kindly allowed further investigations. Three more urn burials not covered by sandstone, and also remains of a cremation, were found. One urn is badly broken, the two others are in good condition, though cracked about the rims. The contents have not yet been investigated.

One good flint knife 1ins long, seven eighths ins wide, three sixteenths ins thick, leaf shaped and burnt, was found among charcoal and bones near one urn. Several other flints (rough scappules) were found near another urn. A piece of sandstone saddle quern was found in association with the burials.

All the urns found were with the highest position about 14ins below the surface. The urns etc. are now in the Warrington Museum. The excavation was directed by Mr Leslie Armstrong assisted by Messrs. F.Dale, Massey, Ridyard and Colonel B. Fairclough.

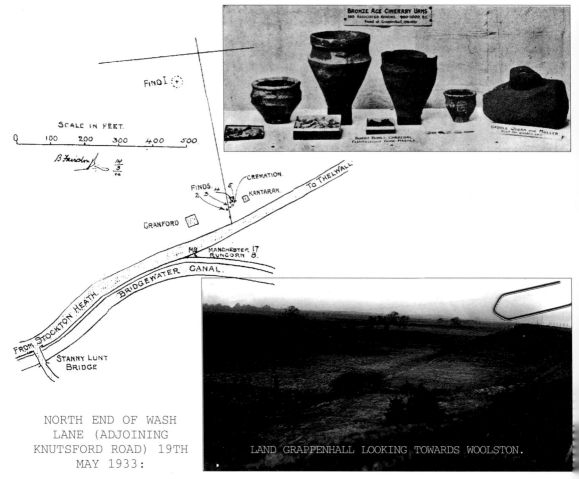

NORTH END OF WASH LANE (ADJOINING KNUTSFORD ROAD) 19TH MAY 1933:

Messrs Bolton and Lakin, Contractors, are cutting a sewer along WASH LANE and across KNUTSFORD ROAD to BROOK PLACE and beyond. At the end of WASH LANE a shaft is being sunk, 6 feet square.

At a depth of 7ft 6ins the workmen came upon a flat surface which proved to be a number of blocks of red sandstone laid down side by side. Apart from some yellowish clay found in their vicinity, there was no evidence of binding material, and they rested upon sand.

The blocks vary in length from 2 to 3 feet, but their width and thickness are roughly 10 to 11 inches respectively. There are indications of further stones, not yet uncovered. They were lying the long dimension in a direction approximately E-W. A line across the exposed ends runs approximately N-S. (A similar shaft is being sunk near this corner, near BROOK PLACE, but the foreman says that he has encountered nothing but sand and clay).

The section on both sides of the road shows:-
Road material: 1ft 6ins.
    River sand: 6 to 8ft (8 feet at BROOK PLACE).
       Clay:?

FURTHER REMARKS ON BLOCKS

There was a slab of stone resting across the ends of the pavement stones found below ground, its dimensions are 36 x 12 x 3inches. All stones except the above show tool marks on both sides, very clearly, without any signs of rubbing or wear.

Blocks. Pavement comes to an end 9 feet from manhole. Total length 12 feet (more probably 15 feet). The Resident Engineer, Mr Booth took two photographs; one from north end, showing side end exposure and one from above. (Photo's now lost).

Decided to have one stone brought to Museum yard with the object of ascertaining date from tool-markings. (Stone now lost).

Author's Note: Warrington Museum has Find No: 39'32, charred wood from the site which remains to be carbon dated, and Find No: 45'33.5, a bone needle.

29th AUGUST 1933: Account by Col.B. Fairclough.

16th OCTOBER 1933: Present Col.B. Fairclough and D.Ridyard. While laying a sewer up EUCLID AVENUE, GRAPPENHALL, running south from KNUTSFORD ROAD, at a point about 160 yards from the S. side of KNUTSFORD ROAD, a layer of sandstone was found to cross the line of the trench.

The length exposed, N and S, was 15 feet on the East side, and 9ft 2ins on the West side. The highest point of the sandstone was 15ins below grass level on either side of the trench. On standing in the trench, 20 feet north of the highest stones, and looking south, there shows a bank of dark, poor sand, about 14 ins below the surface. The band is about 6 ins thick. Where the sandstone appears it seems to take the place of the black bank, and as the bottom of the

MORRIS BROOK GRAPPENHALL NORTH SIDE M.S. CANAL 1935

sandstone is from 33 to 29 ins below the surface, at the sandstone highest point, the curve in the band is easily seen.

Author's Note: Diary accounts come to an end at this point and the rest of the investigations are assembled from fragmented archaeological reports compiled at a later date.

In 1934 further detailed investigations on the original large burial mound of 1930 revealed it contained a 'cyst' or stone burial chamber 4ft 6ins (1.4m) long and 18ins (45cm) wide lined with stone slabs but not containing any human remains. However, flint arrow heads were recovered from the grave and burnt bones and ashes found close beside it.

More secondary burials were also found added to the burial mound at later dates indicating long term use of the sacred site and the final diameter of the mound was confirmed at 36 feet (11.4m) ringed with large stones having a single gap which may have formed the entrance.

As with the mound at Euclid Avenue, a later 'urnfield' was found to surround the site which surrendered another burial urn, four flints and at least one cremation burial without an urn. More flints were recovered from the areas on and around the sites, some of exceptional quality.

During an aerial photographic survey of the Grappenhall area undertaken by N.J. Higham in 1986 another potential Bronze Age barrow was located in the form of a 'ring ditch' or 'crop mark' which appeared as a circle in a field on a photograph taken from the air. This feature is noted by Cheshire Sites And Monuments as: "possibly a ploughed out round barrow" and is located behind Oak House near Pickerings Bridge off Weaste Lane which heads out of Grappenhall village in the direction of Lymm.

16th NOVEMBER 1998:
Bringing matters right up to date, it occurred to me that, despite a time lapse of 65 years, some of the sandstone blocks from the burial mounds around 'Cranford' and 'Kantarah' may still exist as part of the gardens of either house so a field survey was undertaken.

A house has been added between the two, next door to 'Cranford',

EUCLID AVENUE AND MOUND SITE 1998.

and is currently owned by Mr Johnny Davis who is aware of the prior existence of the mounds. He assures me that nothing has been found since his house was constructed by Mr Massey in the late 1930s or since Cranford's recent rescue from dereliction; now renovated in a modern style.

He has, however, still got a small front rockery in which we could discern a number of apparently 'hammered' sandstone blocks of very ancient form and 'Kantarah' also has similar blocks mixed in with rockery formations in the front garden. Sadly these represent the only possible remains of a very rare and valuable 3000+ year old cremation site and barrow cemetery lost to history but for the sake of 65 years!

A LAND OF DITCH AND MOUND, FOREST AND CHURCH

The discovery of these large burial grounds at Grappenhall (and other similar finds in Cheshire and the Mersey Valley) suggest settlement from Ireland, Yorkshire and the Pennines from about 2000BC up to the Roman invasions starting in 55BC and almost continuous between these dates. However, no Roman activity has yet been noted directly in the Grappenhall area, only lower down on roads leading to and from the river crossings at Latchford and Stockton Heath.

RAY ALLCOCK COLLECTION

WATERCOLOUR OF THE VILLAGE C 1860-1880

The name GRAPPENHALL is thought to originate from the Old English GROP, GREP or GREPE meaning a 'ditch or drain' combined with the word HALH meaning an 'area of flat land by the side of a river'. In this case the GROP's may have been the ditches which surrounded the many Bronze Age mounds in the area and the HALH possibly the Mersey Eyes between Latchford and Thelwall. These were probably used for farming by the early inhabitants of the village which sits on the crest of a gentle hillside and would have had woodland beyond it into Cheshire even in Medieval times.

A less likely origin for the name still worthy of mention is the word GRAPPE which was thought to be derived from a GRAPE or GROPUS otherwise known as an 'iron hook'!

The name GROPENHOLE appears in the Domesday survey of 1086AD and GROPENHALE in *The County Court, City Court and Eyre Rolls of Chester for 1288AD*. The

Taxatio Ecclesiastica of 1291AD and a painted heraldic panel in the church vestry also feature the name GROPENHALE with the same spelling, which has remained unaltered for a thousand years or more. The Domesday entry reads:

"Osbern Fitz-Tesson owns Gropenhole and Edward of him. The same and Dot were two free men held it as two manors. There is one hide and half a virgate of land rateable to the Gelt. The land is two caracutes, one half of which is the desmesne, and there are two serfs, one villein and three bordars. There is a wood one league long and forty perches broad. There are two bays. In King Edward's time it was worth five shillings. It was waste."

It can be deduced from the above entry that the "two manors" probably comprised Latchford Manor and Grappenhall Manor. The "three bordars" were three cottages standing at that time and most of the area beyond Grappenhall village was deer forest. The "two bays" were 'V' shaped enclosures made from the boughs of trees into which hunted deer could be driven to be speared or killed by hunting dogs.

Of the two Saxon landowners, Edward and Dot, at least one would probably have lived close by the site of the present church and the other probably somewhere closer to Latchford.

There is a traditional list of village rectors displayed in the church which begins in 1189AD with Robert de Gropenhale and continues with 1258AD John de Gropenhale, then 1294AD Richard Roulesham, 1302AD Williemus de Rodyerd, 1311AD Richard Fitz William de Doncaster, 1346AD Roger de Shipbroke, 1377AD William Steresacre, 1423AD William de Hethe (of Stockton 'Hethe'), 1450AD Thomas Byrom, and 1466AD Robert Stanley. The list carries on right up to date but is known not to be completely accurate.

Sir Peter Leicester states that the church of Grappenhall was a rectory in the time of King Henry III (1216AD to 1272AD) and a charter of 1334AD records the erection of a chantry chapel added to the south side of the already existing structure of Grappenhall Church, which was dedicated to Sir William Fitz William Boydell (Knight) and his family.

A survey of land in Grappenhall undertaken by Sir Peter Legh in 1465AD shows the basic village to be in existence and refers to 'Catriche Lane', 'Lumme Brook', Midilhurste', 'Marfenne Medo' and 'Stanylandys'. Features of great interest which have dissappeared but are listed in the survey included Grappenhall Cross, the Fountain of St Leonard The Abbot and two water mills, the 'Herr' (higher) and 'Lagher' (lower). These were probably at either end of the Parish and presumably powered by the two brooks of the Parish. A very important 'scratch drawing' of the church and the village cross exists in shallow outline on the lid of the pre-Norman church chest discussed later under the section on the village church of St Wilfrid.

Some time in the late 1920s a carved base described as "possibly the socket of a cross shaft" was recorded in *The Transactions of The Lancashire and Cheshire Antiquarian Society* XLVII for 1930-31. It was "found behind the Old Rectory" which stands immediately to the east of the church (now an old peoples' home). My own feelings are that this find is actually the medieval 'stoup' discussed in the next section on the church and which has often been misidentified as a small cross base.

Local historian Dr Baguley also informs me that a 'Celtic style' silver cloak clasp has recently been found by a local resident in the area of the village but no further details are presently available.

In later years Grappenhall mainly developed along the cobbled Church Street, with thatched cottages on both sides and a village green where the Parr Arms public house now stands. Mixed in with these cottages were a butcher's shop, general stores, post office and smithy, at the opposite end to the church, near Broad Lane, and owned by George Fairhurst who placed his initials 'G.F.' on the ironwork he produced for the church doors. All the thatche cottages have now gone as those on the south side of the road were demolished over a 160 years ago to build the hall opposite the Parr Arms and the few remaining cottages (including the post office) were demolished or re-roofed at least fifty years ago in the 1940s. Some photographs and paintings of the original quaint Cheshire village do still exist but it would have been far better if the original village had survived! One set of

C.1855AD

thatched cottages were demolished to build the tarmac play ground of the present infant school.

A LAND OF SAINTS AND KNIGHTS, CARVINGS AND CATS

There is little doubt that a church stood on the site of the present Church of St Wilfrid in Saxon times, possibly as long ago as the missionary activities of St Chad in Mercia during the seventh century (600AD to 700AD).

Interestingly, St. Wilfrid (born 634AD), represented the Roman Church at the Synod Of Whitby at which St Chad represented the Celtic Church and both saints were tutored at Lindisfarne during the same period. It appears however, that St Wilfrid was not entirely satisfied with the ethos of Celtic Christianity and left Lindisfarne to study at Canterbury, going on to Rome in 654AD where he studied under St Boniface, Secretary to Pope Martin.

By 660AD he had returned to Britain to become the Abbot of Ripon at the request of Aldfrith of Northumbria (son of King Oswiu). From this position he attended the Synod Of Whitby in 664AD and won the day in favour of the Roman Church. Aldfrith then appointed him Bishop of York but Wilfrid insisted on being consecrated in Compeigne, France, by twelve Roman-Frankish Bishops and returned to find St Chad appointed as Bishop by King Oswiu in his absence.

This was resolved in 669AD when St Theodore, Archbishop of Canterbury, ruled that St Chad had been consecrated as Bishop by mistake (as one already existed) and St Wilfrid was restored to his post at York.

Following political and geographic changes in Northumbria St Wilfrid fell out of favour with the Northumbrian Kings and, after many adventures, found himself exiled to his monastery at Ripon and in charge of the Mercian diocese of Hexham. It was while visiting the monasteries of Mercia that he died in about 709AD or 710AD and was buried at his beloved monastery at Ripon. The church at Grappenhall is one of those dedicated to him.

The 'scratch drawing' of the church and cross on the Parish Chest is the oldest evidence of the church to come to light from this period and I reproduce a fair copy of it here. This shows what appears to be a timber Anglo-Saxon church building with a raised, sloping roof topped by a small cross and, just next to this, a small extension wing beyond which stands a (possibly Celtic) cross set in a socket stone. If the view is looking north then the cross stood in the grounds of the Old Vicarage, if looking south (which I favour) it shows the cross on the old village green (now under the Parr Arms) and the raised roof with the cross would have been roughly over the present chancel where the later Norman stone tower was said to have stood.

The consequence of this discovery also dates the main timber and clasps of the chest to a period before the Normans rebuilt the church in stone and, therefore, probably to the Saxon/Danish period of local history between 900AD and 1100AD. After 1120AD chests began to take on a more traditional form and it is known that oak logs were used for a

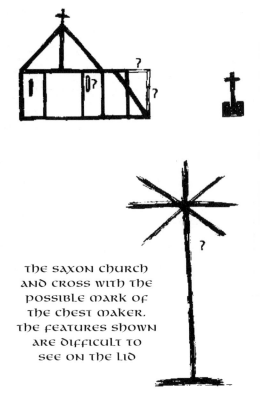

THE SAXON CHURCH AND CROSS WITH THE POSSIBLE MARK OF THE CHEST MAKER. THE FEATURES SHOWN ARE DIFFICULT TO SEE ON THE LID

great many purposes by the pre-Norman cultures including the making of chests. The chest was returned by Warrington Museum in 1939, where it had been an exhibit for sixty five years, and has had three hinges added by the village black-smith in the late nineteenth century (about 1880) and only one of the original hinges remains. It measures 5 ft 6ins (1.7m) long and 12 x 13 ins (30 x 32.5cm) in section with a cavity about 2 ft long (60cm) by 8 x 8 ins (20 x 20cm) and was probably used to keep communion vessels and documents in, the three keys being kept by the Minister and two Wardens in later times.

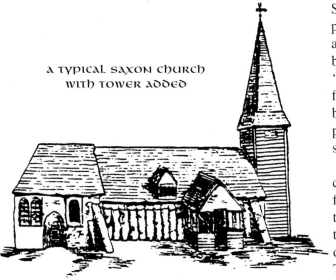

A TYPICAL SAXON CHURCH WITH TOWER ADDED

It has often been suggested that the Saxon church had a tower over the present chancel and a semicircular apse area where the altar now stands but this is not supported by the 'scratch drawing' on the chest or finds uncovered during various building phases. Instead of a tower it probably only had a raised roof as shown on the drawing.

Next in the line of discoveries comes the Saxon font which was found lying three feet (90cm) under the ground near the second pillar at the south west end of the church during restorations in March 1873. The font is damaged where it once

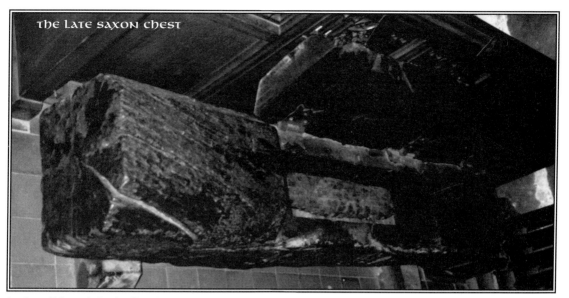

the Late Saxon chest

had a lid and lock fitted to stop people pinching the holy water used for baptisms. This prohibition, introduced in 1236AD and removed in the Elizabethan period, indicates that the font was probably in use up to the outbreak of the Civil War. It was probably buried between 1643AD and 1651 AD to stop Cromwell's men from breaking it up after their victories at Stockton Heath (1643AD), Warrington (1648AD) and Warrington Bridge (1651AD).

No traces of the original base have been found and the lead lining has been added after it was rediscovered in 1873, but the design of arches carved on it indicate a date before 1070AD for the original stone basin as they are executed in an art style contemporary with that of the famous Bayeux Tapestry. Adult baptisms were conducted with the person standing in the font, which was originally sited close to floor level, and water being poured over them, hence the fact that Saxon fonts were made square and only placed on token bases.

Looking at the dedication of the church to St Wilfrid, much activity was under way with regard to the establishment of this saint after his relics were taken from his grave at Ripon in Yorkshire to Canterbury by Archbishop Odo in 958AD, another attempt to make Canterbury the supreme Christian centre over York.

The next hundred years or so saw several churches in this area collecting dedications to St Wilfrid and Grappenhall probably became St Wilfrid's when it was rebuilt in stone during secure and prosperous times in Cheshire under the rule of Hugh Lupus (the Norman 'Wolf' also known to his friends as 'Hugh The Fat', nephew of William the Conqueror) who died in 1107AD. This fits the evidence so far gathered well, and supports a church building phase in stone between 1070AD and 1100AD. No church is recorded in the Domesday survey completed in 1087AD so an almost exact date of 1097AD (±10 years) can be arrived at for the building of the stone Norman church of St Wilfrid's at Grappenhall.

William Beamont observed in 1873 that Grappenhall used to hold their Wakes on the last Sunday of October to coincide as near as possible to the original date for the festival of St Wilfrid on the 12th October. He then observed: *"But neither the 12th October nor any later day in the same month will suit the orientation of the church, which agrees more nearly with the 15th April or the 29th August."*

The April date coincides only with the Roman spring festival of Venus but the August date is St John the Baptists day, martyred by beheading, and said to be the Saint of the Knights Templar and earlier Celtic Christians who both had a certain obsession with severed heads (often from which 'female spring life' blossomed)! From the abundance of Norman and Medieval knightly evidence on the site this connection is not suprising.

During the building excavations of 1873 it was discovered that the north aisle wall rests on the original Norman foundations for the former external north wall. Further evidence for the Norman church are the five gargoyles still in place over the first three arches of the south aisle (in front of the present main front door as you enter).

It has often been said that these appear 'Celtic' in style but closer and more exact examination reveals late Saxon and more probably early Norman influences dating them to the period of rebuilding in stone under the Normans at about 1097AD. The stone masons were probably local Celts working to reproduce Norman designs.

These are not the only gargoyles attached to the building. There are eight gargoyles below the battlements on the tower which appear to date from two time periods. The human heads on the north, east and south sides appear to be from the Saxon/Norman church while the grotesque

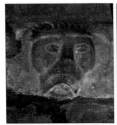    

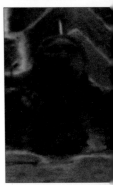

creatures on the four corners and the west side appear to be from the much later Tudor church, the tower of which was first constructed between 1529 AD and 1539 AD (and revised to its present form after 1850).

Two smaller heads were added lower down the west side of the tower, either side of the window over the tower door, both of which appear Tudor or later. The left head appears to be a 'green man' or similar, spewing the characteristic 'ridges' of foliage from the mouth (see photograph).

One stray Saxon/Norman head of human form exists lower down on the north side above the roof marks (see photograph), marks which denote the former school house building which was pulled down in 1846 and replaced by the present village school.

At the time of the Norman church it is known that the church had two entrances, the main one of which probably faced north from the base of the tower

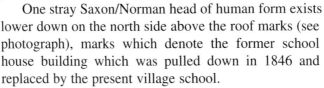
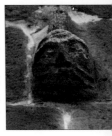

(probably where the Saxon entrance also stood). There was an ancient footpath connecting Grappenhall with Thelwall Lane, via Bradshaw Lane, which virtually came to this door, and only fell into disuse after it was cut across by the Bridgewater Canal between 1759AD and 1776AD.

On the reverse side of the buttress, to the left of the present south facing front door, there is a badly worn block of Cheshire sandstone, which has an ark and about four lines still visibly cut into the surface. This represents the poorly preserved remains of one of only five scratch-clocks or 'Mass Clocks' surviving in Cheshire and is obviously not in its original position as it cannot be seen. It would have been at its present height and by the south priest's door, but it worked like a sundial on the same south wall as the gargoyles inside the church are now. A downward curved spike, or 'gnomon', of some kind would have come out from between the mortar above the centre of the stone and cast accurate shadows down the block along the lines which denote the seven 'Canonical Hours' of Matins, Prime (6am), Tierce (9am), Sext (noon), Nones (3pm), Vespers (evensong) and Compline (from the latin 'completorium' - completion of services). Scratch dials are of Saxon origin and only fell out of use in Tudor times with the invention of clocks. This example is probably Norman.

I have been reliably informed that it has long been thought that an 'ossuary' or 'bones chamber' once existed under the raised cemetery platform in front of the south side of the church, deeper than the level of the existing graves and instead of the traditional church 'crypt'. The favoured location is behind the stocks opposite the present front door where slight discrepancies in the masonry of the outer graveyard retaining wall may indicate a former entrance. A badly worn date inscription at the bottom of this wall, about half way down its length and by the road, used to read 1612AD.

This ossuary chamber was used for victims of the plague (Black Death 1349AD and the Plague which hit Warrington in 1665AD) and apparently comprised a relatively small chamber accessible from above at ground level or from the road. These external ossuary chambers are a feature of many continental churches and this one may well be of Medieval origin, built in a continental French style. It probably still lies intact under the southern cemetery platform filled with bones gathered together in ages past.

Back inside the church, on the wall immediately to the left of the chancel, just next to the right side of the nativity window on the north east wall, there are three objects of interest; two sandstone 'shelves' set into the wall and a small white octagonal 'bowl' of chalky stone. It is thought that the pre-reformation chapel of the Barry family once stood here.

The octagonal bowl is identified as a 14th century 'stoup' used to hold Holy Water with which the congregation crossed and blessed themselves as they entered the church. It is significant that it is made from chalky 'Caen stone' found in Normandy and may have been a personal possession of the Boydell family who had family ties in France before the Norman invasion. It is decorated with eight different geometric shapes including squares, circles and triangles and recent opinion places its age older than originally thought, in the Norman period of 1070AD to 1200AD.

It was found in the late 1920s by Mr Houghton Morrey of Carr House Farm, who was engaged in levelling a rubbish tip behind the rectory at the time, and it has often been wrongly identified as a cross base. Sloping details carved inside the bowl, between sides and base, rule out the possibility that it was intended as a 'socket'. The sides would be vertical and at ninety degrees to the base had it ever been designed for use as a base.

The upper shelf with a flat top and downward pointing pyramidal base is a 'credence' or 'side table' used by a priest requiring extra space for items during mass and is probably Medieval in origin although

difficult to date. Some authorities place it

earlier as part of the Norman church.

The lower shelf, with a depression in the top, is a 'piscina' or 'washing basin' for the priest to wash his hands and communion vessels in, and it may be older than the 'credence'. The presence of both in this part of the church may indicate a 'missing side altar', which once stood below the present nativity window against the north east wall, although they may also have been moved here from the east end of the earlier church during the rebuilding of 1529AD.

LEGENDS WRITTEN IN GLASS

There is a magnificent 'jigsaw puzzle' of Medieval glass images, which have been assembled in the furthest window from the present main front door but on the same wall, along the south side of the church where the Boydell Chapel once stood. This glass is thought to date from about 1316AD to 1318AD. The window as it exists today was created during the reconstruction of 1850 to 1851 when this corner of the church was first built and the Medieval glass remaining in the church was collected together. Extra features were added to fill gaps and it was releaded in 1964. There was a local legend, recently confirmed, that the rest of the Medieval glass from the church was transported to York Minster and refitted there, but which glass this is remains to be discovered.

The 'Randle Holmes Manuscript' (MS 2151 p.78) in the British Museum contains a sketch of a window from the Boydell Chapel showing a knight and his lady kneeling with the Norman-French motto below: *"Priez pour Sire William Boydell et Nicol sa compagne sil vous plest"*, literally translated this says: *"Please pray for Sir William Boydell and his companion, Nicol"*.

Moving up the window remaining at St Wilfrid's, the surviving fragments show:
- St. Peter and his keys and a pilgrim to the shrine of St James (wearing an escallop shell in his hat but without a halo), in the left hand light.
- St. John the Baptist in his camel hair coat, with 'the Lamb of God', is in the centre light (his crosier is an addition from 1851).
- St. Thomas above St Bartholomew (who holds a flaying knife and his own skin(!) to show how he was martyred), is in the right hand light.
- In the upper left quatrefoil St Philip.

- In the upper right quatrefoil St Mary Magdalene with her alabaster box to anoint the feet of Jesus.

- The figure in the upper left hand corner of the window remains a mystery. It could be Jacob gazing at a now missing ladder but it would be nice to think of him as a romantic depiction of St Wilfrid himself still pointing his church-goers towards heaven.

This represents all the Medieval glass which is known to exist, except for some later 15th and 16th century fragments in Warrington Museum, and one large fragment of a lady displayed in an illuminated glass case mounted on the inside wall by the tower. She

is often wrongly judged to be St Mary Magdalene who would not be depicted with blond hair and royal ermine robes! So who is she?

This figure is almost certainly St Barbara who was supposed to have lived between 235AD and 313AD somewhere in the Roman Empire. Legend has it that she was shut up in a tower by her father (Dioscurus) to protect her from the many suitors who sought her great beauty. In time she became a Christian and was tortured and killed on the orders of her anti-Christian father who was then reduced to ashes by a lightning bolt. As a result she became the Patron Saint protecting against lightning strike, fire, thunder storms and sudden death. Her emblem (which she often holds) is the tower in which she was imprisoned.

It is thought that St Wilfrid's has had a prominent 'tower' or 'raised roof' feature of some kind almost from its first construction. It was believed, in later times, that ringing church tower bells could break up hail and thunder storms, a custom still pursued in France up to forty years ago if a hail storm threatened the vines. A traditional English verse contains the lines: "Men's death I tell, By doleful knell. Lightning and thunder, I break asunder. On Sabbath all, To church I call".

The figure of St Barbara in St Wilfrid's is simply pronouncing a protective blessing on church-goers with her hands.

In history her story appears to be religious fiction and only became known in the 7th century reaching most popularity as a cult in the ninth century which fits well with the Saxon and Norman aspects of Grappenhall church. Her feast day is December 4th and she has become the patron saint of military gunners and miners. This fair, blonde-haired depiction of St Barbara may also live on as one of the original inspirations for Lewis Carroll's 'Alice' character in *Alice in Wonderland* (who was in reality Alice Liddell, later Mrs Alice Hargreaves. More in Book 3 under Daresbury).

In its early days the church boasted the possession of more stained glass than any other in the County of Chester and still has an amazing collection of unusual early and later windows today.

'WE ARE DUST AND SHADOW' - MYSTERIOUS MEDIEVAL FRENCH KNIGHTS

The final Medieval item connected with the Boydell family, displayed in the church, lies under an arch to the left of the main altar in the sanctuary - but is possibly the greatest mystery of all. This is the carved stone knight known as 'The Boydell Effigy'. I will try to solve the mystery here.

The effigy has a long and varied history. At some point (possibly during the building of the north isle in 1529AD) it was found buried in the churchyard and was brought into the church where it remained until the building of the vestry in 1851. Being in a very broken and dilapidated state by this date it was removed to the Geological Room of Warrington Museum. In 1875, under instruction from the church, the effigy was placed with a local sculptor for restoration, the details were recarved, missing parts replaced and the finished work returned to the church and placed at its present location with the dedication panel which reads: "*Within the wall of this church rests the body of Sir William Fitz William le Boydell, Knight, who died about AD MCCLXXV (1275AD). This, the monumental effigy, was restored and placed here AD MDCCCLXXV (1875AD).*"

At this point archaeological problems abound. During all the construction work which has taken place on the site of St Wilfrid's church (inside and out), no knightly burial has ever been recorded, no characteristic stone coffin over which this effigy would have been placed has been located, as well as no finds of armour or weapons customarily buried with knights. Most of the burials within the church have simply been noted as male skeletons, with one female found somewhere in the chancel area. If it still exists the knight's burial site remains to be located.

The recarving involved the chain mail, leg greaves, surcoat, sword pommel, parts of the head, face, arm, legs and feet destroying the original character of the effigy. Only the base

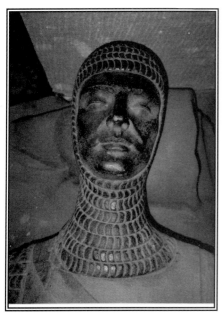

helmet, shield and animal under the feet remain original and untouched.

All considered the effigy shows no signs of being a knight of 1275 AD but rather one of about 1350 AD or later and traces of a crown can just be seen either side of the original helmet indicating Royal service. The crossed legs are often considered a sign of service on a Crusade and the animal under the feet is thought to have been a dog (which can be a sign of a Templar Knight) or a lion (sign of service to the Crown). The last Crusade took place under Louis IX of France ending in 1272AD and the order of Knights Templar was dissolved in Britain (but not Scotland) by 1350AD further adding to the confusion in identifying this knight.

One theory suggests that the effigy was carved during a later period in the style of armour then current - but heraldic sculpture was a fine art during Medieval times and historic detail was usually strictly adhered to, intended to communicate exactly the period, rank and circumstances of the deceased knight.

From 1337AD King Edward III went to war with France, a war known as the 'Hundred Year's War', which only petered out in 1453AD. Major battles included 'Sluys' in the English Channel in 1340AD, 'Crecy' 1346AD, 'Poitiers' 1356AD, 'Agincourt' 1415AD and the final battle of 'Castillion' 1453AD. This raises the questions: for whom did the originally Norman/French family of Boydell fight at this time (if at all), and at which battles? If the crown on the helmet of the effigy indicates service under a Royal then only two battles are a possibility; 'Crecy' under The Black Prince (who also wore a similar crown) or 'Agincourt' under Henry V.

From the available evidence it would appear that the effigy is that of a member of the early Boydell family, depicted wearing armour of the 1350AD period, having served under The Black Prince and for Edward III who declared himself king of Britain and France in 1340AD thus solving the Boydell's problems of ancient loyalty to France.

In 1346AD Templar knights were still permitted in Britain (although not in France) and would have fought alongside Edward III's newly formed 'Order of the Garter' at Crecy in 1346AD. The Boydell family were using the characteristic 'cross patee' of the Templars (in yellow on a plain green field) as their arms at this time and Templars dying during this later period were buried only in cloth robes. These would have decayed long ago leaving the only remaining knightly clue as the legs of the skeleton crossed at burial and easily missed when skeletons are found.

This narrows the effigy down to one of two Boydells. Sir William Boydell (Knight), Lord of Dodleston, still lived in 1340AD but used the 'cross patee' as his coat of arms and Robert le Boydell of Catterich in Grappenhall, who died around

1367AD, having served the Earl Of Stafford in 1347AD. It is possible that he was the Boydell who first had three 'pentagonal stars' on a 'bar' as his coat of arms which developed into the Grappenhall Boydell arms of today.

While not recorded as a knight, I still favour Robert le Boydell as the man depicted in the effigy and his known service date of 1347AD is very close to Crecy at 1346AD. Robert may have served at Crecy and been made a knight by The Black Prince as a result, the fact not being properly recorded due to the confusions of war, and he returned to his post in Cheshire the following year.

It is also highly likely that he was responsible for the building of the Boydell Chapel, along with his brother Sir William Boydell, which would make this effigy, the effigy of one of the major early church builders on this site.

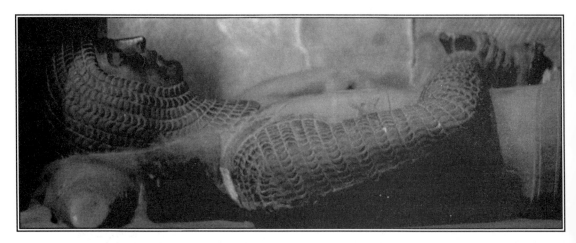

As far as is known, he died without marrying and left no children. Only his effigy lives on enabling him to be restored to his original position in history and credited as he deserves to be, as a knight of the realm and a 'founder patron' of the present church. I am reminded of the inscription which once adorned the, now stolen, 1714AD sundial in front of the church door:

"Pulvis et umbra SUMUS" - "We are dust and shadow".

Sir Thomas Danyers was another knight who undoubtably had much influence during the building of the Boydell Chapel in 1334AD and would certainly have worshipped at his local Parish Church of St Wilfrid (and probably knew Robert and Sir William Boydell).

There exists within the church a brass plate in memory of him of considerable interest to local historians, but which reflects the Victorian tendency for their enthusiasm to be greater than their knowledge. It reads: "*In Memory of Sir Thomas Danyers of Bradley within Appleton, Knight, who died A.D.MCCCLIV. (1354AD) He was present at the Battle of Cresey, the IIVth. (14th) day of May, A.D.MCCCILVI, (1346AD) and there rescued the Standard of Edward the Black Prince from the hands of the enemy, and made prisoner the Comte de*

Tankerville, Chamberlain to the French King. To preserve the memory of so gallant a Soldier this monument was placed here, A.D.MDCCCLIIVI. (1876)"

This plate was placed here after the last major renovation of the church, by a "noted expert in heraldry", however the said battle in which Sir Thomas Danyers rescued the standard took place the 26th day of August not "the 14th day of May". The date of the battle of Crecy is well recorded and widely known!

In other respects the monumental brass plate tells the complete story as known except to add that the 16 year old Black Prince showed gratitude by granting Sir Thomas Danyers a life pension of £20.00 and an estate in England on his return (which he never received from King

Edward III, father of the Prince - probably just as Robert Le Boydel! is not 'officially' recorded as a knight).

Sir Thomas returned to his home in England, Bradley Hall in Appleton, to become 'Justice of Chester' and to rise to the office of 'Sheriff of the County of Chester' by 1350AD. But in 1354AD he died leaving only a daughter, Margaret, who married three times and finally demanded (at the prompting of her third husband Piers Legh), and obtained from King Richard II, the estate promised to her father. The estate granted was Lyme on the Cheshire/Derbyshire border and the Legh family has resided there ever since, returning frequently to Warrington for burial at Winwick Church in ages past. They also adopted Sir Thomas Danyers coat of arms as their own.

It is also of interest to note that a little known connection existed between St Wilfrid's at Grappenhall and the major monastic site of Norton Priory (covered in Book 3 of this series), Norton supplying ministers to the church during the Medieval period. In 1423AD William De Hethe was sent to Grappenhall by the Abbot of Norton and served as the last minister from Norton. The advowson then passed to the Byrom family and Thomas Byrom took over as minister in 1450AD.

BEFORE LEAVING GRAPPENHALL

Starting in either 1525AD or 1529AD, the church was extended with the Norman church being reduced to its foundations and the chancel, north aisle and present tower being added to the Boydell Chapel which was left standing. Possibly the Norman structure had become unsafe over the previous four hundred years and the new building began with the tower (under the watchful gaze of St Barbara), which originally had eight pinnacles of which only the bases now remain.

In 1539AD the next phase of Tudor building got under way with the south aisle extended to its present length and removal of the dividing wall between the nave and the Boydell Chapel, with the creation of the columns and arches in the old Norman external wall below the gargoyles. The west door of the Boydell Chapel also became the present main south door.

The floor must have had various levels at this time as the base mouldings on the pillars are at different heights and some pillars in the north aisle are not perpendicular! The date of 1539AD can be seen inscribed on the reverse side of the pillar nearest the main south door and the church registers begin in 1573AD.

The oldest surviving gravestone in the churchyard is of the Drinkwater family of Thelwall, who also had ties at the same period as this gravestone, of 1624AD, with Warburton Church (see Book 1 in this series). This grave can be found at the south east side (front) of the church. Peter Drinkwater and churchwarden John Platt tried to remove Thomas Bradshaw, the presbyterian minister (appointed under Cromwell from 1653AD to 1660AD) from the church, but were physically rebuffed by Mr Bradshaw and five sturdy bell ringers. Peter Drinkwater was knocked to the ground losing his hat and stick. It took an arrest warrant issued on Christmas Eve 1660AD to remove Mr Bradshaw and restore William Seddon to his pre-Cromwell post at the church. William Seddon died in 1672AD and Mr Bradshaw went on to become the vicar of Lymm living to 1685AD.

The last major work to be undertaken at St Wilfrid's Church commenced under Rev. Thomas Greenall in 1850 and continued with the complete restoration of 1873 and 1874 by Messrs Paley & Austin of Lancaster, using local red sandstone from Cob's Quarry situated near Lumb Brook. At this time the local stocks had just fallen out of use (by order in 1837) after use

for small offenders and drunkards. However, having had the bench removed early this century and being hit by a car in 1971, the timbers were brought into the church, the stonework rebuilt and fitted with a replica set of timbers to prevent further deterioration.

There is also known to exist a secret tunnel running from below the vestry on the north east corner of the church to below the old vicarage (now an old peoples' home) just beyond the graveyard to the east. It is said that this continued and linked with the famous Warrington tunnels at Bridge Foot beyond Latchford, but was broken by the construction of the Bridgewater Canal, and then finally blocked up for safety reasons within living memory.

Despite becoming illegal in 1827, huge iron man traps were still in use in estate woodlands around Grappenhall Haze (also known as 'Pickford's Mansion') right into the early part of this century to deter poachers. Used in conjunction with hidden 'spring-guns', these huge, iron, spring-loaded jaws were buried at the bottom of pits surrounding the estate and some are still thought to remain hidden to this day. Several fine examples of small traps designed to break legs are displayed in Warrington Museum but larger examples could cut a man in half.

A COMPENDIUM OF CATS OR "OU EST MA CHATTE?"

"One needs not go far to account for a Cheshire cat grinning. A cat's paradise must naturally be placed in a county like Cheshire, flowing with milk." Cheshire Folklorist Egerton Leigh

Back to the outside of the tower walls at St Wilfrid's church Grappenhall. On the lower part of the west face of the tower, above the main window, is plainly seen a long carving of a crouching cat ready to spring (see photograph below) probably placed there during the Tudor building phases of 1529AD or 1539AD and dating from an earlier period. There are several possible reasons for it being there, which leads us nicely into an important voyage of Celtic discovery once again tied to the River Mersey.

ROMANO-CELTIC MOSAIC OF BRITISH WILD CAT C 150 AD

The most local reason for the cat being at Grappenhall states that it was a Medieval stone mason's joke, a pun on the name 'Caterick' relating to Robert de Boydell of Caterick, one of three sons of Sir John de Boydell, represented also by the Boydell effigy. It is said that one of

Sir John's other sons, William de Boydell, built the family chapel on to the Norman church in 1334AD, at which time a charter records: *"Be it known that I, William Boydell Junr, do agree to find an honest chaplain to celebrate forever the divine mysteries for the souls of William Boydell (my father) and Nicolaa (my mother) and for the souls of all the faithful departed, in the chapel of Gropenhole, built by the aforesaid William, my father."*

Although William took responsibility for supplying an "honest chaplain" and his father is credited with its construction, the chapel would not have been built without the involvement of Robert, who owned a property in the parish called 'Caterich'. There is a lane close by called 'Cartridge Lane' which has been suggested was once 'Catridge Lane' or 'Caterich Lane' as it passes the site of the Boydell's Medieval moated residence (dealt with under High Legh).

One of the illustrations in the original *Alice In Wonderland* appears to be an exact copy of the cat on Grappenhall church tower in outline, but a great many more 'Cheshire cat' connections abound, which are equally important in the discussion of local Celtic sacred sites.

"CATS BORN IN MAY - BRING SNAKES TO THE HOUSE"
A BRIEF EXPLORATION OF THE CHESHIRE CAT

The title of this section is from an old North Wales proverb taken from Elias Owen's 1896 book *Welsh Folk-Lore,* and, while on the surface it relates a belief in the nature of May kittens, may hide a mystery about the journey of the Welsh Gawain (Hawk of May) down a 'road of cats' to face the Green Knight and return to King Arthur's house with tales or even Saxon followers (snakes) from the region of the 'serpent river'! If you are mystified then read on:

TEFNUT

Over on the Wirral exists a very important image of a cat carved into the rocks on Bidston Hill, close to the Observatory. Here can be found a collection of rock carvings thought to date from the second century (100AD to 200AD) and to be of Romano-Celtic origin.

The one of interest to us is that of a goddess with the moon at her feet and the face of a cat. She is known as the 'Moon Goddess' and may be related to the Egyptian lion-headed sun goddess 'Tefnut' of Heliopolis who represented the moisture in the air, clouds, mist, dew, rain and later possibly the rivers of Britain (and nowadays, probably the weather in Manchester!).

She was the partner of 'Shu', god of the air, son of 'Atum' (or the great creator sun god 'Ra'), personification of the "Breath of Life" who held up the sky goddess 'Nut' from the earth god 'Geb'. In form this would make 'Tefnut' a perfect female equivalent or partner to the male Creator-God of the early Christians and Celts.

The moon symbol is undoubtably a later Celtic addition, possibly added to indicate that this version of the middle eastern goddess 'Tefnut' is associated with the river 'Belisama' (Mersey) whose original Egyptian/Phoenician name was 'Rhebelisama', goddess of moon and heaven. While there is nothing to say a river can not be represented by both the sun and moon, this might explain why cats and cat goddesses of the moon are associated with the distinctly 'solar boat' shaped river Mersey. The Egyptians and Phoenicians also tied their major solar and lunar dieties to rivers such as the famous Ra and the River Nile association.

While they are renowned for trading tin from Cornwall, a Phoenician ship has been found as far north as Scotland raising the possibility that the Phoenicians first gave the name 'Rhebelisama' to the Mersey as long ago as 650BC, well before the Romans used the name.

One of the ancient Celtic tribes living in the region during the Roman occupation were the Cornovii of Cheshire and Staffordshire whose symbol has always been thought to have been a cat, which may explain the presence of many cats in Cheshire and Staffordshire. They were known as the 'People of the Cat', and it is said that some Celtic tribes like the Cattraighe (cat folk) worshipped the goddess 'Catha' or 'Cata'.

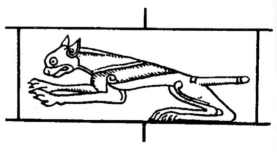

In his book *Earth Mysteries of the Three Shires,* Doug Pickford is of the opinion that a tribe worshipping Catha centred their worship on a rock feature known as the 'Cat Stones' which are part of 'The Cloud', a dramatic hill on the way into Leek from Macclesfield. It is said locally that sacrificial victims were thrown down this sheer rock face, to be dashed to pieces on an altar somewhere below, at the spring equinox (Easter time), and the rock face does indeed have a natural image of a giant cat's face formed from time-etched cracks and curves. As Doug says: *"The cat's face comes and the cat's face goes. Now you see it, now you don't. Surely a magical and mysterious sign to the worshippers of the cat goddess?"* In a similar sacrificial vein the 'Cheshire Smile' or 'Cheshire Grin' was a term once widely used in the area for death by the cutting of the throat from ear to ear or by hanging.

The first instance of the 'smile' surviving in Cheshire is probably represented by the garrotted remains of Lindow Man or 'Pete Marsh', the Celtic sacrificial peat bog body thought to have been sacrificed in about 61AD by local Druids in an attempt to avert the impending Roman attack on Anglesey (which came in 63AD).

The term, as it survives today, comes entirely from the days of capital punishment and execution by hanging.

St Christopher's church in Pott Shrigley, just north of Bollington, also has a famous 'Cheshire cat'. Inside the church, under the chancel arch close to the altar and built into the wall, there is a very large representation of the famous Alice in Wonderland Cheshire cat as it is usually depicted today.

It is possible that Lewis Carroll may have known of this and other 'Cheshire cats' via his father, Rev. Charles Dodgson (vicar of Daresbury 1827 to 1843), who was a travelling Cheshire clergyman with relatives living in Cheshire.

On the outside of the church there is another representation of a grinning stone 'Cheshire cat' and a head which resembles the 'Queen Of Hearts' character from *Alice In Wonderland*. The arms of the 'Pott' family of Pott Shrigley are also topped by a representation of a Cheshire wild cat chained up and patiently sitting.

High on the front wall of Birkenhead Priory, towards the end by the original entrance arch connecting cloisters to church (now completely destroyed), there is the face of a grinning cat, a small gargoyle, with characteristically pointed ears, that gazes down on all who have entered the site since it was first established in about 1150AD.

Who knows how many more of these representations may have existed on this and other ruined Medieval sites along the Wirral, Mersey Valley and into Cheshire? One thing is certain, this motif still appears often enough to suppose that all Cheshire sites once featured it along with other 'standards' such as the 'Green Man', 'Dragons', 'Kings and Queens' and 'Gargoyles'.

Birkenhead Priory was founded by Hamo de Mascy, the founder and builder of the estates and hall at Dunham Massey, and is covered in more detail under that section later in this book.

There is a story of King Arthur, Sir Gawain, Merlin and a monster cat, contained in a Cambridge manuscript version of *The Vulgate Merlin* edited by Mr Wheatley, and told by Lady Wilde in her 1887 book, *Ancient Legends, Mystic Charms And Superstitions Of Ireland*.

In the story a fisherman vows to devote his catch to God but breaks the vow three times catching a black kitten on the third trawl. This kitten then grows, kills the fisherman and his family and moves to a cave in a hill overlooking the 'Lake of Lausanne'. Arthur hears of this and arrives with Gawain and Merlin to find the surrounding country deserted and the giant cat hiding in its cave on the mountain. There follows the conflict between Arthur and the giant cat in which it looks like Arthur may lose and much royal blood is spilled. A short extract of the battle will suffice:

"Then the King ran at him with his sword, but the cat stood on his hind legs and grinned with his teeth, and coveted the throat of the King, and the King tried to smite him on the head; but the cat strained his hinder feet and leaped at the King's breast, and fixed his teeth in the flesh, so that the blood streamed down from breast to shoulder." Eventually two of the cats feet and claws become embedded in Arthur's shield and Arthur cuts them off and wins the day.

"Then Merlin and the others ran to him and asked how it was with him. "Well, blessed be our Lord!" said the King, "for I have slain this devil, but, verily, I never had such doubt of myself, not even when I slew the giant on the mountain ...."

Although this story is often placed in Ireland as part of the 'Cuchulling Saga', given the connections of Arthur and Merlin with Wales and Gawain and the cat in Cheshire, the stories conclusion is geographically interesting.

"So the King let the shield be with the cat's feet; but the other feet (of the cat) he laid in a coffin to be kept. And the mountain was called from that day 'the Mountain Of The Cat', and the name will never be changed while the world endureth."

Inevitably this leads us to look at our own local geography.

In his 1947 book, *Companion into Cheshire*, J.H. Ingram has no hesitation in labelling Cheshire as the "County of Cats and Cheeses" and rightly so. He adds:

"Around the headwaters of Todd Brook rise the highest hills in Cheshire south of Soldier's Lump. Cat's Tor's 1700 feet curve round in a saddle-backed ridge to Shining Tor, whose 1833 feet make it the highest hill in the western part of the Peak District." (Author's note: One possibly linked to the 'Cheshire cat' of the land or the Arthur story, the other to the 'shining bright' of the River Mersey and the Goyt.)

"It is only a stone's throw, one might say, to the Cat And Fiddle Inn - second only in height to Tan Hill Inn in England - which crowns the windswept crest of the Macclesfield-Buxton road at a height of 1690 feet. The Macclesfield-Buxton highway is popularly known as 'the Cat road', so named after the Inn which crowns its summit. There are several explanations of the name, the most popular being that it is derived from 'Le Chat Fidele', the faithful cat. A London merchant is said to have built the first inn on the site, and to have called it after the tavern of that name which he owned in London. Or it may have been derived

from the old nursery rhyme, there being some subtle connections between Cheshire and cats. Anyway, for what it is worth, there is a carving over the door of a cat playing a fiddle."

It is most likely that the Macclesfield banker and prominent Freemason, John Ryle, who actually built the inn in about 1830, was fully aware of local connections to Cheshire cats.

Over the last few centuries a view developed that the cats in Cheshire were so tickled by the thought that it was a County Palatine, (a County with some measure of independent ecclesiastical and civil government) that they couldn't help but grin when they thought of it. If this was the case then they stopped grinning in 1830 when the Palatine administration structures came to an end, and positively cried

PRIZE CATS AT THE CRYSTAL PALACE

when the designation 'Palatine' was finally dropped in 1974!

This may also have been connected in some way to the local saying recorded last century in *Stockport Notes and Queries:* "To grin like a Cheshire polecat" (Cheshire polecats being quite large, wild and very independent in former times).

In days gone by it is said that Cheshire cheese was sold to visitors in edible cat-shaped pieces with bristles introduced for whiskers - was this a symbol of Cheshire's former glorious independence.

The large Cheshire family of Egerton, connected to Tatton Park and Arley Hall, have a rather feline looking Syrian lion on their coat of arms which used to be painted on the signs of Cheshire inns owned or identified with the family and their workers. The African lion has a mane but the Syrian does not, consequently it is thought that rather talentless sign painters depicted it as a cat with an inscrutable smile which developed into the 'Cheshire cat'.

This same process of evolution was also said to have taken place with regard to many inn signs and other heraldic carvings depicting lions, leopards and the arms of the City of Chester which contain the 'Lions of England', body side on but face turned towards the onlooker, very much in attitude like the 'Cheshire cat'.

The first writer to enshrine the 'Cheshire cat' in a written composition was not in fact Lewis Carroll (Charles Lutwidge Dodgson) but Peter Pindar (John Walcot M.D.) who wrote the words: "Lo! like a Cheshire cat our court will grin" between 1794 and 1801. And finally to Lewis Carroll's Cheshire cat:

"Cheshire Puss", she began, rather timidly, as she did not at all know whether it would like the name: however, it only grinned a little wider. "Come, it's pleased so far," thought Alice, and she went on, "Would you tell me, please, which way I ought to walk from here?"

The Rev. Charles Lutwidge Dodgson was born at the Old Parsonage (now demolished) in Newton-by-Daresbury, Cheshire, on the 27th January 1832, five years after his father (also the Rev. Charles Dodgson) had taken up his post there as vicar of Daresbury.

In 1843 the family moved to Croft near Darlington where Charles junior attended school at Rugby. He later obtained a First Class B.A. in Mathematics in 1854 followed by an M.A. in 1857 (his first book was on advanced mathematics) going on to be ordained a deacon in 1861. He never proceeded to priest's orders as he spent the rest of his life writing and lecturing at Oxford and wrote a substantial part of Alice's adventures while on holiday in Llandudno. He died at Guildford in Essex on January 14th 1898, just before his sixty-sixth birthday.

In the 'Wonderland' series, under the pseudonym Lewis Carroll, he published *Alice's Adventures in Wonderland,* in 1865, *Songs From Alice's Adventures in Wonderland,* in 1870, and *Through the Looking Glass and What Alice Found There,* in 1872.

The 'Cheshire Cat' first appears in 'Pig And Pepper', Chapter VI of *Alice's Adventures in Wonderland,* playing what today would be called in the movies a 'bit part' or a 'link'. It simply acts as a sort of 'sign post' from the kitchen of the Duchess to the madness of the Mad Hatter's tea party.

Today the 'Wonderland Cheshire Cat' lives on in the bottom right hand panel of the 'Lewis Carroll Memorial Window' (installed in Daresbury All Saints Church in 1932 on the Centenary of his birth) peering happily out from oak tree foliage between the Knave and Queen of Hearts, over whose head can just be seen the tiny circular spider's web which became the trade mark of Lewis Carroll.

"All right," said the Cat; and this time it vanished quite slowly, beginning with the end of the tail, and ending with the grin, which remained some time after the rest of it had gone."

THE MERSEY CELTIC PILGRIM ROUTE REVEALED

There is no doubt that some of the evidence presented thus far points to the existence of a developed and very ancient Celtic religious route from North Wales and the Wirral, down the Mersey and Goyt valleys, over Axe Edge and Wildboarclough, ending somewhere in Staffordshire.

The first part of this route was identified, in North Wales and other places, by Anne Ross and Don Robins in their book on the Lindow bog sacrifice, *The Life and Death of a Druid Prince,* where they state that: "*Watling Street ....cuts through the Trent-Severn passage to Wroxeter before heading north to Chester and then around the coast of North Wales to Anglesey. In linking sites such as Mancetter, Penkridge and Wall, and driving between Vernemeton and the gyrus of the Lunt, Watling Street reveals itself as the Roman overlay of an ancient Celtic route marked by holy places. This runs through the Trent-Severn passage to the Vale of Clwyd and thence across the Menai Straits to Anglesey.*"

This same route is identified, and driven even further south into Wales, by Martin and Nigel Palmer, in their Sacred Land Project book *Sacred Britain, A Guide to the Sacred Sites and Pilgrim Routes of England, Scotland And Wales.* They start at Chester and include Holywell, Llanasa, The Gop, Dyserth, St Asaph, Llandegai, Bangor, Anglesey, Caernarfon, Tudweiliog, Aberdaron, and end on Bardsey Island.

The route identified in both of the above books forms the first part of our own, starting at The Gop in North Wales, and the other Welsh sites where Gawain began his quest before he crossed to the 'Wilderness of Wirral'. Our Mersey pilgrim route can clearly be found and followed using two ancient key images:

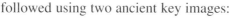

1] Man made and developed mounds, and

2] Images of the Celtic goddess in the form of 'Cheshire Cats'.

Starting on the Wirral we find the distinctive cats at Bidston Hill and Birkenhead Priory. Staying on the south side of the Mersey we pass the hills of Helsby, Frodsham, Runcorn and Halton, followed by the largest Medieval monastic site in North Cheshire at Norton Priory, and the associated smaller site at Daresbury (with Lewis Carroll), all covered in Book 3 of this series.

Next along the line comes Hill Cliffe at Appleton, Stockton Heath, with its Roman settlement, and Warrington, with Town Hill and Motte Hill, at the river crossing site. Further on comes Grappenhall, connected to Norton Priory, and with the cat again, Warburton with its missing Priory, and the mounds of Dunham Castle, Bowdon Castle and Rostherne Church marking the link with Watling Street at the Manchester end.

Then, much further out, come ancient Urmston, Stockport, Chadkirk, and the mounds east of Marple, at Werneth Low, Ludworth and Sun Hill.

Leaving the Mersey of today and following the Goyt as Gawain would have done, we encounter the strange mound behind Erwood Hall at the foot of Shining Tor. This is followed by Cat Tor, the 'cat road' by the Cat and Fiddle pub in the lands of the Celtic cat people, and the source of the Mersey, Wildboarclough, ending at Lud's Church to face the 'Green Knight' on the Staffordshire Roaches just outside Allgreave on the A54 to Congleton (which also later passes the 'Cat Stones' on The Cloud).

At this stage the final end of the route remains to be firmly identified but there are a great many ancient sites surrounding Ludchurch and The Cloud which point to that area as the end of the route.

Thus grew the tale of Wonderland;
Thus slowly, one by one,
Its quaint events were hammered out -
And now the tale is done,
And home we steer, a merry crew,
Beneath the setting sun.
Alice! a childish story take,
And with gentle hand
Lay it where Childhood's dreams are twined
In memory's mystic band,
Like pilgrim's withered wreath of flowers
Plucked in a far-off land.

Lewis Carroll

It is time to leave the picturesque Victorian village of Grappenhall. Continue along the cobble Church Lane and over the canal bridge on to Bellhouse Lane. This meets the A50 Knutsford Road where we take a right and sharp left onto Cliff Lane, which plunges under the Bridgewater Canal immediately after which we turn left on to Weaste Lane. The last Bronze Age barrow cro mark mentioned in Grappenhall is in the fields to the left and this whole area of countrysid possesses a true Cheshire charm, seldom found so close to Warrington.

After only a quarter of a mile take the first road to appear on the left, Halfacre Lane, whic takes us back under the Bridgewater canal to a junction with the A56 Stockport Road. Here w go right and sharp left again down Bell Lane, but be careful as this is a bad junction.

Bell Lane leads us down to the Celtic Cross war memorial where we turn left to park at th Pickering Arms on the left. Just down the road ahead (Ferry Lane) are the Old Hall and ferr and All Saints Church is further on along Bell Lane (B5157).

THELWALL

"IT IS UNQUESTIONABLY A PLACE OF VERY GREAT ANTIQUITY, AND SO MEAGRE AN ACCOUNT HAS BEEN HITHERTO PUBLISHED AS TO ITS EARLY HISTORY AND POSSESSORS, THAN AN ATTEMPT MORE FULLY TO ELUCIDATE THE SUBJECT, AND TO CONCENTRATE, AND THEREBY PRESERVE, THE SCATTERED FRAGMENTS WHICH YET REMAIN AS TO IT, FROM THE GENERAL WRECK OF TIME, CANNOT FAIL, IT IS ANTICIPATED, TO PROVE BOTH ACCEPTABLE AND INTERESTING." James Nicholson in 'The Topographer And Genealogist 1846'.

Little documentation exists on the village of Thelwall, to which the local historian can resort, so I am indebted to a small collection of private papers brought together in 1984 by J. Reginald Leah (who was then over seventy years old), the article from 1846 quoted above, and the few scanty records of the *Cheshire Sites and Monuments*.

The present Thelwall village enters upon the stage of history with a collection of stray axe head finds perhaps lost in a prehistoric area used for hunting and obtaining building materials, for settlements probably situated back towards present day Warrington to the west. Up to the Bronze Age, Thelwall must have been a wooded area bordering the 'Mersey Eyes', formerly marsh land areas, contained by the bends in the river, which have changed very considerably over the years.

THE ANCIENT WISH OF THE HUNTER

In November 1989, Mr Marcus Verschuren was using a JCB digger to excavate a sceptic tank at the rear of Beech Farm on the B5157 Lymm Road, when he brought up a Neolithic/Stone Age polished axe head from a depth of about 4 to 5 feet (1.3m) where it had been preserved in the clay. This axe was made from smooth fine grained white stone (possibly from the Lake District) and was perfect except for a few chips and scratches. It measured 198mm long, 59mm wide and 39mm thick.

Examination of the find revealed that it was almost certainly made for ceremonial use and is effectively 'new' being probably deposited into the River Mersey as an offering where it sank into the silt. From the curved blade end, it is parallel-sided until half way along its length, where it starts to slightly taper to a rounded butt. The 'top' side is highly polished to a smooth finish, but the bottom side is finely crossed with crisscross lines which appear deliberate. It is acknowledged that the shape of

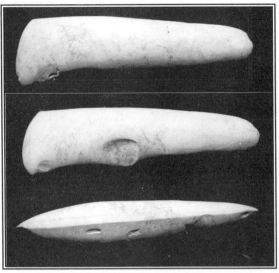

these axes corresponds well to that of long barrow burial mounds, and crisscross lines have been found cut into the chalk under some of these mounds in southern England.

It is possible that such ceremonial axes represented the tomb and were ritually discarded in Neolithic times in the hope of avoiding death. Picture the scene:

The hunter turned aside from the ridge path through the trees and made his way down to the bank of the rushing river where he dropped the axe, which he had taken several seasons to produce, into the swirling waters in the hope that he would survive, even as the unchanging river survives.

P.J. Davey records in his 1972 book, *Studies In Bronze Age Metalwork,* the discovery of a half-flanged bronze axe in the grounds of Chaigeley School. This is probably the same Bronze Age palstave given as found roughly where the Little Manor now stands in Thelwall and recorded in *The Archaeology Of Warrington's Past.*

The County Treasures Record also lists the find of a prehistoric spindle whorl somewhere in the Thelwall area but this is the only information available on this find and it is highly likely that all these finds have their origins elsewhere, probably at the Grappenhall or Latchford settlement sites.

It is certain that Thelwall sits on the continuation of the ancient road 'Thelwall Lane' from the ford at Latchford, a lane which may have existed in Roman times (and most certainly did during the Medieval period) possibly as a direct route connecting Latchford, Thelwall, Lymm, Broomedge, Millington, Rostherne, Tatton and Knutsford. There is every possibility that a Celtic Saxon settlement (possibly with its own manor house and chapel) existed on this site from about 860AD to 923AD, and it has been suggested that the name Thelwall may come from the name of King Ethelred (E-THEL) who ruled Britain from 866AD to 871AD. It may be to this settlement that King Edward came, but this does not mean he built his fortification specifically on this site as the evidence to follow shows.

THE LEGEND OF THEL'S BURGH IS BORN

Although Thelwall cannot claim to be the oldest name still in use in the areas around Warrington it is the only name to appear in written records before the Domesday survey of 1086AD. Thelwall first appears in written history with this statement from the Anglo-Saxon Chronicle:

"*DCCCXXIII. (923AD) In this year King Edward went, after Autumn, with a force to Thelwall and commanded the burgh to be built and inhabited, and manned, and commanded another force also to the Mercian nation, while he there sat, to reduce Manchester in Northumbria and repair and man it.*"

Another recent translation from the Anglo Saxon gives the same account in slightly different terms: "*This year went King Edward with an army, late in the harvest, to Thelwall, and ordered the borough to be repaired, inhabited and manned. And he ordered another army also from the population of Mercia, the while he sat there, to go to Manchester in Northumbria to repair and man it.*"

From this single entry has developed the elaborate legend that a 'City-Burgh' existed o the site of the present village, a timber fortress with a bank around which a Celtic settlement developed. This view gained increasing popularity during Victorian times and had become sufficiently well established to be included in the *English Historical Review* of 1938 and pretty much accepted from then on. In 1988 the 'City-Burgh' was listed in the *Cheshire Sites And Monuments* at one of three possible locations:

1] Under the present village.
2] In the grounds of Victoria Park, Latchford.
3] On the promontory between two valleys lying to the east of the present village.

Taking number 1], not surprisingly no evidence of the burgh has ever been found in the area now known as Thelwall, because a lot has changed since King Edward left the place where "he there sat" in the spring of 924AD. The translation given as 'borough', meaning the entire area, is just as valid as the singular interpretation of a fort or 'burgh', and the ancient 'borough' of 'Thelwall Chapel' stretched from Lymm (probably Statham), through the present Thelwall village, to Nether or Lower Walton and included all the land encompassed by the Thelwall Eyes - a collection of large loops in the river Mersey.

Taking the evidence of the entry in the Anglo-Saxon Chronicle, it would appear that King Edward was fond of utilising Roman fortifications such as the one in Salford, Manchester, and that he created a new fortification somewhere in the region known as 'Thelwall' over the winter months between 923AD and 924AD.

By Domesday in 1086AD this area was defined as the 'Manor of Grappenhall' lying in the 'Bucklow Hundred' and including the areas of Latchford and Stockton Heath. Using this information to create the borders of the ancient 'Thelwall' region, it is justifiable to say that King Edward's fortifications could be found anywhere in this area. Bear in mind that Domesday took place only 162 years (less than three generations) after the burgh was first constructed.

The site of the present day Thelwall is strategically least likely to contain a fortification, although the popular theory over the years is that it was sited in the grounds of Chaigeley Manor Special School next to Laskey House on the Lymm Road. It is also unlikely that an experienced warrior like King Edward would have chosen a site so close to the River Mersey on which to build a timber fort during the wet winter months.

Taking number 2], a theory advanced by G.A. Carter in the Warrington Guardian of 3rd November 1967 produced the headline, 'Saxon King May Have Camped In Victoria Park' and that King Edward's fortifications may be found in the region of the traditional ford at Latchford. From the evidence, it appears that the Danes probably had tight control of any crossing place here in 923AD, ruling out this possibility. The early Roman bridge at Howley (thought to have been mainly a timber structure) had probably also collapsed and the ford itself is only a legend.

So far there is no hard evidence for site number 3] listed by *Cheshire Sites And Monuments*, although it does commend itself well as a possible site. Looking again at the evidence I think we should look elsewhere.

It appears most likely that King Edward fortified or rather 'repaired, inhabited and manned' existing structures at Stockton Heath and possibly Appleton, which were both military stand-off points, and probably still had an alternative river-crossing bridge from Roman times, giving direct access to Mercia down the A49 King Street (now London Road).

It is interesting to note that if we stick to the carbon-dates as given, the probably Danish/Viking log boats found in the Mersey at Walton all date to after 924AD, between 958AD and 1190AD, after the crossing at Stockton Heath would have come under Saxon Mercian control. The Roman bridge at Stockton Heath may also have been destroyed as a result of conflict or neglect at the time of King Canute (1016AD to 1035AD) necessitating the continued use of log boats into Norman times.

As has been established in the section on Stockton Heath, the existence of features such as: the Roman site, the banked enclosure later used in the Civil War (and now under the Mulberry Tree pub), the border with the Welsh/Britons, the evidence from the name STOCC, and evidence from maps, commend it as the most probable location of King Edward's 'City-Burgh', more convincingly than anything so far discovered in modern day Thelwall or Latchford. There may also have been other fortifications in Appleton which are dealt with in Book 3.

Many writers note that King Edward was preparing defences against Danish/Viking invasion, but he was also at war with Ethelwald, son of the former King Ethelbert (died 866AD), who disputed Edward's right to the Crown. Ethelwald made his headquarters at York and enlisted the support of the Northumbrians, who continued to fight King Edward after Ethelwald's defeat. It took the defeat of the next two Northumbrian Princes, Reginald and Sidoc, to place Northumbria under King Edward's control and this was probably also in is mind when he chose to fortify the Northumbrian/Mercian border along the Mersey. The Danes occupied the lands opposite modern day Thelwall (eg. Rixton or ERICS-TOWN) over marsh land in the river bends, but the Northumbrians probably still controlled the old Roman roads at Warrington through which any attack would have come.

As has been said, the name of King Ethelred, who ruled from 866AD to 871AD, has been suggested as one root for the Saxon (E) THEL making THELWALL, King ETHEL's ancient WALL, which could be called a 'burgh'. However a 'burgh' could also mean only the existence of a fortified manor house (usually with a moat) just to further add to the confusion. This may be all that was in the area of the present village before the arrival of King Edward in 923AD Thelwall Old Hall, built in 1618AD, may be on such a site, with a lost moat formerly fed from the river which flows behind, or the present church may also be close to the site of a 'burgh' which may have stood near the, now demolished, Thelwall Hall (now a site of open park land)

THE REAR OF THELWALL OLD HALL FROM THE FORMER RIVER MERSEY BED

The name THELWALL of 923AD is also supposed to derive from the activities of King Edward with THELL's interpreted as the tree trunks used to build timber stockades and WALL as in a high barrier, a barrier made from upright tree trunks, in Old English. In 1846 it was put like this: *"It was so called, as Florilegus testifies, by reason of its being surrounded by a fortification composed of stakes and stumps of trees, the boughs being cut away; for the Saxons called in their tongue the trunks and bodies of trees DELL, and the word WALL signified, as it does now, a fence."*

Another interpretation often quoted locally is that THEL was the name of the owner of the WALL after its construction, and WAL(L) can also mean a Welshman, Briton, foreigner, serf or slave in Old English (the same as the WALH or WEALH which begins the Old English name for WARRINGTON and WALTON). This would make THEL-WALL the 'Briton's Stockade' and, all considered, the presence of a fortified Saxon manor house at Thelwall is likely and King Edward may have used Mercian/Welsh among his builders.

However, respected Warburton family historian Norman Warburton interprets the whole name THELWALL as a 'pool by a plank bridge' and the later use of the 1231AD name THELWELL also supports the possible existence of a pool or Old English WELL, possibly again owned by THEL. Such a pool once existed a little further out of the village past All Saints Church, behind the shop on the right hand side at the corner of New Road and Alderley Road, under what is now Wilmslow Crescent, and known as Long Acre Pit.

Fishing rights on the Mersey, which flowed behind the old village Post Office opposite the Pickering Arms, were granted to the Abbot of Evesham in 1068AD but Thelwall is not named. Significantly Thelwall is also not mentioned in the Domesday Book of 1086AD lending support to the theory that it was either a large area ,rather than a settlement which could be recorded and quantified, or that it may have been recorded as part of another area. Neighbouring Lymm and Grappenhall are both recorded in their own right and Warrington is treated as covering a large area.

STAG-LEATHER GLOVES FURRED WITH FOX

Thelwall first reappears in writings of 1118AD and 1231AD. Sir Geoffrey de Dutton and his son Adam de Dutton settled at Thelwall in the mid 13th century taking land formerly owned by the Abbot and Convent of Evesham for which the annual rent was *"one pair of stag leather (buckskin) gloves furred with fox, (given) at the festival of St. Michael (29th September)."*

At this time, the first 'ecclesiastic' is recorded at Thelwall in records belonging to the Duchy of Lancaster as, "Thomas de Thelwall, clerk", chancellor of the Duchy and County Palatine of Lancaster 17th April, 51st Edward III (1377), appointed by John of Gaunt, Duke of Lancaster. This may be the first indication for the existence of a very early Medieval chapel in the village.

The court-leet for Thelwall manor, as part of Halton and the Duchy of Lancaster, was held in Thelwall every year, on the eve of Palm Sunday, by the steward of the Marquess of Cholmondeley under the Crown. This court was known to be of very ancient date, from the time of Henry, Duke of Lancaster under Edward III, who maintains his right to hold this court at Thelwall in about 1350AD.

The de Dutton family were followed a hundred years later by Ralph Clayton (about 350AD). Adam Clayton's rent at Thelwall a generation later was one shilling or, once again, a *pair of stag-leather gloves, furred with fox"*. Randal (or Randle) de Calyton helped to rebuild the steeple of Lymm St Mary's Church in 1521AD. John de Clayton acquired the fishing rights in 1542AD then sold his property to Richard Brook of Norton in 1561AD by which time a small village was developing generating documentation between 1551AD and 1663AD.

When Leland, the royal itinerant under King Henry VIIl (1509AD to 1547AD), visited Thelwall he said of it: *"Thelwaul, sumtimc u havenet and little cite, as it apperith by the Kinges records. Now fische garthes marre the haven and the old towne, now a poor village. It standith a ii miles upward from Warrington."*

In other words it was nothing more than a small fishing village and, at this time, the Mersey frequently flooded the village area at high tides. Richard Brook's son, Thomas, Sheriff of Cheshire in 1578AD and 1592AD, built the present Thelwall Old Hall in Ferry Lane on a raised site next to the banks of the Mersey in 1618AD, and his memorial chapel on the site of the present All Saints Church (last rebuilt in 1843). It is clear that an older chapel had also existed on this site to serve the other Thelwall Halls which both stood a little way further up All Saints Drive. They resided on the opposite side at the end of Parry Drive, on the park field which now has some wooded areas and a childrens' playground.

The fine Georgian hall was allowed to collapse into ruin in about 1945 after military use during the Second World War. It was originally built by Thomas Pickering in about 1750AD and was described as being: *"....near the site of the ancient manor house, which was then taken down"*. This ancient manor house and the original All Saints Chapel probably dated from Medieval times although no deed of consecration has been found for the original chapel as it was probably domestic in origin belonging to the original hall.

The Brook family sold out to Thomas Moore in 1621AD and, in turn, John Moore sold out to Robert Pickering 'Counsellor at Law' in 1666AD, after the Civil War had ended completely in 1651AD. Sufficient existed at Thelwall during the English Civil War for musket balls, buttons, buckles and coins from local conflict to still turn up on farmer's fields today.

It must have been during this period that the Pickering Arms public house was constructed with the inscription along the roadside timbers which reads: *"In the year 923AD - King Edward the Elder founded a cyty here and called it Thelwall"*.

One of the Legh family of Ridge visited Thelwall in 1650AD and recorded: *"Thus we find Thelwall, that great and ancient city, built and possessed by King Edward, now a little village, by which examples of the kind we may, with the Romans, conclude, that cities go through infancy, youth, maturity, and old age: 'Non indignemur mortalia pectora solvi, Cernimus exemplis oppida saepe mori'. 'We cannot wonder sure that mortals doe decay, We see e'en cities of dissolve away'."* The end wall of the Pickering Arms (below) containing this inscription was damaged in the earthquake of 1984, bulging outwards and cracking before being repaired, and i is still thought that Thelwal village remains the smallest Roya 'City' in the world. The Pickering family, after which the pub i named, remained as loca landowners into the Victorian era

Pickering Arms, Thelwall

SARAH GRIFFITHS

OPPOSITE PAGE
TOP: THELWALL OLD HALL IN 1900 AND TODAY
MIDDLE: THELWALL HALL c 1900 AND ALL THAT REMAINS TODAY
BOTTOM: ENTRANCE TO THELWALL HALL AND CHAPEL 1885 AND THE OLD POST OFFICE 1998

WE SHALL MEET YOU WHERE REASON WILL BE HEARD AND RIGHT WILL BE DONE US" - IN SEARCH OF THE ANCIENT CHAPEL

An ecclesiastical legal case broke out in 1663 between the keepers of Daresbury Church (Peter Dunbabin and Richard Eaton) and Thelwall Chapel (Peter Drinkwater and Robert Legh) regarding Thelwall paying towards the upkeep of Daresbury. Daresbury lost the case on the basis that Thelwall could be proved to be older and to have been used, along with closer churches like Grappenhall, for some considerable time.

Two quotes from the many locals interviewed at the time will serve to illustrate the point.

That the chapel of Thelwall is very ancient, and he (this deponent) can remember the same twice repaired, and has known three ministers successively maintained there. That Mr Pickering is the present lord of the town, and is a Protestant. Sayeth, that the chapel stands within a field or croft belonging to the manor house of Thelwall, and he believes it was many years ago consecrated." Robert Lawrenson De Browneshawe (age 68).

"That the chapel is of very ancient date. Sayeth, that Thelwall chapel stands in a field belonging to the lord of the manor, and adjoining to the hall, and that the chapel yard (grave yard) lies open to the field. Sayeth, that since the wars began (Civil War) the said chapel did fall much into decay, but is now well repaired again."   Johannes Bate De Latchford (age 61).

These repairs were done by Robert Pickering Esq., Lord of Thelwall, in 1663AD, and his initials were then placed on the old belfry as '16 R.P. 63'. Rev. James Wood was the first minister after the restoration, appointed by Robert Pickering, but he died in 1666AD. Justice had been done, the residents of Thelwall had proved that they had their own chapel to support and, as they said, *"We shall meet you where reason will be heared and right will be done us"*! Unfortunately this lasted barely a generation.

The chapel lapsed back into ruin until the Presbyterians tried to obtain use of it in 1719AD but were refused, and the building became unusable by 1731AD. Thomas Pickering Esq. inherited a chapel used *"only as a wood-house, jointly tenanted by bats and owls"* in 1748AD, and Commissioners under the Bishop of Chester were sent to repair and refit it in 1782AD at which point it reopened. Only the structure could be saved however, and even this was dismantled sixty years later to make way for the present church which stands: *"immediately adjacent to the ground upon which the ancient chapel stood"*.

Another clue to the location of the original chapel is the fact that: *"The vault of this family (Pickering), which was situate in the interior of the former chapel, is now open to the rest of the churchyard."* A recent search failed to locate the vault but it may have been swallowed up by the later church extension. The oldest surviving gravestone lies to the left, by the wall just through the lych gate, and is possibly that of Robert Legh (name damaged) who died in 1674AD. The "ancient chapel" of possibly Celtic/Medieval origin remains to be found.

When I visited Marcus Verschuren, to examine the Neolithic Axe head he found in 1989 he showed me two old English oak doors which he had recovered from the attic of his old Victorian house on Halfacre Lane and fitted to his new house on Lymm Road. Originally the doors would have been three panels high but only the lower two had survived so Marcus cut the peg fixed frames down to their present size to make them usable. The small upper panels feature 'Puritan farmers' sowing seeds (Christians sowing the Gospel) while the two lower panels show Bishops or Saints with 'crosier' staffs, one with a book and another with a two-stranded 'whip' or 'scourge'.

The figure with the book presents problems as it could represent any of the four Evangelists, six or more saints or any bishop or saint who evangelised or whose life reflected the

Gospel precepts. Given the circumstances he could be St Chad. The figure with the 'scourge' can only be the Celtic Saint Guthlac who fits amazingly well into the picture of early Thelwall.

Guthlac was born in about 673 AD in Mercia (Cheshire) and became a member of the Mercian royal family gaining distinction through his military exploits as a youth in the army of King Ethelred of Mercia (674AD to 704AD). He left military service aged about 24 and entered the monastery of Repton where he gave up alcoholic drink and was introduced to the idea of becoming a hermit. After some time he departed for the Lincolnshire Fens where he settled at a hermitage in Crowland on a bend in the river Welland and died there in 714AD. Because of his spiritual trials, temptations and heavenly visions he is represented holding his 'scourge' with which he flogged the Devil and a prosperous monastery developed at the site of his hermitage, later becoming Crowland Abbey.

Could it be that the Mercians who came here in 923AD founded a chapel to 'St. Guthlac and All Saints' which was fitted with a cabinet (having carved doors) by Robert Pickering during restorations in 1663AD, doors that had become partly rotten by neglect in 1748AD and were removed to the Victorian house on Halfacre Lane in 1843 when the old chapel was taken down?

A COLLECTION OF OLD CURIOSITIES

It is thought that an ancient ford of some kind once existed on the Mersey at Thelwall, possibly close to Thelwall Old Hall, but this was destroyed by the construction of the Howley weir by the Mersey and Irwell Navigation Company in about 1770AD. Before the activities of this company salmon weighing 19lbs and measuring *"one yard and a half a quarter long"* were caught here twice in 1749AD followed by an even bigger one weighing 24lbs the same year at Thelwall Lock.

Navigation possible on the Mersey at this time, ended at Laskey Lane, Thelwall, which is named from 'Last Quay Lane', the location of the last quay where boats could be moored without being stranded. At the corner of Laskey Lane and Lymm Road stands Old Hall Farm which is a fine example of Tudor timber and brick construction with its own surviving ice house at the rear and a detailed plaster frieze on the ground floor dated to the 1680s. Sadly the front has had to be rebuilt since the photo here taken in 1857.

MARCUS VERSCHUREN

EXAMPLE OF MAYPOLE PROCESSION AND DANCING (BEDFORDSHIRE)

In living memory, a Mrs Roebuck, organist at the church, used to organise the ancient local tradition of Maypole Dancing as part of the village sports day for the children. Few of them must have realised that the Maypole reaches back into the Stone Age and to ancient Egypt as a fertility ritual known as the 'raising of the Djed column' or 'world tree' around which the central pole axis of the world revolved displayed by the changing seasons. The same tree 'Idrasil' would have been familiar in legend to the Danes and Norse at the time of King Edward, but the Thelwall Maypole Dance no longer takes place.

Out of the village to the east, at the junction of Bell Lane and Lymm Road, stands the war memorial which has been cleverly designed as a grey granite standing cross of the early Saxon/Danish period with the face of King Edward in the centre.

Edward may have reigned for a time as a lesser king under his father King Alfred 'The Great' as he signed charters "rex" in 898AD. He spent the early part of his reign fighting wars against the Danes assisted by his sister Ethelfleda, Lady of Mercia, and the later part consolidating his gains with Ethelfleda fortifying Warburton and Runcorn in 915AD and his own fortifications of Thelwall and Manchester in 923AD. Before his death he was acknowledged as "father and lord" by most of England, parts of Wales and Scotland and also by many of the Danish and Norse leaders. He died in 924AD shortly after leaving his 'City-Burgh' at Thelwall.

Opposite the war memorial stands 'Bell Cottage' which was formerly known as 'Rachael's Cottage' and had a well in the garden by the path. Here in the early part of the 20th century, it is said, lived 'Old Rachael' who survived to a hundred years old and was 'said to be a witch'!

A curious little ferry exists down the dirt track at the end of Ferry Lane, where the elderly ferry man will row travellers across the Manchester Ship Canal for the present fee of 11 pence a trip. He was of the opinion that this was expensive when I talked with him this year as it used to be a 'h'penny' in old money or 'half-pence' when decimalisation was first introduced!

From the Pickering Arms, take Bell Lane back to the Celtic Cross war memorial and follow the bend round to the left on to the B5157 Lymm Road and on to the junction with the A50 Stockport Road. Turn left and then first left again on to Warrington Road heading for Statham. Stay on this road for about a mile until it takes a ninety degree right bend and rises up a hill to a crossroads. Here turn left on to Dane Bank Road, drop down the steep hill and park anywhere at the bottom. Lymm village is probably best experienced on foot. (Should you not wish to walk, driving directions continue at the end of the Lymm section and also pass through the village).

LYMM AND STATHAM

"Lymme exhibits a description of scenery varying altogether from either that of the neighbouring district, or the county in general."   Historian George Omerod.

Despite the tantalising absence of ancient remains (which obviously once existed in the Lymm area) the remaining village and surroundings still retain something of the atmosphere of age that compels any traveller to explore hidden paths and curious remains. It is worth noting some of these sites of interest along the valley of the rushing 'Hlimme' - now the Bradley and Slitten Brook, Lower Dam, Dingle, Upper Dam and The Bongs.

Having parked the car, a modern iron gate on the right side of the road begins the footpath into a deep valley partly created by the cutting of sandstone for building.

Approximately half way down this valley lies the ruins of a 'slitting mill' and ice house dating from the early days of the industrial revolution. This was originally used for metal working but converted to textiles in 1800AD. The stone taken from such quarry sites as this holds the evidence to our first and probably oldest mysterious discovery.

SHADOWLANDS

Wind lashing orange sands across the flat beach of a vast salt lake drove roaring reptilian dinosaurs like giant, drunken, newts toward sand mounds of huddled turtles. Tiny lizards like bald chickens cried to pterodactyls screeching in the rushing rain clouds overhead while lumbering, crocodile like, sea giants slid silently away from the shoreline leaving a cascade of swirling wakes behind them. It was the time of the first formation of Cheshire.

An unimaginably long time later early builders came to cut the red Cheshire sandstone in the area around Lymm and encountered the signatures left by the prehistoric drama, which had unfolded on the beach of that vast salt lake millions of years before. Two names for the characters involved then developed.

One name created for these beasts was Labyrinthodon, because the dinosaur remains found had a labyrinth of complex teeth. The other name created was Hand Animal or Chirotherium; a crocodile-like ancestor of a great many later dinosaurs that left five fingered hand-prints behind in the soft sands in two sizes, small front and large rear pair.

In 1841 the footprints of Chirotherium Aff Storetonense (to give it its full name) were dug out of the Keuper Waterstones, now known as the Tarporley Siltstone Formation, at the quarries in Lymm. They had also been found in Germany in 1833, Birkenhead in 1838, Liverpool in 1840 and were then found at Runcorn in 1843 and continued to be found in Lymm right up to 1900. In 1925 Wolfgang Soergal identified Chirotherium as a 'Pseudosuchian' or 'false crocodile', a very early type of dinosaur. Further finds were also reported in the Storeton quarries on the Wirral, at Weston and at Daresbury.

Warrington Museum are presently displaying three specimens of Chirotherium prints and have one stored in a draw, all found in the Windmill Quarry, Lymm. These also show fossil rain spots, sun cracks, worm-casts and ripple-marks, as do other print specimens of prehistoric turtles and other small animals found in the same sandstones at various of the sites. Apparently there are hundreds of such specimens in the cabinets and store rooms of British museums, most of them originating in Lymm, but now they only turn up on older sandstone constructions such as those recently found on the stones of Warburton cross.

If you are following the walking route through the old quarries you are standing on the very shore of Cheshire's prehistoric salt lake. The path then crosses the rushing Slitten Brook and a mysterious cave can be seen high up on the cliff face to the right, out of which a flow of water has poured for many centuries. A large flight of steps ascend to the canal side from which vantage point can be seen the entrance to a tunnel on the opposite bank, down which barges were

moored for maintenance purposes. This long tunnel has occasionally collapsed leaving holes in the gardens above!

A left turn under the canal bridge takes the path into the village where another left turn reveals the Lower Dam, a picturesque artificial pool at the village centre. Next to this, the path leads into the Dingle Continue left on the road to reach the village square, stocks, cross and the Lymm Hall site behind it (which is private). We now turn our attention to the history of the village and surrounding areas.

SHADOW OF A PREHISTORIC PAST

Two prehistoric implements of red deer antler were found at Lymm while excavating was under way on the Manchester Ship Canal. These were assigned by R. Newstead to the early Neolithic period and were in the possession of Mrs C. Griffiths of Helsby in 1899 but have since been lost again in the mists of time. The OS map reference is given as the Lymm area and indicates that the find came from the stretch of the canal behind the barrow shown on the 1873 OS map in Rixton or just beyond Lymm Golf Course.

Whitbarrow House Farm (literally 'White-Barrow') in Statham is recorded in the OS Record Cards as the site of a possible round barrow, but a survey in 1964 found no traces of the barrow after which the farm may have been named. It may be that the Rixton barrow was on the farmer's land and was known by locals as the White Barrow.

The find of a possible prehistoric burial site is noted in the County Treasures Record for 1934 and in the OS Record Cards in 1964, in the area behind Tanners Pool on Cherry Lane B5158 opposite Cherry Hall Farm. A visit to the site in 1964 again revealed nothing on the ground and no more details are available.

In 1971 Dr N.N. Hancock found a late Neolithic or early Bronze Age flint 'plano-convex' knife made of pale grey brown flint in the grounds of 119 High Lane, Lymm. It was 2 ins (5cm) in length, had heavy wear on one side and had been reworked for scraping or cutting. In 1979 Dr Hancock also found a flint scraper of similar age in his garden, but it has been suggested that the finds may have been imported with top soil brought from Sale.

The name LYMM was thought to be an Old English development of LIMITAE from the Roman/Latin word used for 'the boundary of an area' (LIMIT) but is recorded simply as LIME in the Domesday survey of 1086AD.

The *Concise Oxford Dictionary of English Place Names* suggests instead that it was situated on a stream called HLIMME or HLIMMA meaning 'roaring brook' or 'resounding noisy stream' in Old English which became LIME and then LYM. This brook is now called the Bradley Brook. It must be noted that the name LIME presents several other problems in translation. It can be taken to be 'the area named from an elm grove' (Old English LIM, LIN, Primitive Welsh LIV, LIVN, British LEMO, LEMANO) or 'bare place' (Old English LIM, Primitive Welsh LIM(M), British LUMMIO), and J.M. Dodgson favoured primitive Welsh pre-English origins (before 700AD) in his 1967 article 'The English Arrival in Cheshire' in the *Transactions of The Historic Society of Lancashire and Cheshire.* The village was still known simply as LYM as late as the 17th century before the permanent addition of the extra 'M'.

The 'hlimme'

Lymm became part of the 'Bucklow Hundred' and the 'Shire of Chester' at the start of manorial organisation in the tenth century and probably included parts of Grappenhall, Latchford, Warburton and High Legh at various times. Lymm has been credited as one of only a few pre-conquest parishes identifiable in Cheshire. Other local examples also include Great Budworth and Rostherne (including High Legh, Knutsford, Over Peover and Mobberly). It is at this time that evidence of concrete settlement in Lymm begins to emerge from the mists of time.

SHADOW OF A SAXON HALL

Ownership of the Lymm Hall site directly overlooking the present village has been traced back into Anglo-Saxon times (pre 1066AD) by Liverpool archaeologists, and it is likely that a member of the Dutton or Venables family adopted the name Limme at some point just after the

Norman invasion. A Gilbert de Limme was living in the reign of King John (1199AD to 1216AD) with a family bearing this name still residing in Lymm when Edward III ended his reign in 1377AD.

The last Gilbert de Limme lived at the moated site of Lymm Hall, just off Rectory Lane, before it passed to the Dumvyle or Domville family who were responsible for major rebuilding there during the Tudor period and were still descendants from the original De Limmes. The Domville coat of arms, a white lion rampant on a black shield, can be found over their pew in Lymm church and on various items around the hall. The Lymm branch of the family died out in 1719AD but other family members still survive in the Warrington area to this day.

Liverpool archaeologists explored the site in the 1970s, especially the main house platform and the front garden of the Tudor Moat House. At the Moat House they first found a layer of sand similar to that lining the moat and probably dating to the Tudor Domville family rebuilding of the sixteenth century (1500 AD to 1600 AD).

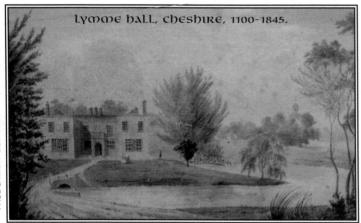

Lymme hall, cheshire, 1100-1845.

PAUL & MARY COTTRILL

Below the sand they found 293 pieces of various pottery dated between 1450AD and 1550AD including cooking and ale pots, flagons, fine Tudor green pottery and the base of a baluster jug of possibly French origin. They also found three and a half lead spindle whorls, a decorated stone whorl, a decorated lead ampulla, a whetstone and nine bronze pieces including a button and at least two bowls, all between 1975 and 1976. They concluded that they had found a Tudor 'midden' or rubbish dump and evidence of two earlier re-cuttings of the moat.

Today the hall still stands in wonderful Gothic splendour, within the north and west sides of the original Medieval moat (now dry), and possesses a much archaeologically-explored ice house, a hidden wine cellar below the present kitchen (accessible only through a narrow outside opening),the original moat bridge below the later added facia, a magnificent Tudor Moat House sat over the Medieval 'midden', a sloping-sided hexagonal font dated 1401AD removed from old St Mary's church during the rebuilding of 1851, and two cock fighting pits sadly damaged by drunken soldiers in the Second World War.

When local historian Harry Boscow visited the site, for Cheshire Life Magazine in November 1935, the cock fighting pits were in perfect condition and still clear of weeds. Each had a central stone table: *".... about two feet high, shaped like a mushroom, on which the birds fought."* He continues: *"Lymm must have been a great centre of the sport. Old records in the neighbouring parish of Warburton refer to a cock mister, his duty being to collect the cocks and prepare them for the fray."* Cock fighting and bull baiting continued in the area until 1821 and were known to be the last in England to come to an end.

LYMM HALL AND FEATURES IN THE GROUNDS 1998

THE TUDOR MOAT HOUSE

REAR VIEW OF LYMM HALL

It is said that a stone found on the side of Rectory Lane, opposite the entrance to Lymm Hall and next to the former site of the Dingle Hotel, frequently walks down the hill to the village centre and back again! In Lancashire and Cheshire this kind of story is typically told of such boulders which did indeed 'walk here' under glacial ice sheets thousands of years ago.

SHADOW OF A SAXON VILLAGE

In the latter part of 1998, the final demolition of the old Dingle Hotel took place, which stood up a drive immediately opposite the gates to Lymm Hall on a flat area overlooking the gorge of the Lower Dam.

There was much debate associated with the age and need for preservation of the building, especially with regard to its ancient cellar, but I was privileged to be allowed to attend and photograph most stages of the demolition and some conclusions can be reached.

There were several local legends which placed the date of the original building back to the days of the Medieval Lymm Hall. It is certainly true to say that there were many ancient timbers used in its construction - but all the timbers had been reused from other demolished buildings, possibly barns and out-buildings associated with Lymm Hall and its estate. The building as it stood in 1998 was nothing more than an elaborate jigsaw puzzle probably begun some time after the Civil War, about 1670AD, using materials from other buildings derelict or damaged by the conflict.

The legendary secret tunnel from the site to the Church of St Mary was never found and the

cellar probably defined the extent of the main building of 1670AD. Glass and pottery fragments recovered from builders trenches in front of the Hotel date from the 1680AD to 1720AD period (at the earliest) and one interesting early Victorian Greenall Whitley bottle was also recovered complete with cork stopper (see photograph).

LYMM VILLAGE CROSS ABOUT 1900 BEFORE RESTORATION (R), AND TODAY (L)

Opinions about the age of Lymm Cross differ so much that some experts place it in the 14th century (1300AD to 1400AD) while others ascribe it to the 17th. The prominent red Cheshire sandstone outcrop on which it sits is undoubtably the centre point round which the later village has developed. It would not surprise me in the least if a far older site of some kind were to be found under the present cross structure if future technology allows for such investigation (maybe a socket for an older cross or slot for a Maypole).

Three local legends support this view. One states that the first monument to stand on this spot, including the worn steps of today, was constructed by the Romans to honour the Cheshire salt workers. This may be supported by the name of Pepper Street, just behind the cross, which is a name known to be often given to Roman roads.

The second legend (asserted by Rev. Thurston, a former rector at Lymm who died about 1917) states that St Paul came to this spot and preached to the local heathen inhabitants using the outcrop as his pulpit. It is known that St Paul left Jerusalem on his missionary journeys to the Roman world in about 45AD, travelled round the Mediterranean for about ten years before he upset the Roman authorities, arrived in Rome under 'house arrest' in about 55AD and probably died there in about 67AD. This leaves little time for him to have come to Britain unless he caught a ship to Warrington some time between 45AD and 55AD and the fact was not recorded!

The third legend was proposed in 1970 by local historian Norman Warburton who records: *"It is held that Lymm Cross dates back to the early days of Christianity and is said to have been built as a memorial to the coming of the Christian Faith into this area. It is highly probable that the Cross was a Roman shrine adapted to this purpose."* (Possibly one location for the Roman altar found in St Mary's church). It is almost certain that the cross is a 'preaching cross' rather than a boundary or market-type cross and may well represent the close location of a Roman highway probably roughly following the A56 from the ford at Latchford to Watling Street at Rostherne.

In 1987 Martin Patch of the Manchester Museum Celtic Heads Study informed me that a small metal fertility figure of an 'impish' Roman character with an enlarged male organ had been found on a local farmer's field and handed in. At the time its age and origin were being hotly debated, but it could be a Roman/Celtic fertility figure find quite unique in this area.

Back to the walking route. Return to the Lower Dam and take the path to the right of the pool into The Dingle. Massive and ancient trees still grow from this valley floor but the high road bridge at the southern end of The Dingle has now been used to form the dam, behind which the relatively modern lake has been formed. Fish still spawn in the brook here and a kingfisher has been seen.

Up another long flight of steps and across the road leads us to the circular path surrounding the Upper Dam. An artificial cave is said to pass under the road here from The Dingle below and local residents still remember an alcove with seats and a table cut from the stone by quarry men last century, just to the right of the long flight of steps but now walled up.

Turn left to visit St Mary's Church, which is clearly visible dominating the waterside on a sandstone outcrop, or carry on along the path opposite, on the right hand side of the dam. This is a circular walk which will eventually bring you round to the church unless you have the time to explore the dark and dismal marshes known as 'The Bongs' through which modern pathways do pass - but beware lest you are spirited away by a Will-o-the-Wisp or Peg-o-Lantern!

VIEWS OF THE DINGLE A CENTURY APART

Most of the existence of this area is due to the activities of the Victorian soap giant Lord Lever who intended to create a village for his workers here, but ended up building it at Port Sunlight in Birkenhead, due to objections from the already established Crossfields factory and others in Warrington. The bridge to and from nowhere situated at the upper end of the dam (known locally as Devil's Bridge), and the rows of poplar trees, are the only remaining testament to his intentions, as the project was abandoned. The most striking feature round the dam is the imposing site of St Mary's Church.

SHADOW OF A SAXON CHURCH

Nothing much remains of the various ancient churches which have graced the site of the present St Mary The Virgin at Lymm, which overlooks the Upper Dam and the A56 Church Road. The church is currently open, however, between 9am and 5pm daily and still well worth a visit.

This church was one of only nine churches recorded in Cheshire during the Domesday survey of 1086AD, and was held, along with the village, as part of the lands of the Saxon Ulviet before the Conquest. There are several entries in Domesday covering the Lymm area which list three Saxon landowners, Edward, Wulfgeat and Ulviet, and the two new Norman owners, Gilbert and Osbern (who also owned Warburton).

After the Conquest, the church fell under the control of the two Norman lords, who probably replaced the timber Celtic church with a Norman stone structure and both then appointed ministers. Lymm had two ministers for over 800 years until the founding of St Peters in Oughtrington in 1873. Local tradition states that the Norman church was replaced by a Medieval one in about 1320AD during the reign of King Edward II (1307AD to 1327AD). While only a tradition, the first hard evidence of a church on the site comes from this period.

SKATING ON THE DAM C 1920S. NOTE UNIDENTIFIED BUILDINGS IN FRONT OF CHURCH.

THE STONE HEADS LIVE ON

Opposite the church, and a little further up the hill, stands a jigsaw puzzle house called 'Rivington Cottage' (No. 7), which appears to owe some of its existence to the period around 1550AD and up to about 1850. Built into the road-facing walls are three heads which probably came off the Medieval church when it was rebuilt in 1521AD and again in 1851. The front wall and window to the left are also the remains of an older building.

The head furthest up the hill is that of a woman or 'fair man' with hair resembling ears of corn hanging downwards, earrings of clustered grapes or continental cob corn (favoured by the Romans)

and a quite obviously severed neck with protruding bone. This head probably comes off the original Celtic church structure and looks to be a fertility god or goddess associated with corn crops of great age.

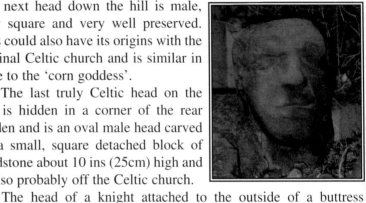

The next head down the hill is male, very square and very well preserved. This could also have its origins with the original Celtic church and is similar in style to the 'corn goddess'.

The last truly Celtic head on the site is hidden in a corner of the rear garden and is an oval male head carved on a small, square detached block of sandstone about 10 ins (25cm) high and is also probably off the Celtic church.

The head of a knight attached to the outside of a buttress supporting the oldest visible part of the cottage looks like it could have fallen off the present church structure only yesterday. The owners of the cottage say that some features have been added to the property by previous owners so there is a definite need for caution when identifying the later heads on this site with any former church. The style of the helmet and visor suggest it may be late Medieval. The lower face is missing which is a shame and it looks like this damage was done during demolition of the structure to which it was formerly attached. This head may come from the inside of the

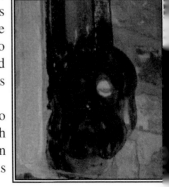

Medieval church of St Mary's when the tower was rebuilt in 1521AD as it is unlikely that anyone would take the trouble to cut into the buttress just to mount a head. It was probably placed here when this part of the building was constructed in about 1550AD.

At the rear of the building are two heads either side of an ex-church window arch which has obviously been fitted as a new feature by the previous

owners. One head is the traditional King, the other, the Queen, and they are Victorian in origin.

Inside the living room are two more heads recently added to the stonework either side of the stone fire place (which is also a recent added feature). The left-hand head is a well executed crowned King and the right-hand head, set in the corner of the room, is a very attractive head of a 'fair maiden' with flowing hair, and these are also both from the Victorian era. These four heads are not from the church of St Mary site.

Moving back inside the church, another damaged stone head of female form, and with curling hair, was said to have been dug out of the foundations of the 1320AD church during later rebuilding making it either from that church or the Norman/Celtic structure. Today it is set high into the interior wall of the vestry which is kept locked, but I can reproduce probably the only photograph taken of this head here and state that it appears Celtic in origin, possibly from the base of a window arch.

Four more heads, a tomb canopy arch and a 'Roman' altar stone are set into the south aisle outer wall. Looking at the arch, the bottom right head (which is quite worn) represents a male face with swept back and tapering long hair under which an hour glass replaces his left ear.

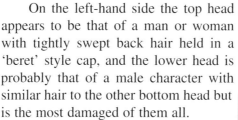

Above him, and still on the right hand side, is the face of a courtly lady with hair in a net which is then covered by a head and chin cloth held in place by a thick cord head band adorned with three 'four-petal' flowers.

On the left-hand side the top head appears to be that of a man or woman with tightly swept back hair held in a 'beret' style cap, and the lower head is probably that of a male character with similar hair to the other bottom head but is the most damaged of them all.

The whole tomb canopy with heads certainly dates from the 1320AD building period but now contains no tomb or any clues as to who was buried within it.

I feel that the central 'Roman style' altar is more important than has previously been suspected. It appears to pre-date the Medieval structure that

houses it and possibly the Norman church before that. The letters 'IW' have obviously been carved into it at a much later date and may actually represent the Greek letters 'I' and 'E' (turned side on) which were used as a first and last letter abbreviation for IHEOYE, the Greek for 'JESUS'. What we may be looking at here is a 'Christianised' version of an actual Roman altar found locally and included in one of the later church buildings. It may have been part of the reason for the church being built on this particular spot, on a prominent rise by a road.

arch and roman altar

From the available evidence I propose that a native Celtic track probably followed the course of the Bradley Brook (the HLIMME) all the way into the village and the site of the cross, and that a Roman road came from the ford at Warrington and roughly followed the A56 to a crossroads by the church, then on along Higher Lane to Rostherne. This would go a long way to explaining the layout of the village.

Two hoards of Roman coins are recorded found in the areas just outside Lymm. The first was found to the north at Statham in Georgian times (approx. 1700AD to 1800AD) and corresponds to the suggested direction of the native Celtic track.

The second hoard was found at Agden to the east in 1957, and corresponds to the suggested A56 Roman road (covered in more detail in the Dunham section of this book). Three other coin hoards at Bowden, Ashley Heath and Sale were also found close to the ancient Roman road.

From about 1320AD the Domville family of Lymm Hall had a chapel attached to the church which occupied the site of the first eleven pews of the present north aisle and is now noted only by the black shield containing a 'rampant' white lion on the north wall, above the pews and between the windows, which was the family coat of arms.

At some point the Norman church was given the hexagonal, sloping sided font dated 1401AD now being used for flowers in the gardens of Lymm Hall and probably removed during the rebuild of 1851.

A "steeple of stone for Limme church" is recorded as added to the Norman church in the earliest surviving church document of April 24th 1521AD. Notes and sketches of the windows in the Medieval church of 1320AD were made by a Thomas Challoner in 1580AD and these are reputed to be currently housed somewhere in the British Museum.

The church possesses an early seventeenth century musicians' box which was used in the church for sixty years by Thomas Hill, a bassoon player, who died aged 84 in 1831.

Victorian 'vandalism' resulted in the demolition and rebuilding of the entire church in 1851 leaving nothing of the ancient structures to be seen except those items listed here. The improved tower of 1851, based on the structure of 1521AD, then became so unsafe that it was taken down and the tower of today only dates from between 1887 and 1891 when it was dedicated.

ChANCEL DOOR (NOW DESTROYED)
SURMOUNTED BY AN ANGEL holDING A
ShielD CONTAINING The ARMS OF The
BARON OF halTON OR LIMME OF LIMME.

In former times Lymm had its ancient 'Rush Bearing' to the church, on the Monday after the second Sunday in August, which was revived in 1970 in an altered form, and was formerly a village holiday. Originally the garlanded rush cart, drawn by six dapple-grey horses, went round the village behind a troupe of Morris Dancers and a 'fool', before the evening ceremony of scattering the rushes on the church floor took place to the sound of the church bells.

The village also had a Mummer's Play at the end of October in the run up to 'All Hallows Eve' (now Hallowe'en). This troupe visited local houses preceded by the 'Hodening Horse' head on a pole ,and a story goes that this was obtained from horse slaughterers at Warrington except on one occasion when they dug for three nights looking for one buried by a local farmer!

To return to the driving route simply retrace the walk back down the 'Hlimme' brook to Dane Bank Road and carry on by car to the junction with Rushgreen Road (A6144).

For our final look at Lymm village turn left down New Road and over the canal bridge to the Cross. Here turn left and to the right on to Rectory lane which takes you past Lymm Hall on the left and up to St Mary's church. Here turn left on to the A56 Higher Lane and the house with the Celtic heads is just on the left. Stay on this Roman road for a couple of miles through Broomedge and Agden until it becomes Agden Brow and the Lymm Road, dropping downhill into Little Bollington. The entire area to the left and right of the Lymm Road contains dozens of ancient Celtic sites from this point on, so a firm base of operations is suggested at Dunham Massey Park despite the slight detour from a circular route.

The Lymm Road meets a large traffic island at which we turn left and stay on the A56 'Watling Street' Roman road up the hill. At the first set of traffic lights we turn left on to Woodhouse Lane. After about a quarter of a mile a car park exists on the right-hand side of the road (almost opposite the east gate to Dunham Park) and another National Trust car park serves the Hall and Gardens about half a mile further on at the west gate, on the left.

LYMM CROSS
ABOUT 1870

SARAH GRIFFITHS

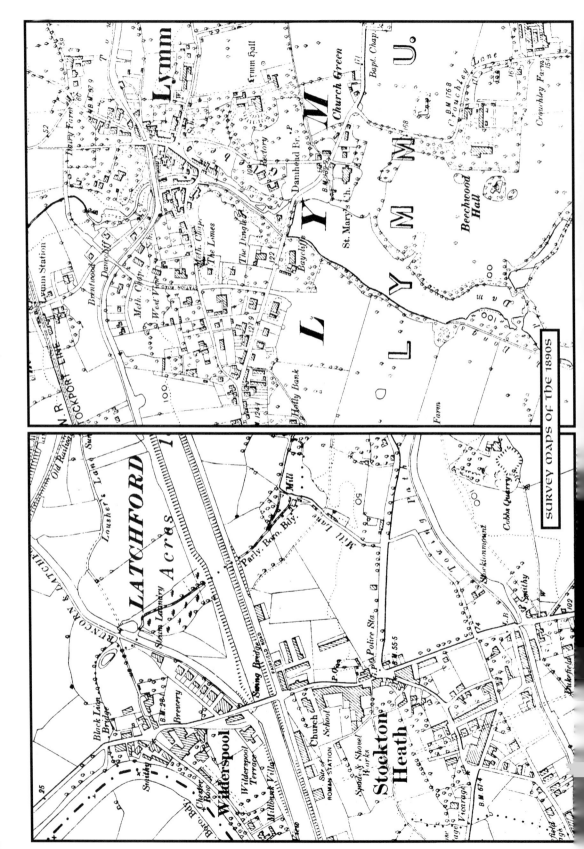

SURVEY MAPS OF THE 1890S

DUNHAM MASSEY AND LITTLE BOLLINGTON

ROSTHERNE

TATTON AND KNUTSFORD

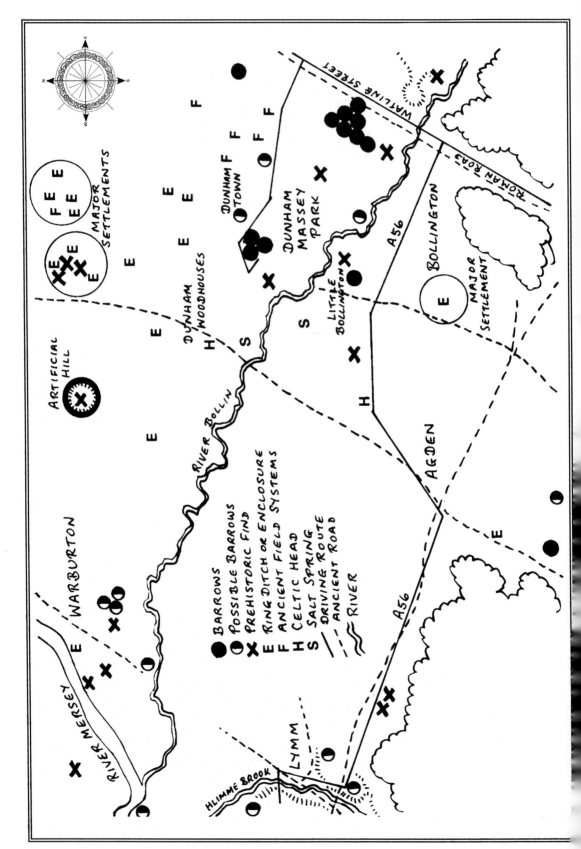

Map Legend:

● BARROWS
◐ POSSIBLE BARROWS
✗ PREHISTORIC FIND
E RING DITCH OR ENCLOSURE
F ANCIENT FIELD SYSTEMS
H CELTIC HEAD
S SALT SPRING
- - - DRIVING ROUTE
—— ANCIENT ROAD
〜〜 RIVER

Labels on map:
WATLING STREET
ROMAN ROAD
A56
DUNHAM TOWN
DUNHAM MASSEY PARK
DUNHAM WOODHOUSES
LITTLE BOLLINGTON
BOLLINGTON
MAJOR SETTLEMENT
MAJOR SETTLEMENTS
AGDEN
ARTIFICIAL HILL
RIVER BOLLIN
RIVER MERSEY
WARBURTON
LYMM
HLIMME BROOK

ÓUNHAM MASSEY AND LITTLE BOLLINGTON

In 1994 the National Trust began a complete survey of their large estate at Dunham Massey, at about the same time as the Celtic Warrington Project began to survey the south east Warrington area. Robert Woodside completed the draft version of the National Trust survey in summer 1998 at the same time as I completed the Celtic Warrington survey of the same area. Not surprisingly, when we compared notes in January 1999 we had covered very much the same ground and interviewed the same archaeological sources on ancient history to whom we are both indebted.

Consequently, the contents of Robert Woodside's report, intended for the eyes of the National Trust, are very like the contents of this section covering the ancient history of Dunham Massey intended for the eyes of the general reader. I apologise for any apparent duplications here and would just like to give full credit to all those, including Robert Woodside, who have helped compile information on Dunham Massey and surrounding areas.

I would just like to add that at this stage it appears the National Trust report is not intended for release to the general reader; Celtic Warrington, however, is.

ÓUNHAM MASSEY PARK

The earliest evidence for human settlement around Dunham Massey and the River Bollin omes from prehistoric times. During the Mesolithic period (10,000BC to 5000BC) there is ·vidence in the area for human hunting activities mainly in the form of stray flint and bone finds,

such as the single flint found at the centre of Dunham Park, the two arrow heads found just outside the park, and the shaft scraper found in fields below Pool Bank Farm close to 'Watch Hill'. (The obvious exception to this is the major flint working site on Tatton Park dealt with in that section). These sites have revealed animal bones belonging to aurochs ('urus' or large cattle), red deer and elk which would have formed herds grazing along the Mersey Valley in prehistoric times. The deer found in Dunham Massey Park today have been introduced and are sadly not native to the area despite the frequent appearance of the much sought after Celtic 'White Stag', sacred up to Medieval times when it became the prize of the hunt!

Moving nearer in time to the Neolithic period (5000BC to 2000BC), Mike Nevell's excellent 1997 book *The Archaeology of Trafford* contains the result of a Palaeoecological Analysis of the surviving remains of Warburton Moss to the north west of Dunham Massey. Results showed that the area was dry and heavily wooded from about 3000BC, until traces of charcoal indicated the arrival of human activity during the Bronze Age (about 2000BC).

By the Iron Age (800BC), cereal pollen and weeds found on compacted ground enter the analysis, indicating prolonged settlement and farming practices, along with wet land pollens such as heather, bog myrtle and sphagnum moss. This situation remained until the drainage activities of recent times.

Neolithic finds have also come to light in the surrounding areas including flint arrowheads at Altrincham, Little Bollington and Sale, and a scraper at Altrincham. Prehistoric finds on or near the Altrincham ridge or close to the A56 Roman Watling Street hint strongly at a pre-Roman north east to south west route through the Mossland Crescent east of Trafford, possibly taken over and used by the Romans, like the A49 London Road in Appleton south of Warrington.

ENGRAVING OF DUNHAM HALL AND PARK IN THE LATE 1850S

During field walking, over a rectangular enclosure, crop mark and other features along the Caldwell Brook in the far north of the Dunham estate, prehistoric stone tools, including axes, and two flints were found. There are at least six square and rectangular crop features in the fields either side of Red House Lane, one of which has been identified as clearly prehistoric. Others may be Iron Age or Romano-British and some Roman pottery has been recovered from the fields and sites. The marks appear to show at least three settlements with fields and buildings occupied during two different time periods. A crop mark off Dairyhouse Road, at Sinderland Green, north of Dairyhouse Farm, may be yet another circular enclosure or a Bronze Age barrow.

Between Sinderland Green and Dunham Park there are a total of fourteen enclosures, crop features and earthworks (two identified as prehistoric). Combined with this, there are five Medieval field systems recorded in various forms along Oldfield Lane to the east of Dunham Town and one next to Little Bollington to the south west.

Another major settlement site exists just a little further south of Little Bollington along Reddy Lane opposite Arthill Farm. This consists of a series of sub-rectangular enclosures and field boundaries identified on aerial photographs by archaeologists at Manchester and excavated in 1987 and 1988. An enclosure ditch with two internal post trenches indicated a small defended site with four internal round and two rectangular buildings. The round buildings gave carbon-dates of 2879BC to 2581BC and 2280BC to 2036BC giving a late Neolithic or early Bronze Age date to the site of about 2458BC.

ALTRINCHAM IN 1913

Archaeologist Nick Higham has suggested that two tribes of Celts inhabited this area from the later Bronze Age, the Brigantes predominantly north of the Mersey and the Cornovii, south into Cheshire. After the Romans left the area it probably became partly reafforested until Trafford was settled by the Danes who invaded from east of the Pennines. The lack of Pagan Saxon burials also suggests a great deal of Celtic Christian activity here during the dark ages. ALTRINCHAM, or ALTRINGHAM, as a name, is most probably Saxon in origin and is derived from the Old English ALDHERINGE-HAM meaning the homestead called 'Aldhere's Place' or 'The Village Of Aldhere's People'.

SACRED BURIAL GROUNDS OF THE BOLLIN VALLEY

Archaeological evidence in the area begins to increase during the Middle Bronze Age (2000BC to 1500BC). Having examined the River Bollin junction with the Mersey at Warburton in Book 1, it comes as no surprise to find that the Bronze Age inhabitants of North Cheshire made use of the other flat areas, further back along the Bollin Valley into Cheshire, to bury their dead.

Overall it would appear that burials in round barrows were made close to the river, probably for sacred reasons outlined elsewhere in this book, and that settlement took place on the ridges to the north and south.

The first small group of burial mounds to be recorded were noted by the early eighteenth century antiquary, Horsley, as being in the Dunham Park, north of the present hall, beyond the 'moat' feature, and containing an urn unearthed by workmen (now lost). This site was still just barely visible in a report of 1934 but has now disappeared.

On the 1805 to 1873 OS map a large tumulus is clearly shown at the centre of Dunham New Park (now the golf course), but this site was improved during landscape work by the 5th Earl of Stamford between 1770AD and 1785AD and nothing more is known about the site.

The same OS map shows 'Fairy Brow', south west of Dunham Park over the Bollin, as an ancient site which had a long folk tradition as a 'haunted graveyard' - a 4000 year folk tradition in fact!

In 1983 the site of a possible barrow was excavated here by South Trafford Archaeology Group and the cremated remains of a sturdy young man were unearthed buried in a shaped deposit reminiscent of a 'leather bag' which gave a carbon-date of about 1435BC. Despite being known now as the 'Dunham Bag Burial' no actual leather bag was found. This burial was accompanied by a single riveted tanged Bronze Age dagger or razor, about 3 ins (8cm) long, placed just above the flat top of the burial, and six flint tools typical of the 2000BC to 1500BC period. One unworked flint was found burned in the cremation remains which are now stored at Chester.

Over the centuries sand had been removed from this barrow site and the stones from the burial structures were found at the bottom of the hill on the Bollin flood plain where they had been discarded. It is also felt that further burial remains constituting a 'cemetery' and a possible settlement site are present in this area for future excavation.

A little further south of Fairy Brow there exist significant crop marks at Arthill Farm, Bollington, one set of which indicate a possible early Bronze Age enclosed settlement of 2120BC to 1730BC, and another set representing an enclosed field system from the Roman period 100AD to 300AD. Field walking has also produced worked flints from the area of Arthill Heath Farm, even further to the south, and the ring ditch of a Bronze Age barrow has been identified on the ground at Broad Oak Farm on Peacock Lane.

In his report, Robert Woodside notes that a mound shown in the south west corner of Dunham Park, on the 1839 Dunham Massey township tithe map, may represent the site of yet another group of potential barrows to the north of the site at Fairy Brow. On the 1876 25 ins OS map, three contour circles are shown, but it is unclear if these are mounds or water filled depressions.

In 1979 Manchester University undertook a successful season of aerial photography which revealed a concentration of at least seven crop ring features in fields between the A56 Roman road and the south east boundary of Dunham Park above Home Farm. These have all been interpreted as ploughed-out Bronze Age barrows in a 'cemetery' formation.

The same season revealed a barrow crop mark in a field just north of Dunham Park and east of Dunham Village which has also been identified as a ploughed out Bronze Age Barrow

Various OS maps from the 1930s to the 1950s also show a tumulus situated on raised ground next to the small farm building 'feature' on the field rise north west of the walled cottage garden at Dunham Town.

The biggest tumulus (or barrow) type structure that I have so far encountered in Cheshire can be found at the most northern extremity of the area covered by this book, north west of Reed House Farm and Mosshall Farm and clearly visible from either Dunham Road or Gorsey Lane. This mound has given up a stray prehistoric stone axe head but a trench dug through it to lay pipes revealed no finds. However serious investigation of the site remains to be done.

This huge mound lies just beyond the boundary ditch dug between the 'Booths' of Dunham Massey and the 'Warburtons' of Warburton in 1446AD following various ownership disputes between both estates. William Massy, John Nedham and Roger Legh arbitrated and decreed that: *".... the meres (boundaries) cross the moors and mosses in a direct line from a great stone to be set up on the north side of the moor, in the west corner of the 'Gale Slakke' and 'Bruesshaghfeld', by the side of the moor, to two great stones to be set up on the south west side".*

It is interesting to note that Peter Warburton II inherited the Warburton estates in 1448AD and moved the family seat to Arley Hall in 1469AD, just after this arbitration, and a massive stone exists on the Arley estate on Sack Lane by Arley Green (see Arley chapter) which may be a continuation of the "great stone" boundary concept.

If this is the case then the Warburtons controlled Warburton, Lymm, High Legh, Antrobus and Arley in about 1470AD, and the Booths controlled Dunham, Bollington, Millington, Mere and Tabley - and therefore a much longer estate boundary should be searched for. The Dunham stones are gone but a later ditch can still be traced along the approximate course of the old boundary.

THE ROMAN TREASURE HOARD

The south eastern boundary of the Dunham estate is marked by the A56 Roman Road known as Watling Street which ran from Viroconium (Wroxeter), provincial capital of the Celtic Cornovii tribe, towards Mediolanum (Whitchurch). Here it turned north west to Deva (Chester) and north east to Salinae (Middlewich). From Deva (Chester) the roads then led to North Wales or Veratinum (Warrington). From Salinae (Middlewich) roads led to Condate (Northwich) and Mamucium (Manchester) - the road which passes Dunham Massey as the A56.

The Roman Road almost follows the path of the modern road except where it is still visible crossing the River Bollin in fields about 100 yards north west of the present A56 main road.

A stray find of a Roman amphora handle (100AD to 250AD) was found here during field walking, and South Trafford Archaeology Group excavated the road after flooding in 1987 and found a substantial construction with a number of unidentified wooden post holes possibly not of Roman origin. There is a good possibility that more road has also survived higher up on the golf course in the 'New Park'.

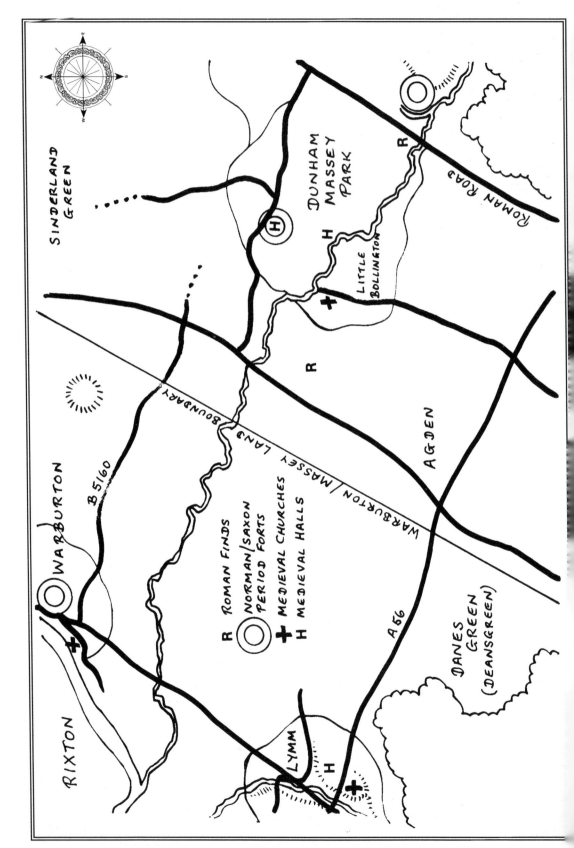

In 1957 a hoard of 2450 Roman coins were found buried in an earthenware jar at the south end of a strip of land overlooking Agden Brook on Woolstencroft Farm west of Dunham Park (previously mentioned in the Lymm section at Agden). The coins ranged in date from Valerian I (253AD to 260AD) to Probus (276AD to 282AD) with the majority being of Terticus I and Victorinus.

Most of the coins are bronze with a few of a silver/bronze alloy and some showing signs of silver coating. Some are 'barbarous radiates' and 'minimi' otherwise known as local copies of the official coinage produced under licence to the governor. Further investigation of the site during the 1990s has not brought any more discoveries to light.

Don Bayliss records another hoard of Roman coins found further along the River Bollin to the east at Ashley Heath, yet another on the north west side of the A56 Watling Street half way between Altrincham and Sale, and a collection of loose coins south east of the A56 at Bowdon.

If the dates on these match those from Dunham Massey then a very serious upheaval was taking place in this area in about 280AD, probably related to the Admiral of the Roman fleet, Carausius, breaking away from Rome to become 'sovereign of Britain' from 286AD to 294AD.

The owner of the coins may have travelled from Warrington or Manchester and there can be no doubt that the coins were buried on purpose. Does this date signify the last days in the final decline of Roman Wilderspool and Manchester and the start of the Welsh/Briton reclamation of their Mersey Valley territory? By 290AD the power of Rome was weakening.

OWNERSHIP OF DUNHAM PARK THE PRESENT DUNHAM MASSEY

This owes much to the special vision of Sir George Booth (1675AD to 1758AD), the 2nd Earl of Warrington, who designed the park with its radiating avenues and intricate tree patterns. He built the stables and clock tower, rebuilt the house, and furnished the entire property inside and out, adding his own library collection to its book shelves. Legend says that he planted over 100,000 trees (although only about 60,000 have so far been accounted for) probably including the famous 'Dunham Oak' which stands, supported by concrete, in the centre of Dunham Town.

The 'Oak' today and in 1932

By adding his vision to Dunham Massey, Sir George Booth was simply building on a long tradition of developers at Dunham Massey stretching back into the Dark Ages.

In the first division of Briton by the Romans this area was included as part of BRITANNIA SUPERIOR, which was divided again becoming FLAVIA CAESARIENSIS. After the Romans departed, and the Saxons invaded, the Saxon King Ethelfred defeated the Britons in 607AD to 613AD, captured this area and marched on up the Dee to massacre the Celtic monks of Bangor. However Celtic rule had been maintained here almost two hundred years longer than in Saxon south east England and Anglo-Saxon colonisation came very slowly. From the study of place names it appears that the English (read 'Saxon') arrival in Cheshire was probably made along Roman roads before 650AD at the latest.

The Celtic name DUNHAM or DONEHAM, found in Domesday 1086AD, means 'hill-village' or 'homestead on a hill'. Some other possible Celtic place names thought to survive around Warrington are: Walton, Grappenhall, Stretton, Lymm, Mowpen Brow (High Legh), Bollington, Dunham Massey, Dunham-on-the-Hill, and Crosstown (Knutsford).

King Alfred (871AD to 901AD) placed Cheshire in MERCENLEGE, and about 980AD the Mercian remains of the Cornovii tribe parcelled twelve 'hundreds' south of the Mersey into the shire of LEGECEASTER which later became CHESTERSHIRE or CHESHIRE.

The Vikings began to attack along the Mersey in about 902AD and King Canute brought Danish rule in 1016AD. It is thought that Altrincham was then part of the northern kingdom of Northumbria making the Bollin valley a very important border region.

Dunham Massey can be traced back to this late Saxon period when it was held, along with the manors of Little Bollington and Bowdon, by Eluard (Alweard or Alfward) the Saxon. Nine manors are mentioned in Domesday as being owned by Eluard before 1066AD, but he had his centre at Dunham, his food production at Hale and his church at Bowden.

The primary Medieval settlements recorded in early documents are Dunham (1086AD, and Castle 1173AD to 1323AD and Park 1362AD), Bowdon (Bogedone 1086AD and chapel 1307AD), Hale (1086AD), Ullerwell Castle (in Hale 1173AD), Altrincham (1290AD), Oldfield (Aldefeld 1293AD), Sinderland Green (meaning 'Separated Land' about 1350AD to 1400AD) and Little Bollington (1086AD and Mill 1088AD/1363AD).

After Eluard the Saxon, the lands were then given to the Norman Hamo de Mascy (from Massey in Seine Inferieure, France) by Hugh Lupus who ruled Cheshire on behalf of the Normans at that time, and once again this linked the Mersey valley to the Seine areas of Northern France. The original estate spread over much of North Cheshire and South Lancashire, raising interesting questions about the relationship between Dunham, Rostherne and Tatton, but the Anglo-Saxon Dunham Town is yet to be discovered; the mill and church are both

A MISTY BRICKKILN LANE, DUNHAM

recorded in Bowden.

The family of Hamo de Mascy held the huge Barony of Dunham Massey until about 1342AD but little is known of this mysterious family thereafter.

Sir Peter Leycester calculated that six generations of the family all called 'Hamo' (!) had elapsed between 1086AD and 1340AD, although the generational gap implied is improbably long. It may be that the name 'Hamo' translated more as a title than a first name in Norman times. The last Hamo de Mascy died in about 1342AD and, after a hundred years of argument over ownership, the estates then passed to Sir Robert Booth early in the fifteenth century (about 1433AD).

The earliest description of the Hall in Dunham Park occurs in a review of the manor dated to about 1410AD or 1411AD. The manor had a hall surrounded by a moat and adjoining fish pool and included: a high chamber (private bed-sitting room of the owner), chapel and other small

chambers, treasury, stable, gatehouse and a thatched granary within the moat, and a ruined dovecot, orchard and meadow outside the moat.

The Booth family secured their position by marrying into prominent families such as the Venables of Bollin and the

Ðunham Mill 1910

Ðunham Mill Today

Traffords of Trafford. Sir George Booth senior (1566AD to 1652AD) was made Sheriff of Lancashire and twice of Cheshire, and built the New Hall around 1616AD. Sir George junior (1622AD to 1684AD) joined his grandfather George senior in the Civil War conflict and spent time in the Tower of London for his part in the uprising of 1659AD. Sir Henry Booth (1651AD to 1694AD) also spent time in prison for his part in the Duke of Monmouth's rebellion and was only given back his political position as the st Earl of Warrington after the 'Glorious Revolution' of 1688AD. Sir Henry Booth (1675AD to 758AD), 2nd Earl of Warrington, inherited the Dunham estates in 1694AD. He found them in state of virtual dereliction, and so began a long period of restoration from which most surviving aintings of the park originate.

Dunham Massey stayed in the Booth family until 1758AD when it passed by marriage to he Grey family of Stamford in Leicester. The Earls of Stamford then kept the estate until it assed to the National Trust in 1976.

CASTLES IN THE AIR

Two chroniclers, Benedict of Peterborough and William of Newburgh, record that *'Hamo de Masci held castellum at Duneham and Ullerwell'* (translated from the latin in *Gesta Regis Henrici Secundi,* B. Stubbs, London 1867). These castles mentioned in 1173AD are a mystery, further complicated by the presence of 'Watch Hill' which is yet another primitive castle close by at Bowden.

The site of the primary castle held by Hamo de Mascy after 1086AD has always been thought to have stood somewhere on the Dunham Park estate. Cheshire historian, George Omerod, believed that the site of Dunham Castle was represented by the mound feature, surrounded on two sides by water, found at the north west corner of the hall, when he examined

it in about 1816. The castle is mentioned as still standing in: *"the sixteenth year of the reign of Edward II (1323AD) when Robert Massey of Tatton pleaded that Nicholas Audley held the Manor of Tatton of him by knight's service at his castle at Dunham"* (Omerod 1882 II, P 440). This quote raises questions again regarding the relationship of Tatton to Dunham as Robert Massey was Lord of Tatton but had one of his knights holding Dunham Castle on his behalf.

From this point written evidence only hints at the existence of the castle which may have been replaced by a new moated hall some time between 1323AD and 1362AD.

Three hundred years later a large earthwork over 35 ft (11m) high is clearly shown on paintings and engravings of Dunham Park, beginning in 1697AD with a four stepped 'prospect mound' garden feature with a summer house on top. By 1751AD it had been cut back to form five steps with an urn on top and was then reduced to the present flat dome ringed with trees at the turn of the century (about 1905).

EAST AND WEST VIEWS OF DUNHAM HALL AND 'CASTLE MOUNT', JOHN HARRIS 1750/51.

In 1972 suggestions were made that this mound may not have been the Norman motte and this caused local historians and archaeological groups to further investigate the site in detail. Despite a geophysical survey and Paleo-Environmental research nothing conclusive could be found as the site had been modified beyond recognition. Nevertheless Dunham is specifically specified as the site of the Norman castle in ancient documents and the original mound appears too large and badly situated to have started life as just a garden feature.

A site for Ullerwell castle has been located in Hale in the Ringway area of Manchester but is outside the geographic area of this book.

The suggestion in 1972 was that Watch Hill, on the east side of the A56 overlooking the River Bollin, was the actual site of the Norman castle of Dunham Massey, the moat at Dunham belonging to the later Tudor hall and the mound being only a garden feature. All eyes turned to Watch Hill (also known as 'Yarwood Castle' and 'Castle Hill').

THE CASTLE HILL MOTTE

Archaeological investigation was undertaken in 1976 by K. Brown and B. Johnson who found evidence for a timber structure and possible hearth on top of the motte, but the only datable find so far from the site was a silver Henry II penny (1154AD to 1189AD) which came out of a rabbit hole on top of the mound in 1993 and may represent a link to the rebellion of barons (including Hamo de Mascy) against the King in the uprising of 1173AD. It was also established that the mound had been artificially raised by about 2m. of earth being piled on top, when the ditch separating the natural promontory from the bailey site had been dug, and some of the defensive banks surrounding the bailey 'village' were just visible in 1976.

THE MOTTE FROM THE BAILEY

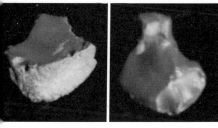
BOTH SIDES OF THE SHAFT SCRAPER

Little work has yet been done on the bailey platform field to the south east. A stone age 'finger and thumb' flint tool formerly used for stripping arrow and spear shafts was found by myself during field walking in January 1999 by the lower foot path style below Pool Bank Farm (the next field south east from the bailey). Sadly other parts of this area have been artificially raised over recent years.

The great age of the surrounding human remains and the fact that 'Watch Hill' certainly has a commanding view over the Roman crossing point of the River Bollin to the north west, leads me to suspect that the late Norman date given to this castle site is probably not the point at which it was first constructed. I am fairly certain that the castle has its origins in the Celtic/Saxon Dark Ages of the tenth century (900AD to 1000AD) or before, and is certainly too small and too far removed from Dunham Park to be the Norman castle of Dunham.

TBE MYSTERIOUS PRIORY OF BAMO DE MASCY

The castle at Dunham Park built by Hamo de Mascy may have disappeared but fortunately it was not the only structure that he commissioned. It is a little known fact that he was also responsible for founding and constructing the Priory at Birkenhead in about 1150AD and a lot can be deduced about the man and his beliefs from the ruined Priory that remains.

The first generations of the de Mascy family probably arrived with William the Conqueror in 1066AD, having been born in northern France. Scandinavian Northmen or 'Vikings' were granted the Duchy of Normandy in 911AD and it is from this background that the Norman/French family of Hamo would have been descended, therefore a 'Hamo de Mascy' probably existed in some form for over 300 years. Either the Hamo who first came to Britain had discovered the secret of eternal youth or the name 'Hamo' became more a title than a first name. Eventually his 'potion of youth' must have run out and the last 'Hamo de Mascy' appears to have died in about 1342AD leaving a hundred year dispute over the ownership of his lands, including Dunham.

Birkenhead Priory was constructed by Hamo (III) on an isolated headland on the Mersey protected by the river to the east, 'Wallasey Pool' to the north and 'Tranmere Pool' to the south and was initially established with sixteen monks. There is some disagreement as to whether these monks were Augustinian Canons, as recorded in the manuscript at Corpus Christi College Cambridge, or Benedictine Monks, as stated in all the present literature on the site. I favour the Augustinian monastic rule as this occurs at other sites along the Mersey Valley associated with the Knights Templar, who may have first encountered the rules of St Augustine during their activities in North Africa and the Middle East in the Crusades. Of course, the monks of Birkenhead could have been Augustinians following the rule of St Benedict!

These monks ran a ferry crossing from here to the developing town of Liverpool and entertained a great many travellers including King Edward I during his Welsh campaigns in 1275AD, and again with his Queen Eleanor in 1277AD, when he received envoys from the King of Scotland at the Priory, including the son of Robert the Bruce. In 1282AD the King ordered carts and wagons from the Priory to carry food to his English armies fighting the Welsh, a conflict which amounted to nothing more than the Normans attempting to subdue the Celtic/Britons.

how bamo de mascy may have looked at the time of henry ii

INTERIOR ENTRANCE TO THE WEST RANGE WITH STONE 'MONK'S HEAD' WINDOW DETAIL
FROM THE RANGE AND A 'FEMALE PATRON' WINDOW DETAIL FROM THE NOW
DEMOLISHED PRIORY CHURCH. THE FEMALE PATRON WAS 'DE-FACED' DURING THE
DISSOLUTION OF THE MONASTERIES.

FOR MARCH, 1785.

An Account of BIRKHEDDE PRIORY, *in* Cheshire: *With a fine* VIEW *of its venerable Ruins.*

THIS Priory, as appears from different Writers, was also called Bricheved, Byrket, and Burket-Wood Priory. It was founded in the latter end of the reign of Henry the Second, or in that of Richard the First, by Hamon Maffey, third Baron of Dunham Maffey, who placed therein fixteen Benedictine Monks. A Manufcript in Corpus Chrifti College, Cambridge, makes them Canons of the Order of St. Auguftine. It was dedicated to St. Mary and St. James.

In the Monafticon are two Charters of the faid Hamon Maffey. In the firft, he grants to this Monaftery in free alms, half an acre of land at Dunham, and an acre at Lacheker, with the advowfon of the church of Bowdon; and in the other, the liberty of choofing their own Prior, granted before by Pope Alexander: whence it feems, as if the Papal permiffion for fuch election was not then fufficient without the confirmation of the patron.

At the Diffolution, its revenues were eftimated at 90l. 13s. per ann. according to Dugdale; 102l. 16s. 10d. according to Speed; its reputed value 108l. and by a MS. in Corpus Chrifti College, Cambridge, it was only reckoned at 80l. In the 36th of Henry the Eighth, it was granted to Ralph Worfeley.

This houfe is faid by Leland to have been fubordinate to the Abbey of Chefter; but Tanner does not fubfcribe to that opinion.

In the Vale Royal of England, pub-lifhed in 1656, by Dan. King, there is a view of this Priory, by which it is plain that much of the buildings have been demolifhed fince the time when that was drawn. Annexed to it is the following account: ' Where the paffage lies over into Lancafhire, unto Leaverpool, we ftep over into Berket-Wood, and where hath been a famous Priory, the foundation whereof I am not yet inftruct for; but now a very goodly demean, and which is come, by defcent from the Worfleyes, men of great poffeffions, now to a gentleman of much worth, Thomas Powel, Efq; the heir of that ancient feat of Horfley, in the county of Flint; and one whom our county may gladly receive, to be added to the number of thofe that deferve better commendation than I am fit to give them; though unto him I am particularly bound to extend my wits to a higher reach, then here I will make tryall of.'

At prefent it is the property of Richard Perry Price, Efq; whofe grandfather, Mr. Cleveland, purchafed it of Mr. Powel.

What is fhewn in the annexed view, which was drawn in 1770, feems to have been part of the church or chapel of the Priory. Towards the left hand, under the middle of the tuft of ivy, is the remains of a confeffional feat, the entrance being through the Gothic arch: the fmall window was the aperture, at which the penitents related their tranfgreffions to the prieft.

BIRKHEDDE PRIORY. *by W. B.*

By 1318AD the Priory was becoming run down and applied to King Edward II and later King Edward III to have paying guests, as well as the ferry, and this was granted in 1318AD and 1330AD. The last Hamo de Mascy died in about 1342AD but connections to the Booths of Dunham continued from about 1433AD until Henry VIII dissolved the monastery in 1536AD and the site was abandoned.

THE PRIORY SITE PAINTED IN THE 17TH CENTURY

BIRKENHEAD FERRY IN THE 18TH CENTURY

Although the ferry and estate were maintained, the buildings gradually deteriorated until Cammell Laird's Shipyards threatened the site in 1889 and the area of the former Priory Church was used to build a dry dock in 1956. Charles Aldridge launched an appeal to save the remains of the priory in 1890 and employed masons from Chester to make the remaining structures safe. (Their various marks are all over the buildings today). When J. Cuming Walters visited the Priory for his book *Romantic Cheshire,* with illustrator Frank Greenwood in the late 1920s, he noted that: *"Birkenhead hides its historic old Priory in a dingy quarter and proudly displays its great docks and shipping."* In 1941 the Scriptorium roof was damaged by a stray incendiary bomb intended for the shipyard.

BIRKENHEAD PRIORY TODAY

Fortunately for our study successful restoration efforts since 1890 have saved the original Chapter House and Scriptorium built by Hamo de Mascy, and many other small but important details.

THE UNDERCROFT ILLUSTRATED BY FRANK GREENWOOD IN 1930 AND AS IT IS TODAY.

The site today is well worth a visit by anyone interested in the life and times of the Norman/Medieval Lords of Dunham Massey or the activities of the Knights Templar, and holds more than its fair share of surprises.

Buildings still standing include: the Cloister (now a Victorian cemetery), Chapter House, Scriptorium (now a private chapel), Buttery, Undercroft, and the ruined: Monk's Parlour, Prior's and Monk's Lodgings, Serving Lobby, Refectory, Guest Hall and Guest Rooms.

Buildings which are now missing completely but were known on the site included: the Priory Church (now a dry dock), Dorter or Sleeping Rooms and Latrines (doorway still standing in Cloisters), Misericord, Prior's Chapel, Kitchens, the timber Gate Keeper's Lodge and the West Range 'stairs' (possibly a shrine).

TREASURES OF THE KNIGHTS TEMPLAR

The first building encountered on the site is the West Range which incorporated the Guest Hall, Guest Rooms, Serving Lobby, Monk's Parlour and Prior's Lodgings. The front of this building facing the road has the highest concentration of carved faces on the site, high up along the top lintel, mixed in with the flower pattern. This includes the Birkenhead 'Cheshire Cat' at the east end.

Just inside the Guest Hall is a fireplace with one remaining carved face which may represent a bearded Knight Templar with long hair, or the patron Hamo de Mascy (of the day).

who built the West Range some time after 1250AD. Whoever the builder was, this stone head is very striking and he undertook a peculiar ceremony before commencing construction.

IS THIS THE HEAD OF HAMO DE MASCY OR THAT OF A TEMPLAR KNIGHT?

During excavations a small stone 'cyst' or four-sided burial chamber was discovered under the most easterly buttress of the West Range, where the timber entrance to the Monk's Parlour and "stairs" to the Prior's Lodgings on the first floor are supposed to have stood. This contained the bones of a young wild sheep with horns which must have been sacrificed as an offering of some kind before building of the Range commenced, and then buried with care and consideration in a purpose built 'grave'. No explanation for this can be found. Was it the 'scape goat' for the sins of the people, a Pagan fertility sacrifice, a Christian 'sacrificial lamb' or an obscure Templar sacrifice? We will probably never know but

SITE OF THE 'SACRIFICE BURIAL.

THE FRONT OF THE WEST RANGE.

it is certainly the most peculiar evidence for the possible survival of Celtic sacrificial rites I have found so far. The timber structure which stood here, and was interpreted as *"a two story porch entrance to the Parlour with stairs to the Prior's Lodgings"*, was burnt down. Maybe this was a timber shrine of some kind which every visitor to the Priory would have had to pass by or through in order to enter and which eventually fell out of favour and was destroyed.

Attached to the West Range is the magnificent surviving Undercroft drawn by Frank Greenwood in the 1920s, with a Buttery (now the visitor reception) and the former Guest Rooms on the first floor (now a concert facility). The very high standard of worksmanship used on the Undercroft suggests that it probably doubled as an additional dining room as well as a cellar. The Undercroft now houses an excellent museum which contains the remains of the 'sheep sacrifice', along with other items found during archaeological activity, such as a wild boar's tusk, gold coin of Edward III (about 1361AD), corn grinding bowl and wheel, Medieval French green glaze pottery and later 'Cistercian ware' cup and bowl fragments from 1500AD to 1536AD. There is also a stone slab patterned with superb fossilised sand ripples and the footprints of Chirotherium, the 'Hand Beast' dinosaur of Lymm.

The Chapter House, which is now a small chapel with a spectacular vaulted Norman ceiling, was one of the first buildings constructed in about 1150AD with the Scriptorium (or possibly Strong Room) added as a second floor in about 1375AD. This is probably the oldest building still standing on the Wirral and Mersey Valley.

In the chapel of today lie at least five distinctive gravestones belonging to Knights Templars either side of the altar, along with the tombstone of Prior Thomas Rayneford who died in 1473AD and whose grave originally housed three skeletons when this stone was relocated.

The presence of Templar 'Warrior Monks' on the site is also supported by various records of violent conduct, apart from supplying the armies of Edward I in

1282AD. The Prior and a monk called Geoffrey armed themselves and assaulted John Watson, stealing all his clothes in what appeared to be some kind of revenge attack at the Saturday market in Liverpool in 1350AD. A monk, Robert de Urmston, of Birkenhead Priory, was accused of stealing a silver-gilt brooch and cape from another monk (John de Wigan) but was acquitted in 1423AD. Richard Norman killed a Birkenhead monk in self defence in 1435AD, made pilgrimage to Rome and became Prior at Birkenhead some time after his return. He was then accused of accidentally killing Margaret Belynge (Billinge) with his 'stick' which fell on her from a tree! He was acquitted but his 'stick', worth fourpence, was confiscated.

The Priory Church was originally dedicated to St James and The Virgin

Mary which is typical of Templar sites; St. James being one of those martyred by 'beheading' (along with John the Baptist) and The Virgin Mary being the 'goddess' figure of Christianity. Templars harked back to the Celtic belief of a severed head guaranteeing the fertility of their endeavours and they also had a female concept of God and Divinity (for which they were later persecuted).

The stained glass window above the altar was installed this century to commemorate Robert Sydney Marsden (who was on the restoration committee in 1913 to 1919) and shows images (R to L) of King Edward I, St. James, Jesus, The Virgin Mary and the subject of our searches, Hamo De Mascy himself (as he might of looked at the time of his death around 1342AD).

We leave Birkenhead Priory with just one last tantalising legend. It is said that the priory had amassed great treasures by the time of the Dissolution in 1536AD. Knowing what was coming, some of the monks tried to carry as much as they could and escape down a secret tunnel but a great stone door gave way crushing one of the monks and entombing the others. This sounds remarkably like the work of the Knights Templar who protected their treasures in this way on other 'booby-trapped' sites. It is said that the treasure remains hidden to this day!

THE 20TH CENTURY STAINED GLASS WINDOW BY NINIAN COMPER IN THE CHAPTER HOUSE WHICH FEATURES (L TO R) HAMO DE MASCY (MASSEY), MARY (MARIA), JESUS, ST JAMES (ST. JACOB) AND EDWARD I.

JUST A PINCH OF SALT

Dunham Massey is not generally renowned for its industrial activity, however documentary sources in the John Rylands Library indicate evidence for the Cheshire salt industry beside the River Bollin at Dunham Woodhouses, east of Dunham Massey Hall. Ancient Britons, Romans, Celts and the later Danish and Norse invaders all had need of salt, and the presence of brine springs here in the Bollin Valley would certainly not have escaped their notice. The fields, in which the Dunham brine springs are, have so far given up a hoard of 2450 Roman coins from about 280AD, a Bronze Age stone axe from next to Agden Brook, a Celtic head to the north at Dunham Woodhouses and a Celtic head from the side of the Lymm Road to the south probably both dating from 100BC to 100AD.

In April 1957 a circular hammer stone (axe), with a depression worked into each face, was found in the field on Woolstencroft Farm close to the Bridgewater Canal and Agden Brook. Uniquely for finds in this area the stone was identified as 'greywacke' probably originating in North Wales and possibly Bronze Age.

A Celtic stone head was found in 1995 in the garden of Ivy Cottage at Dunham Woodhouses by the owner while digging a grave for the recently deceased family cat. This head is a one-sided sandstone carving of a face with hair, ears, big eyes, a pointed chin and flat features about 1 foot high (30cm) and looks Romano-British in origin. It is also just north of the most

northerly brine spring and is recorded here in print for the first time.

The other Celtic stone head was found in the garden just to the west side of Brookside Cottage on the Lymm road by the present owner about thirty years ago when, as a boy, he was helping his father to dig out this part of the garden for a flower bed. It is free standing, using the neck as the base, and surrounds a block of grey sandstone creating the effect of a full head. It has hair, ears, an oval face and flat features. Martin Patch of the Manchester Museum 'Celtic Heads Survey' examined and recorded the find concluding that it was probably Late Iron Age Romano-British dating from about 100BC to 100AD. It was found south of the most southerly brine spring next to Agden Brook.

The similarities of style, material, size and features of the two heads leads to the obvious conclusion that they were carved at about the same time. But a word of caution. They were also found about the same distance from each house, 8 to 10 feet (2.5m to 3.1m), at about the same depth under ground, 12 to 18 ins (30cm to 45cm), and both houses were originally built in the late 17th to early 18th centuries. It is also said that they could have been produced by builders on the Bridgewater Canal between 1759 AD and 1776 AD. Nevertheless, any one or all of these finds could represent Iron Age Celtic religious veneration towards the brine springs of Dunham Woodhouses.

While there has yet to be found any ancient evidence of salt working on this site, a lease dated 20th August 1633AD records an agreement between George Bowden of Bowden Hall Cheshire and Christopher Anderton of Lostock, Lancashire, for *"the lives of his three sons, two acres called 'The Bendeye' with all salt-springs, brine-springs, salt-waters and salt-pits therein"* at an annual rent of £3. This indicates an established salt working site probably from some time before 1600AD.

In addition to this are included two acres called Hermytts Faugh and other land 143 yards long and 7 yards wide, with a lane on one side of The Little Broadfield and Hermytts Faugh for *"the conveniency of passage with salt"* for the sum of £200. George Bowden and his sons could also set up two salt pans and sow crops or graze *"any part of of 'The Bendeye' not used for salt making"*.

George Bowden died in 1651AD but salt manufacture carried on under George Booth, 1st Baron Delamer of Dunham who passed the lease to William and Robert Typping of Dunham Massey in 1655AD, with the provision that no more industrial equipment was added to that already there. References to the salt works continue in the Will of Thomas Walton in 1754AD but in 1775AD John Walthew bought 8119lbs of lead and James Hollinworth bought 3516lbs of old iron which probably indicates the final removal of the salt works.

In 1825 Nos. 1 and 2 Bollin Cottages were erected on *"....the site of which, together with the yard and garden, was formerly called the Salthouse Yard"* and recent research concerning the site has shown that even the field names of 1633AD are long gone. Only the access track and two natural springs south of Dunham Woodhouses now remain of this mysterious industrial site.

Back on the road once more we retrace our journey down Woodhouse Lane to the lights and turn right back onto the A56 heading south. At the large traffic island go straight across and continue down the A556 dual carriageway (still 'Watling Street' Roman Road) to the lights by The Swan at Bucklow Hill. There are many ancient sites clustered about this junction.

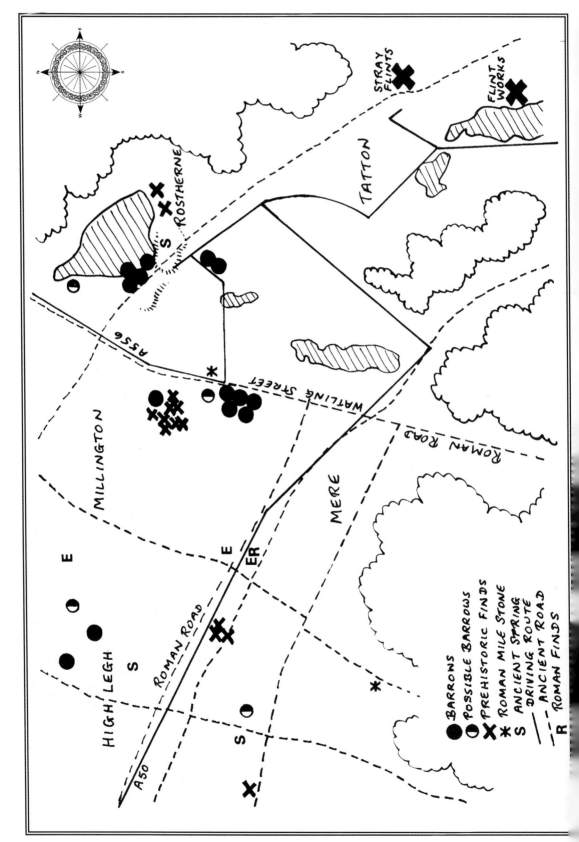

ROSTHERNE

A vanished site is thought to have existed at The Swan pub crossroads with the A556 Roman road between Manchester and Chester here at Bucklow Hill. It is thought that The Swan stands on the site of an old Medieval monastery established as a hospice or 'hostelry' for travellers and the present building alongside the main road has a Roman mile stone set into the side under a cleverly placed double chimney arch.

Aerial photographs have revealed a barrow type crop mark in the field across the road from The Swan and at least a further five clustered together into a 'barrow cemetery' in the next field south on the other side of Bucklow Lane, next to the A556 Roman road. As noted in the section on moated sites there is also a visible mound in the back garden of Denfield Cottage just to the north.

Turn left at The Swan then immediately left again down a small country lane called Cicely Lane which leads on to New Road. At the 'T' junction you have entered Rostherne and will be immediately surprised by the unexpected charm of this hidden and picturesque Cheshire village. Turn left and the main site here, St Mary's church, is about 100 yards on the right, on a hill overlooking the Mere. Park and enter the churchyard on foot and there is a breathtaking view over the Mere just behind the church.

The Lake of the Holy Cross

Set in a hollow a mile or so to the south of Dunham Massey and north of Tatton Park is Rostherne Mere, the largest and certainly one of the most picturesque lakes and villages in Cheshire.

Evidence of prehistoric activity in the area is limited so far to the discovery of two flint flakes (one burnt) during archaeological activity around the Mere in the early 1990s.

Aerial photography has been a little more successful locating a possible 'barrow cemetery' of at least four circular features in a field just north of the church and bordering on the lake. There are also some interesting mound features visible on this shore of the lake. Two more barrow circles exist three fields south of the church on the south side of New Road.

A single fragment of coarse, grey Roman pottery from the late first or early second century (150AD to 250AD) has also been found on the south-east side of the Mere.

ROSTHERNE MERE LOOKING SOUTH TOWARDS THE CHURCH

There are two opinions as to the origin of the name ROSTHERNE. In Ewall's *Origins of Place Names in England* it is said to derive from the old Norse personal name RAVOS and HORNE making it RAVOS-THORNE, the 'thornbush of Ravos'. The more popular alternative is that it originates with the Saxon ROOD meaning 'cross' and THERNE meaning 'lake'. This would mean that Rostherne (CROSS-THERNE) was once known as 'The Lake of the Holy Cross'.

A legend, similar to that at Combermere, tells of a workman who cursed a bell as it was being conveyed to Rostherne Church and was promptly knocked into the water and drowned, followed by the bell which was never recovered. Another version simply states that he left it in the lake after the third attempt to recover it. The Mere is deep in places, over a hundred feet, but is far from being bottomless as was once believed.

Another legend tells how the Mere is connected to either the Red Sea (!), Irish Sea or River Mersey by an underground channel and that every Easter a mermaid swims up stream to the lake and rings the bell hidden in the watery depths. This is not as strange as it sounds as the Mere was the only known location in Britain for a form of freshwater smelt, an esturine fish of the salmon family, which may indicate a former connection to the sea via an estuary. Sadly the last known specimen of this intriguing fish was caught here in 1922.

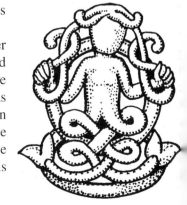

People would visit the Mere on Easter Sunday in the hope that they would see the mermaid, hear the bell or hear the mermaid sit on the bell and sing while combing her hair. A variation of the mermaid legend recorded by G.A. Payne, in his 1904 publication *A History of Knutsford,* combines both stories, so that the mermaid occasionally rises and rings the bell which was dropped by accident into the Mere. He also notes that the mere is 103 feet deep (32m) and 1250 yards (1184m) at its extreme length.

Another local legend states that 21 year old Charlotte Egerton, whose striking white marble monument stands in the Egerton Chapel of Rostherne church, died as a result of drowning in the Mere, but this remains only a legend.

Unlike the 'flashes' to be found along the north side of the River Mersey, the 'meres' are mostly of natural formation and a glance at any map of Cheshire will show a dozen or more in this area, some of considerable size. Rostherne covers over a hundred and fifteen acres (48.5 hectares) yet some, such as 'Ridley Pool', mentioned in the *Itinerary* of Mr Leyland in 1534, and 'Bagmere', which warned

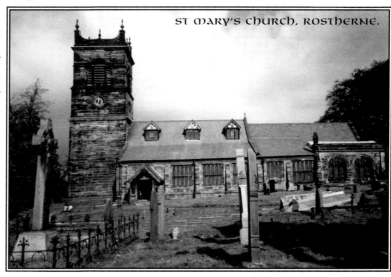

ST MARY'S CHURCH, ROSTHERNE.

the heir to Brereton Hall of impending death by its activity, have been drained away to nothing. In 1961 the 119+ acres of lake and woodlands were bequeathed to the nation by the late Lord Egerton of Tatton and are now managed as a closed wildlife reserve by English Nature (who should be contacted for all access). Otherwise, the closest members of the public can get to the lake, is on the mound on which stands the Rostherne church of St Mary, the original parish church of the Knutsford area.

AND THE PAGAN GODS GAZE ON

Certainly the most remarkable strictly Celtic discovery I have made during the production of this book is the head of the British Pagan fertility god Cernunnos carved on a block of stone and built into a wall retaining the graveyard at the eastern corner of the church building.

While a cult remarkably similar to that of the British Cernunnos existed in European Gaul well before the Roman period, the British cult had a form thought to be unique to the tribe of Brigantes who covered northern Britain from the Mersey at Manchester to regions beyond Hadrian's wall. Here Cernunnos takes four forms; the first is an armed warrior equivalent to the Roman Mars, the second is a form similar to Mercury, the third is a naked phallic deity and the fourth is the form of the horned head as found at Rostherne which is the most interesting as it links directly to the head cults of the Celts.

As a god, Cernunnos may have developed from the combination of the human horned god figure of the European Bronze Age (possibly brought here during the Belgic invasions from about 100BC), combined with the already existent prehistoric British cult which worshipped the bull and bull's heads as a fertility symbol for the land (later becoming the human head cult of the Celts).

It appears that this is a stone representation of a wooden original which would have been carved into the top of a tree trunk pole - poles which were set up in the groves of worship or nemeton often attributed to the Druids. This is consistent with the pattern emerging of a Druidic 'mossland crescent' outlined in Book 1 and it may be that such a grove existed on the raised platform on which the church now stands, close to which the very ancient road to Knutsford ran. It is thought the head carving dates to the 4th century just after the Romans withdrew from Britain, but before concerted Celtic Christian evangelisation began.

A SIMILAR CERNUNNOS HEAD 100AD - 300AD, FOUND AT NETHERBY, CUMBERLAND

THE WELL

This takes us into the age of Pagan-Christian 'ebb and flow' during which time Cernunnos may have shared his hill with a Celtic/Christian cross erected by early missionaries, possibly between 600AD and 700AD, when the Saxons gave the name CROSS to the lake. Archaeologists at Manchester are aware of the possible existence of an unexcavated lake village on the shores of the Mere, and the flat plateau behind the church lends itself well to the site of a timber Saxon village, complete with the well which still flows out of the hillside on English Nature property towards the lake.

The oldest documentary evidence for the existence of a church here is a brief mention in 1188AD when Gilbert de Venables (II) appointed his brother Hugh as rector of Rostherne, but evidence also exists in the Early English-style columns in the nave which date to about 1150AD to 1200AD. These can be found supporting the north side of the church and two detached fragments lie outside the north wall in the graveyard abandoned in past ages after rebuilding.

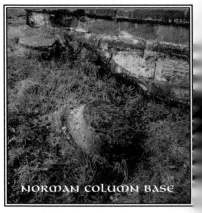

NORMAN COLUMN BASE

WINDOW TRACERY

Some window tracery from this period also exists outside the church against the east wall of the graveyard, along with other detached fragments of masonry around the site, such as the small carved arch fragment in the wall next to the Cernunnos figure.

Just inside the church door, set into the wall high up and to the left, there is a row of seven shields featuring alternate foliage and fleur-de-lis patterns which were part of the Medieval church. These may not have originally been intended as 'shields' but rather 'arches' as the fleur-de-lis are upside down!

The octagonal pillars supporting the south side of the nave are of the decorated style dating from about 1300AD to 1350AD and represent the expansion of the church during the late Medieval period.

MEDIEVAL MASONRY

In 1741AD the original tower (built in 1533AD) collapsed severely damaging the church. During the rebuilding work of 1742AD to 1744AD, the coffin of a Medieval knight was unearthed creating one of Rostherne's least known mysteries. At the present time the stone coffin is outside the church against the eastern corner, opposite the Cernunnos carving, and the lid, carved to represent the effigy of a knight, is under an archway to the left of the altar in the chancel.

The first mystery is the size of the coffin. It is 7 feet 11 ins (240cm) long by 2 feet 10 ins (88cm) wide at the top and 2 feet 2ins (66cm) across the base, with a shaped body cavity 6 feet 11 ins long carved inside it. Even allowing for armour, this is a very substantial human being for Medieval times. It is said that the coffin contained a skeleton which

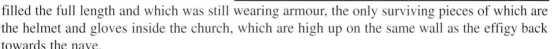

filled the full length and which was still wearing armour, the only surviving pieces of which are the helmet and gloves inside the church, which are high up on the same wall as the effigy back towards the nave.

The helmet (with its unusual 'unicorn' horn) and gloves have survived remarkably well except for the fingers of one glove which have been lost. They were identified by a representative of the Tower of London Armoury as a rare type of ceremonial funeral armour of the twelfth century (1100AD to 1200AD) used by "certain orders of knights". At this time it would have been the Knights Templar. The effigy then presents a problem as it is obviously too small to cover the coffin as a lid but shows a great deal of evidence of being restored on the base and cut down in size.

The effigy is original and carved in a fairly primitive style wearing a full body coat of mail with hood (no helmet), covered by a plain surcoat and holding the hilt of his sword. His legs are straight and his feet rest on a growling lion. He holds a shield with bottom half in blue/black and upper half two horizontal bands of white and two of blue/black.

Considering the effigy has spent time underground it is surprisingly well preserved and can be dated to about 1200AD, contemporary with the helmet and gloves. If the shield was originally intended to be black and white then all the evidence point to him being one of the early Knights Templar or 'Poor Knights of The Temple of Solomon' who were founded in 1118AD (or possibly 1114AD) and had their headquarters next to the site of Solomon's Temple in Jerusalem, hence the name 'Templars'. They were a military order of 'warrior monks', sworn to the defence of pilgrims and the Christian faith during the Crusades, and the lion at the feet of the effigy may show service under Richard I 'The Lionheart' on the third crusade between 1189AD and 1192AD.

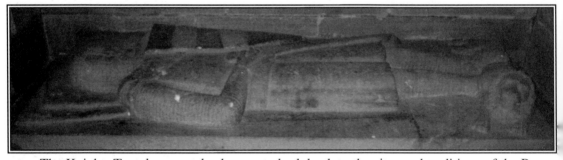

The Knights Templar were also known to hark back to the sites and traditions of the Pagan Celts, who still existed in parts of Britain and Europe at this time, and the dedication of the church to St John the Baptist and The Virgin Mary comes as no surprise on a Templar site.

Another idea advanced locally is that the figure represents Sir Hugh de Venables who died about 1260AD and was descended from the first Baron of Kinderton, Gilbert de Venables, the Norman lord who owned Rostherne in Domesday, 1086AD. From the evidence however, it is more likely to be an earlier Venables if a Venables at all. This Cheshire family did not die out until 1679AD. Further evidence for the age and possible Templar nature of St Mary's at Rostherne is the 'Weeping Chancel' in which stands the altar. This part of the building is noticeably out of alignment with the rest of the building and it is thought that this arrangement was taken to represent the head of Jesus crucified which inclined in the same direction (if the transepts are his arms and the nave his body). This kind of 'sacred geometry' is a trademark of

THE OFF-CENTRE CHANCEL

Templar masons who would also carefully calculate the angle of the building so that the sunrise on the feast day of the church's patron saint would stream in through the east window over the altar. St. John the Baptist's feast day is the 24th June and The Virgin Mary's principal feast day is the 15th August.

The rest of the church is a jigsaw of architecture almost to the present day. The wall of windows and the small door which make up the church front (outside south wall) dates to about 1400AD, and used to be part of the Agden Chapel which is known to have a crypt containing lead and leather covered coffins. The Lister family of Agden Hall have now also died out.

The original tower of 1533AD was replaced by the existing one in 1744AD. The sundial was placed outside the church and the chancel end of the church was extensively restored by Wilbraham Egerton in 1888, with the mosaic flooring added in 1910. The original Tudor stone pinnacles from the outside east wall of the chancel still stand next to the east wall of the cemetery, three here, and two more in the front graveyard close to the Egerton memorials.

It will not have escaped the notice of anyone visiting Rostherne's church of St Mary that the cemetery is entered through a most unusual revolving lych gate ('lych' means 'corpse') operated by a counterweight hanging down one side. This gate is dated 1640AD on a beam under the roof facing the church and, in many cases, these gates had a coffin-table on which the bearers rested their burden, maybe after a laboursome journey across the fields, while the priest recited part of the burial service. If the dead person were from a poor family the body would be removed from the coffin and buried in a simple shroud which at one time had by law to be made of wool to encourage the wool trade. Just such a burial was accidentally disturbed during restoration work on the churchyard in the early 1980s. This body had had coins placed over both eyes. *Folklore, Myths and Legends of Britain* published by Reader's Digest records that this lych gate at Rostherne used to be avoided by newly married couples, as it was believed that one of them would die within a year, or the marriage would be an unhappy one, if they passed through it. Newly-weds beware!

THE EGERTON MEMORIAL

Just before we leave the church we return to a final but later look at the 'Pagan fertility pole' on which Cernunnos would have originally been carved. Rev Adam Martindale (1623AD to 1686AD), a prominent figure in the non-conformist movement in Cheshire, was responsible for allowing his wife to order the destruction of the original village maypole as she and her husband considered it *"a token of homage to the strumpet Flora"*, which indeed it was as the Roman spring festival of 'Floralia' was celebrated in her honour from 28th April to the 1st of May, the day of the maypoles and the month of Sir Gawain.

Rev. Martindale and his wife were removed from Rostherne by the 1661AD 'Act of Uniformity', and moved to become chaplain at Dunham Hall, at which point the villagers replaced their beloved maypole which has vanished again over the last three hundred years. Only the Morris dancers celebrate the May festival in the village now, but a maypole appears on the first Saturday in May at Knutsford's 'Royal May Day' festivities along with the 'Queen of The May' (May Queen), Jack in the Green (The Green Man), Morris dancers and the unique custom of 'sanding' described in the later chapter on Knutsford.

Turning our attention beyond the church one last time, there are only a few minor details of the present day picturesque Rostherne Village that can be included in a book devoted to 'Celtica' and 'mystery'. Directly opposite the church tower is a house which was originally the hall of the Egerton family (a far cry from Tatton Park). In the garden of this house, on the pinnacle of an outstanding mound overlooking the Mere, stands the oldest yew tree in Rostherne, which probably dates back well over a thousand years. Wordsworth may well have had this tree in mind when he wrote:

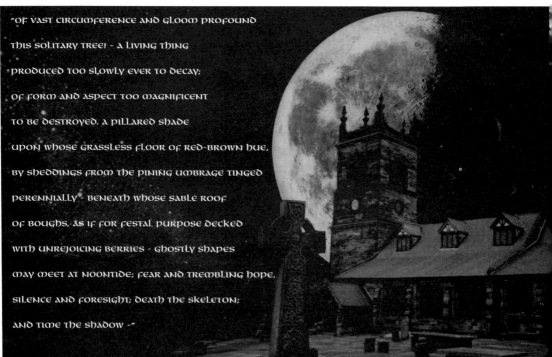

"OF VAST CIRCUMFERENCE AND GLOOM PROFOUND

THIS SOLITARY TREE! - A LIVING THING

PRODUCED TOO SLOWLY EVER TO DECAY;

OF FORM AND ASPECT TOO MAGNIFICENT

TO BE DESTROYED, A PILLARED SHADE

UPON WHOSE GRASSLESS FLOOR OF RED-BROWN HUE,

BY SHEDDINGS FROM THE PINING UMBRAGE TINGED

PERENNIALLY - BENEATH WHOSE SABLE ROOF

OF BOUGHS, AS IF FOR FESTAL PURPOSE DECKED

WITH UNREJOICING BERRIES - GHOSTLY SHAPES

MAY MEET AT NOONTIDE; FEAR AND TREMBLING HOPE,

SILENCE AND FORESIGHT; DEATH THE SKELETON;

AND TIME THE SHADOW -"

VANISHING VILLAGES

At the foot of this mound, towards the hidden mereside, Harry Richards (who lives in part of the Old Hall) can still remember a cock fighting pit - a small horse shoe shaped amphitheatre having flat stone seats on the raised bank, which was removed some years ago by English Nature during restorations to the Mere.

Archaeological activity around the west and south-west of Rostherne and south-east of the Mere has brought to light systems of late Medieval and post-Medieval fields, banks, ditches and furrows accompanied by scattered fragments of Medieval pottery, especially west of the present Egerton Hall and south-east of New Road. Given the activity at St Mary's church during this period this is hardly suprising.

Return to the car and go back to the 'T' junction but this time carry straight on south out of Rostherne Village to the 'T' junction opposite the main north gate of Tatton park.

In the fields, immediately opposite this gate, stood the original village before the days of the developed Rostherne. This Tudor village was known as 'Camp Green' and was entirely demolished by the Egerton family as it spoilt the view at the end of their drive. The entire village was relocated to new buildings at Rostherne, Lady Mary Square being a prime example, built in 1909 by the Lady Egerton of the day without back doors, in order to prevent the estate women from gossiping! (This white square of houses will have been passed on the way out of the village).

ROSTHERNE CHURCH AND MERE ABOUT 1925

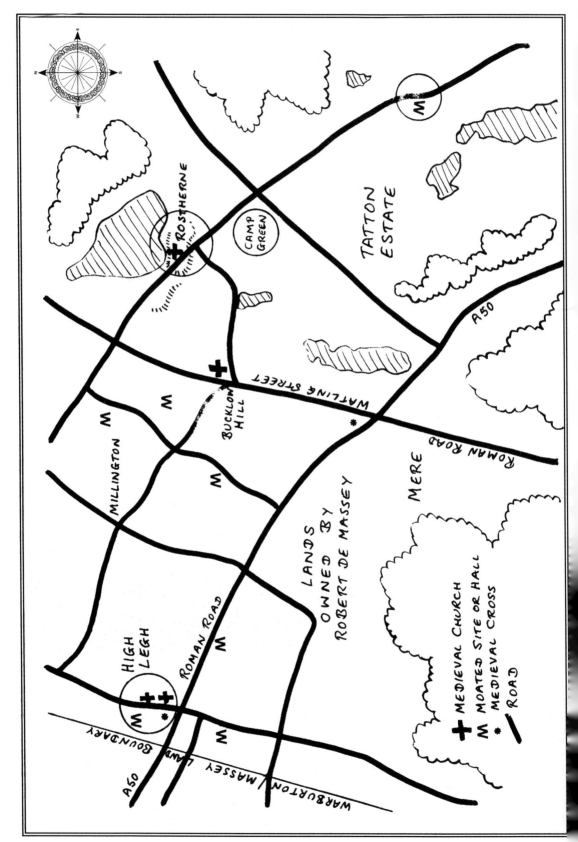

TATTON AND KNUTSFORD

Enter the north gate of Tatton park and we take a minor detour into the lands of the National Trust once again - but the main Tatton Hall is not our objective. Take the left turn at the top of the drive before you reach the stately home and follow signs for the 'Old Hall' where our story of 'vanishing villages' continues. Park by the Old Hall site in order to explore.

The Lost Villages of Tatton

"That village, so often near a Roman road, is sometimes clearly a Saxon hamlet with its great house, its church, and its cottages. There is no question of its death: it is, in fact, a lesson in survival, and a streak of ancient wisdom warns us that it is our duty to keep an eye on the old thatch because we may have to go back there some day, if not for the sake of our bodies, perhaps for the sake of our souls."   *"In Search Of England"* - H.V. Morton.

Archaeological activity took place on the Tatton Park estate from the mid 1970s to the mid 1980s and yet the full report of the findings still lies as a single complete copy in a box in the records office at Chester fifteen years later.

The Old Hall, Tatton

The following sequence of events discovered at Tatton has been pieced together from brief reports which have been printed in archaeological publications at the time and a great deal of on-site research, and probably represents the first opportunity the general reader will have to discover Celtic Tatton.

The Mesolithic Flint Works

The oldest discovery so far made on Tatton Park resulted after a young boy, Thomas Sprott of Knutsford, found a small scattering of three flints on the eastern shore of Tatton Mere in August 962. The site was duly noted, and explored again as part of a renewed archaeological interest in Tatton by Dr David Coombs and a team of field walkers in 1979, and another 30 flints were recovered. The site was then excavated in October and November 1982 under the watchful eye of Nick Higham and a concentration of flints were found at a depth of about 70cm to 90cm with other flints in upper layers which had been washed off farmers' fields higher up the bank (from Medieval times onwards). The shore sands of the Mere were also successfully sieved for flints.

THE MESOLITHIC FLINT WORKING SITE IS IN
FRONT OF THE TREES ON THE SHORE ABOVE

More excavations in June and July 1983 increased the area dug and established that the flints occupied one concentrated site in grey sand over the underlying red sandstone, although no hearth or timber structures were found. It was concluded that this was a tool making site for a settlement still yet to be found.

A staggering 900 flints were recovered in all, about 600 from the dig site and 300 from the mere edge, and these included microliths, scrapers, obliquely blunted points, flint cores, awls, a possible sandstone rubber, an axe sharpener and a saw. All were identified as typical of the early Mesolithic or Middle Stone Age period, probably between 10,000BC and 8,000BC, and the flint used was of southern English origin which accords well with the recent Hoxnian axe find at Millington also common in southern England. Combined with the Knutsford 'tear drop' axe found 26 years ago and other stray flint finds, a picture of a prehistoric 'north west-south east highway' is beginning to emerge along the north Cheshire ridge which runs through Tatton.

FOUR THOUSAND YEARS OF VANISHED VILLAGES

The main archaeological effort at Tatton during the 1970s and 1980s concentrated on one detailed and long-standing site overlooking the ancient but disused sunken road 'Portstrete', to the north east and in front of the Old Hall site.

MEDIEVAL PORTSTRETE LOOKING NORTH (L) AND SOUTH (R) IN FRONT OF TATTON OLD HALL

It is worth noting that this ancient road connects Rostherne in the north with Knutsford in the south, and enters Tatton Park close to the Rostherne Gate where the Tudor village of 'Camp Green' used to stand, before the Lord of Tatton had it demolished, because it spoiled the view. The road was in use around 1300AD but is obviously much older in origin considering prehistoric discoveries made in the area.

Tiny fragments of charcoal collected from the clay infill of the Saxon palisade trench on the archaeological site gave a carbon-date of 7440BC (±180 years), probably indicating background of Mesolithic activity over the whole area.

It is also worth noting that Tatton Mere is a natural feature which probably began life as a marshy valley in Mesolithic times, but Melchett Mere to the north west is the result of subsidence in the 1920s. The oldest features found on the 'Portstrete' dig site were three primitive fire hearths which carbon-dated as late Mesolithic around 4310BC (±100 years). Sadly no artefacts from this period were found.

Next in chronology came a structure which remained only as an irregular group of post holes but gave up evidence of barley cultivation from a pit containing charred remains. Carbon dating placed these items at 2590BC and 2540BC (±100 years), and a scatter of flints, from the same Neolithic or early Bronze Age period, from the entire dig, further confirmed human activity at this time. A group of six post holes forming an arc, and therefore possibly a hut, also gave a middle Bronze Age date of 1580BC (±100 years) but later damage to this evidence made dating uncertain. The route taken by the sunken road 'Portstrete' suggests that it skirted the Iron Age palisaded enclosure to the east, showing that it either avoided earthworks significant for many years or came into being at an extremely early date, possibly in the BC period.

A 'Merrels' stone or 'Nine Men's Morris' board has also been found on the Tatton Estate. This rounded, flat, stone inscribed with squares within squares, dots and lines, represents one of the oldest known games in the world thought to date back as far as 3000BC - but no one knows the original rules! Some later examples have a horse carved in the centre, and diagonal 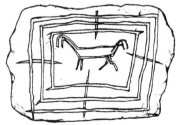 lines joining the corners, and the game was probably played by two players each trying to make up groups of three of their own counters or 'men'. The earliest documented record of the game is in 1390AD, but Norman and Viking finds attest to the earlier origins of the game which was popular in Medieval times and played more recently by Welsh shepherds under the name of 'Trios'.

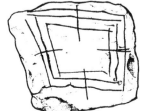

A BRIEF GLIMPSE THROUGH THE VEIL OF THE DARK AGES

Directly next to the sunken road archaeologists found the remains of a cobbled yard and path which had remained through at least three distinct time periods, Iron Age, Romano-British and the Celtic Dark Ages.

Hearths and stake holes by the path were interpreted as a small timber post-late Iron Age round house, and both path and house had been covered by the later Roman deposits confirming this supposition. An Iron Age 'fire-pit' was also discovered on the site in 1982 and carbon-dated to 390BC (±120 years).

A palisade fence was constructed around the cobbled yard and over a much larger area (about 180 x 142ft or 57m x 45m), rectangular in shape with rounded corners with a simple post defined gateway by the south east corner. This signifies a break with the traditional circular Iron Age structures, and carbon-dates from this and associated structures place it in the early Roman period between 80BC and 40AD (±100 years).

Charcoal in the next development layer gave a date of 240AD (±100 years) and contained a fragment of a Roman mortarium or grinding bowl, and some of a collection of grain storage pits gave carbon-dates of 200AD (±110 years). A few sherds of Roman pottery including Romano-British 'white ware' came from the layer covering the Iron Age round house, and the boundary of a cultivated Romano/British field was also identified on the eastern side of the site, just beyond the round house (but later cobbled over).

After the Romans had left, the site continued to be occupied with one end of the cobbled yard being resurfaced as many as five times. Post holes and pits, from the period of last resurfacing, contained compacted maroon powder, possibly a dye based on fuller's earth, and this probably indicates a small scale textile treatment site utilising urine and fuller's earth in wood-lined pits. Sheep bones, a fragment of a late Saxon loom weight, ruts or gulleys in the cobbles and two fence lines running north east to south west, can all be associated in some way with this dye works.

The main structure associated with the dye works on the site was a Saxon post-hole constructed long house which measured at least 46ft x 14ft (14m x 4.6m) with widths of 14ft (4.5m) and 13ft (4.m) at the north and south ends respectively. The long house stood approximately north east to south west and was divided by one internal wall with a hearth off centre in the southern half. The south long side was bowed outward in the centre and the whole structure was raised using untrimmed, close set timbers sealed with daub and initially set into a trench. At this point a dating mystery enters the equation.

Another set of post holes found almost entirely within the long house carbon-dated to 2590BC (±70 years) implying that the long house had stood on the same site as a vastly older timber structure.

A fragment of a rotary quern and sherd of Saxon period 'Chester Ware' pottery (950AD to 1100AD) were also found close by and it is thought that the long house dates between 500AD and 1000AD (if other examples are anything to go by). But the carbon-dates place the structure in the late prehistoric or Romano-British period!

However, a strikingly similar example of three buildings of this type can be found close to the Mersey source at Buxton, Derbyshire, where the basic internal layout is the same and worked flint, pottery, pits, grains and chaff from emmer wheat and barley, a stone axe flake and a hearth have been found, as at Tatton. No other structures of this kind have so far been found in Lancashire or Cheshire although there are at least another four sites so far identified in Wales at Llandegai (North Wales), Clegyr Boia (St David's), Gwernvale (South Powys) and Moel Y Gaer (Rhosesmor). These sites are assigned Early Bronze Age dates (about 2000BC), but there are other rectangular building sites in Ireland dating as far back as 4000BC.

Several phases of timber fence lines led to evidence of at least two other timber structures, one with a possible hearth, which had stood close to the long house and next to the dye works probably in Saxon times. A 'H' shaped building appeared to have a circular working area with a cobbled centre outside it, interpreted as a 'threshing floor'.

The traces of the Anglo-Saxon long house and associated features represent the only Romano-British and Dark Age Celtic evidence so far excavated in the North West region. It is thought that the name TATTON is derived from TATA'S-TUN, the Anglo-Saxon for the town or village, TUN, belonging to TATA and it is mentioned in the Domesday survey of 1086AD. Maybe this site was Tata's Tun?

DORTSTRETE HEADING FOR KNUTSFORD OUT OF TATTON GREEN

After the Norman Conquest the overall site developed into a collection of timber structures probably still associated with farming in the newly developing village of 'Tatton Green'. Some of the Saxon developments still stood at this time but were gradually replaced as the site was rebuilt into Medieval timber residential structures.

Banks and ditches in the area dug during earlier periods formed the basis of later Medieval boundaries suggesting that the site had an established character by about 1100AD.

The next period of activity dates to the 13th or early 14th centuries (1200AD to 1450AD) when the cobbled yard was probably used as a hard standing area for livestock and suffered from sinking and drainage problems. Medieval pottery fragments were also recovered from an area on the northern edge of the yard, and hearths with stake holes, from the same period, probably represent fires used by the keepers of the livestock for additional cooking and heating. The yard fronted on to the sunken road for about 142ft (45m), but the lack of damage to the yard surface adjacent to the road implies that it did not form part of a congested village street, but rather supports the idea that the yard was just one area within a scattered Medieval hamlet strung out along the road. The Black Death would have reached Tatton by about 1350AD and a period of decline set in, however two additional settlements are recorded in the 13th century as 'Northshaw' (or 'Norshaw') some distance to the north east and 'Hazelhurst' between Tatton and Knutsford.

Sheep rearing is recorded on Tatton at this time with fields named after sheep and references to a 'fulling mill' up to 1400AD. The water mill was situated just less than a mile to the north of the Old Hall but only remains now as bits of stonework incorporated into the foundations of a modern pumping station by the side of the lake still called 'Mill Pool'.

The last period of activity on the archaeological dig site surrounds the late Medieval and Tudor periods during which the village of Tatton Green became established and comprised of about fifteen houses and a village green strung out along 'Portstrete'. About five buildings were identified on three locations, and excavations brought up an earthenware jug and a yellow and green glazed cup from one of the house sites, dating from the Civil War period.

ARCHED STONE FROM AN ANCIENT TATTON BUILDING REUSED AS A GATE POST

There existed the possibility that 'padstones' had been used on which to seat parts of the timber buildings, a technique used in the initial construction of the Old Hall, although they had all been removed from the site leaving irregular holes.

Samuel Egerton, Lord of Tatton, had the entire village, fields and ditches removed when he developed the park two hundred years ago but traces are still visible from the air, and documentary evidence for the village still exists. Archaeologists unearthed a series of livestock burials in the area dated to about 1740AD to 1750AD which demonstrate the end of human habitation in the area.

The Old Hall at Tatton

As can be seen, Tatton Green was not a nucleated village but a farming community of cottages and crofts with open fields strung along the vanished 'Portstrete', which connected the very ancient place of worship at Rostherne with the Medieval market town of Knutsford. The greatest concentration of buildings, however, developed in front of the outer wall of the Old Hall, and a continuation of 'manor house' development can probably be implied from the Anglo-Saxon long house to the early Medieval Old Hall, a possible gap of only a few hundred years during the Norman period.

At first glance Tatton Old Hall is an undistinguished red brick farm house with a stone slate roof set within plain grounds, except for a reconstructed crook-timber hay barn and a small visitor centre. There has come to light, however, sufficient architectural and structural evidence to show that it was once, probably, completely a timber framed manor house of some significance.

substance. This almost certainly represents the manorial seat of Richard de Massey who was Lord of the Manor of Tatton in the late thirteenth century (about 1250AD to 1300AD) and owner of the huge game hunting park which surrounded it. He also had a knight stationed at Dunham Castle at this time on his behalf.

Probably the most significant surviving feature is the ornate roof structure over what is now a reconstructed late Medieval Lord's Hall complete with central hearth, tapestries, top table, straw beds and straw floor covering. A date of the 15th century has been ascribed to this roof structure and much of the rest of the hall survives in original 16th and 17th century style (1500AD to 1700AD).

The estate passed to the Egerton family in 1598AD and remained in their care until it was given to the National Trust in 1958. The main hall, ornate roof and other features, located and perceived by archaeologists, suggest that the building was once a house of considerable importance, having an 'E' shape with two wings and an entrance porch (similar to Lymm Hall) or a 'U' shape, and facing the green of Tatton Green village.

An inventory of 1614AD, held at Cheshire County Records Office, lists Tatton Old Hall as follows: "*Parlour, Great Parlour, Great Chamber, Brewhouse (for pickles and preserves), Buttery and House*" with a "*Work House (workshop?), Pottery Kiln and Mill*". There would also have been barns, out-buildings, possibly a yard and stables.

It is not known when the Lords of Tatton (the Breretons or Egertons) moved to the site of the new Tatton Hall but it was probably in the late seventeenth century. The cellar under the library has a date stone of 1718AD and the dining room is in a style of about 1750AD. The new house was finally begun in about 1788AD to 1791AD. Tatton Green was demolished during the landscaping of the park in 1791AD under William Egerton, and the hall

open hearth in the old hall

was completed in 1807AD under Wilbraham Egerton.

The Old Hall was then used to house the gamekeeper who tended the deer in Tatton Park which are said to be descended from the original forest stock of the area, and an interesting tale persists of 18th century deerstealing. It is said that the foresters of Tatton once chased a poacher to his cottage near Swanbrook Hollow but, though they searched the house from top to bottom, they could not find a trace of the dead deer. Much disgruntled they rode off and, when they were well and truly out of sight, the poacher removed the dead deer from the cradle which his wife had been gently rocking as though to lull their child to sleep!

A WORD ABOUT KNUTSFORD

To visit Knutsford simply leave Tatton Park by the south gate or turn right at the Camp Green 'T' junction by the north gate on to Ashley Road and turn left at the next 'T' junction, then first left again on to Mereheath Lane. This will bring you to the same point.

Apart from a short Domesday entry which ascribes the "waste and woodland" to the ownership of Erchebrand "the free man", Knutsford's origins are lost in the mists of antiquity.

The name is said to be derived from the Danish King Canute (Cnut) who forded the Birken Brook or River Lily, which runs through 'Molly Pott's Moor/The Moor here', with his army in 1017AD while on the way either to fight the combined forces of Scotland and Cumbria or on his way back, depending on who you read.

"Let all men know how empty and worthless is the power of kings, for there is none worthy of the name, but He whom heaven, earth and sea obey by eternal laws."   King Canute The Great.

King Canute was the son of the Danish King 'Sweyn Forkbeard' who led a Viking raid on England with Canute in 1013AD when Canute was about eighteen. Sweyn was declared King of England by those he had conquered but various conflicts with King Ethelred the Unready (978AD to 1016AD) and his son King Edmund Ironside (ruled only April to November 1016AD) caused problems which were compounded when Sweyn died. The Vikings proclaimed Canute King and he decimated the forces of Edmund Ironside at Ashingdon in Essex on 18th October 1016AD and Edmund died six weeks later making Canute 'King of all England'.

The change in Canute after his accession to the throne was amazing to the point that it is hard to believe just how much he left his heathen pirate days behind to become a civilised

Christian ruler. He married King Ethelred's widow, Emma (who returned from safe haven in Normandy), he was then baptised a Christian, sent his Danish/Viking army home (except for a small bodyguard) and employed Englishmen in all high offices. He appointed English Bishops, patronised abbeys, divided the kingdom into earldoms which were the forerunners of the Norman feudal system found in Domesday, revised the laws and appointed sheriffs to apply them. He even became accepted as overlord by the Scots and Welsh. Pope Benedict VIII honoured him in Rome and he eventually became King of Denmark in 1019AD and Norway in 1028AD.

Legend has it that it was then he tried to command the tide to stop and got wet feet for his efforts resulting in the quote which started this brief life history. He died at Shaftsbury on the 12th November 1035AD.

It is worth observing here that the Domesday survey was conducted in 1086AD, while King Canute ruled Mercia up to 1035AD, a gap of only 51 years from his death during which time the town name of CVNETESFORD would have had to become established - or even a town established for that matter!

Charles R. Bennett, a Chairman of the Historical Committe of the Knutsford Society, commented in his 1982 book *The Story of Knutsford*: "....it is fairly clear that at the time of Canute's reign (1015 to 1035AD) there was no established community on this site, and all evidence points to the growth of a township from the beginning of the 12th century."

While the Norman Domesday spells the name as CVNETESFORD, it would be an intriguing possibility that this might actually be derived from a Norman mishearing of the highly similar Celtic/Briton CARNUTESFORD. This would actually mean that the Celtic/Briton name was 'Ford of the Druid' or 'Druid's Ford'. Given the proximity to local mosslands used by the Druids (see Book 1 in this series) and the longer time this allows for establishment of a name not based on a settlement, I favour this as a more probable source than 'Canute'.

In his Arthurian book *The Queen and the Cauldron*, Nicholas Gold states that: "*On a fixed date in each year they (the Druids) hold a session in a consecrated spot in the country of the Carnutes, which is supposed to be the centre of Gaul (Chartres)."*

KNUTSFORD VIEWED FROM THE BOTTOM OF THE RIVER LILY

KNUTSFORD VIEWED FROM THE POSSIBLE FORD
SITE OVER THE BIRKIN BROOK

Caitlin Matthews goes further in her *Elements of The Celtic Tradition*: "*Prior to the sack of the Druid's centre at Anglesey in 64AD, it is likely that Druids from all over the British Isles met together periodically, as the Gaulish Druids are said to have done, gathering together at the Place of the Carnutes ....*"

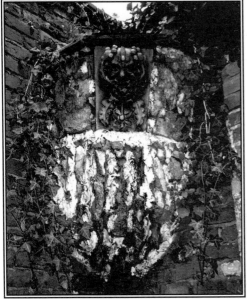
GREEN MAN AT THE COURTYARD CAFE

Stuart Piggott also notes, in *The Druids*, that: "*Caesar also states of Druid teaching that ...'it is thought that this system of training was invented in Britain and taken over from there to Gaul, and at the present time (54BC) diligent students of the matter mostly travel there to study it..... Jackson has drawn attention to an early Irish reference to a 'fili returning from study of the craft in Britain. He* (Caesar) *then goes on to describe annual meetings of a Druid assembly in a sacred place (in loco consecrato) in the tribal territory of the Carnutes believed to be the 'centre of all Gaul'. The holy place believed to be the centre of Gaul has the ring of truth, for as Eliade has stressed, such sacred centres can be many, each with its own mystical validity, and the 'omphalos' at Delphi is merely one of the most famous. But apart from the reference in Caesar we have no other recorded meeting place of the Druids.*"

If this pattern holds true for Britain, 'Home of the Druid', then the consecrated centre of this Druidic/Celtic land could well lie hidden in the Mossland Crescent somewhere between Knutsford and Alderley Edge.

If the adding of a letter 'R' to the name CVNETESFORD appears obscure some other spellings of the name over the years have included CURTSEYED, KNYTESFORD, KNOTTESFORD, KNOTSFORD and the present KNUTSFORD.

After Domesday all Cheshire belonged to the Norman Overlord Hugh Lupus (Hugh 'The Wolf') who continued to allow Erchebrand use of the land but under the watchful eye of the Norman William Fitznigel. By about 1290AD it had passed to the Norman Overlord William of Tabley (under King Edward I) who in turn, granted Nether Knutsford to his vassal Sir Richard Massey of Tatton. Richard applied for a market charter in 1292AD which upset his Overlord William, who only reached agreement over it in 1294AD, dividing manorial rights and profits 38 burgesses to himself and 19 to Richard. This division continued right up to 1590AD when the lands of Knutsford passed entirely into the ownership of the Lords of Tatton.

ALL THAT REMAINS OF THE PAROCHIAL CHAPEL DEDICATED TO ST HELENA

During the Medieval wars it is highly likely that Knutsford provided archers to the nationally renowned Cheshire Bowmen. Just after the Battle of Agincourt a survey of the Bucklow Hundred taken in 1417AD showed that almost a quarter of Cheshire bowmen came from this area making up 107 out of the 439 recorded.

Two chapels existed at Knutsford in early times, a Chapel-of-Ease by the old stocks (now removed) in King Street, built in the 14th century (1300-1400 AD), and the Parochial Chapel dating to the same period, with William le Dene recorded as the first clergyman from 1316 to 1321AD, Gilbert de Legh from 1321 to 1382AD, Nicholas Mynchehull from 1382 to 1396AD and Hugh de Toft from 1396 to 1427AD. For a full list of clergy to the Parochial Chapel I recommend P.J. Hunt's 1979 booklet *For All The People - The Story of Knutsford Parish Church*, in which is also recorded:

"We have a list of incumbents (clergy) *dating back to 1316; this is the date which is inscribed on the restored foundation walls of the Parochial Chapel to be found off Boothfields* (near the junction with Higher Downs) *on the north-east side of Knutsford. "*

This site is a railed-off enclosure in which low walls, now somewhat overgrown, mark the outline of the church. There are several gravestones which were found in various positions all over the site, and these have been laid flat within the outline of the church. The inscriptions on many of these are still legible."

The railings and undergrowth have been cleared away but unfortunately so has most of the chapel, which is now on a grass field in the centre of a housing estate and quite difficult to find. It is generally thought that this ruined chapel was once dedicated to St Helena, the mother of Emperor Constantine who became the first Christian Emperor of Rome, but other authorities ascribe the dedication

to "Blessed Marie of Knutsford" (in 1398AD) or "St. Ellene of Knutsford" (in 1476AD). The plinth and quoin stones from the church of St Helena were re-used in the building of the present St John the Baptist church in 1742-44AD, and the four original bells recast into five, with another added, were first rung in the new church in June 1749AD. It is believed that the four original bells were badly made and in poor repair making them noisy and unsuitable for use at weddings hence, in his *Knutsford: Its Traditions and History* of 1887, Henry Green observes that:

"The bells of the parochial chapel were too far off, and on occasion of a wedding the plan was introduced of announcing it to the neighbours and to the town generally, by sweeping the street before the door of the bride's father, and by garnishing it with a sprinkling of sand. At first the sanding was confined to the bride's house, but in process of time innovations crept in, and her friends in other houses, partaking in the neighbourly joy, partook also in the observance; their houses too put on the bridal adornments, and looking clean and bright shared the festivity of the day."

In his book of 1947, *Companion into Cheshire* J.H. Ingram updates this account by adding that: *"Among the old customs which have fallen into disuse is that of 'sanding', or making pictures in coloured sand in front of the bride's house on her wedding day. When Queen Victoria, then still a Princess, came to Knutsford, the streets were sanded in her honour. Mrs Gaskell (1810-1865, the novelist famous for 'Cranford') tells how verses were written in sprinkled sand when she was married (to Rev. William Gaskell in 1832). An old ballad describes how:*

The lads and lassies their tun dishes hanging,
Before all the doors for the wedding were sanding,
I'd ask Nan to wed and she answered with ease -
' *You may sand for my wedding as soon as you please!*

J.H. Ingram also observes that: *"The May pole is set upon Knutsford Heath and the May Queen is crowned amid scenes of great joy. Does a man in armour, on horseback, still take the part of the 'Cheshire Champion'?"*

FROM AN EARLY BOOK JACKET FOR CRANFORD

To return to the circular driving route for south east Warrington; leave Knutsford by the south gate of Tatton Park taking Mereheath Lane north to the 'T' junction. Turn left on to the A5034 to the junction, then right on to the A50 Manchester Road to Mere Junction where you enter 'Highwayman country'.

high legh

arley hall and arley green

appleton thorn

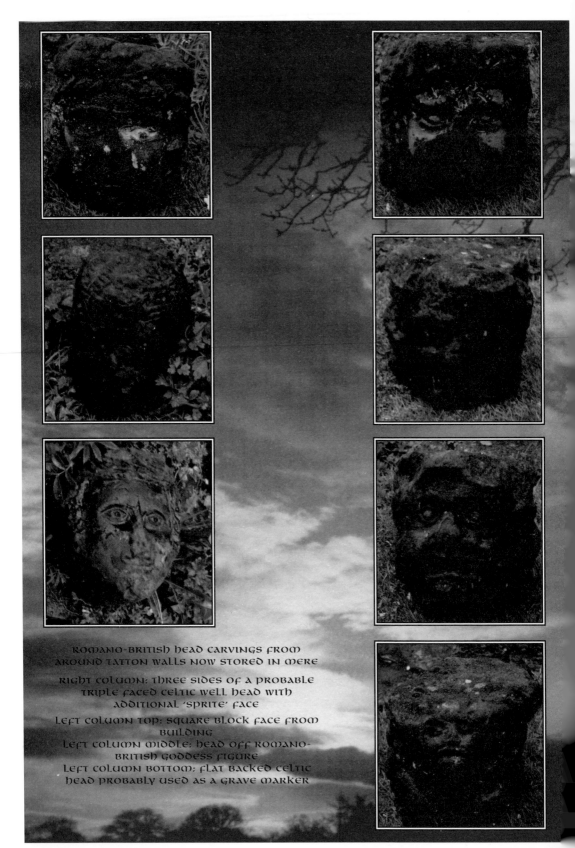

ROMANO-BRITISH HEAD CARVINGS FROM AROUND TATTON WALLS NOW STORED IN MERE

RIGHT COLUMN: THREE SIDES OF A PROBABLE TRIPLE FACED CELTIC WELL HEAD WITH ADDITIONAL 'SPRITE' FACE

LEFT COLUMN TOP: SQUARE BLOCK FACE FROM BUILDING

LEFT COLUMN MIDDLE: HEAD OFF ROMANO-BRITISH GODDESS FIGURE

LEFT COLUMN BOTTOM: FLAT BACKED CELTIC HEAD PROBABLY USED AS A GRAVE MARKER

high Legh

"The roads were so bad we were in Danger of our Lives."
Scratched by a traveller on a window pane in Shocklach Church 1756 AD.

Highwaymen frequented the roads of Cheshire south east of Warrington. For over thirty years the mouldy bones of James Price hung in chains on Hoole Heath, near Chester city walls, for robbing the Warrington mail coach.

Tradition says that Dick Turpin killed a man at Newbridge Hollow close to Altrincham and the story of Knutsford's 'Highwayman Higgins' is told in fact and fiction by De Quincey and Mrs Gaskell. They record how he would use his position to gain entry to society events, dance with rich and attractive ladies, then rob them as their coaches drove home down the dark lanes of surrounding Cheshire, and it is to these dark lanes that we now turn.

At the first set of traffic lights 'dog-leg' right and left. The Roman road runs through fields to the right and two tiny grey flints or 'microliths' were found here, probably originating near Beeston Castle. Staying on the A50 Manchester Road through Mere until it enters High Legh, distinguished by the water tower on the left, followed shortly after by the Garden Centre on the same side and the Village Hall on the right.

Although what follows frequently centres on the roads leading from this area, especially the land through the old East Hall gateway on the right, there is not a great deal here to see. The two chapels can be visited by turning right just after the Village Hall then second right for East Chapel or third right for West Chapel (St John's), but are usually closed.

the old gate to east hall today (L) and in 1900(R)

Carrying on along the A50, the Bear's Paw public house appears on the right after about half a mile and, immediately past the pub, you should turn left down Swineyard Lane which is the road created by the Dark Age Saxon/Celts.

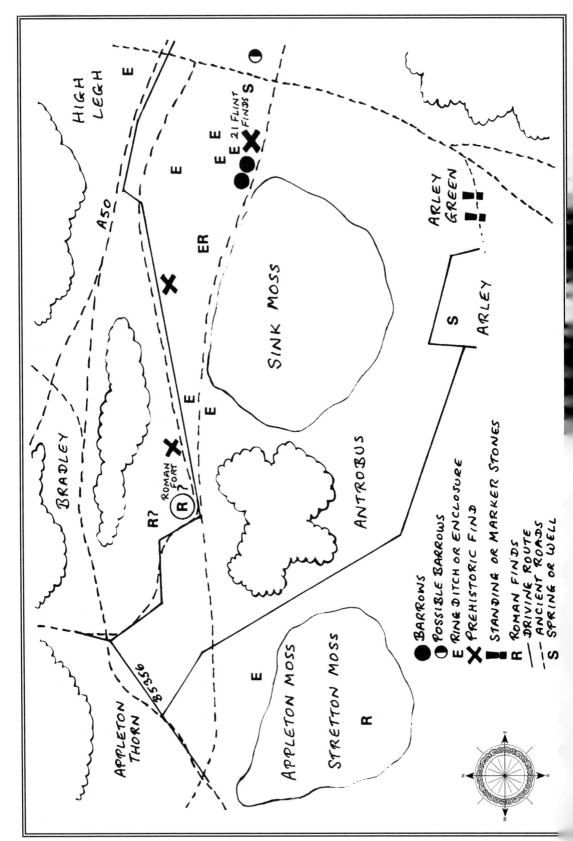

ALONG THE SAXON ROAD

There is now little doubt that another major ancient highway passed through the area known as High Legh, in addition to the paved Roman Road, which roughly followed the course of the North Cheshire Ridgeway and A50 Manchester/Knutsford Road. Evidence indicates that it was further south along Swineyard Lane and New Lane heading for Appleton and crossing the North Cheshire Ridgeway at Appleton Thorn.

There are no fewer than six sites of prehistoric flint finds, twenty one possible barrow crop marks, eight enclosures, ten moated sites and a possible castle platform in a line to Hill Cliffe in Appleton. Starting at the ancient site of Rostherne the moated sites so far identified are: Denfield Cottage, Hough Hall, Dairy Farm, Swineyard Hall, Barley Castle Farm, Bradley Hall, Reddish Hall and a destroyed moat under an industrial estate near Barley Castle Farm.

It would be logical to assume that at least some of these sites had become connected while they were in use during Medieval times, but prehistoric and Romano-British finds have also been made along the same route - and nowhere else in the immediate area.

As has been said in the introduction to this book, a scattering of seven flint nodules were recovered surrounding an early Stone Age 'Hoxnian' pointed flint hand hammer found by Leslie Lowery (the Celtic project photographer) in the corner of the field behind Denfield Cottage during a survey in September 1998. This followed the discovery of another axe head in Knutsford and listed under the section on Tatton Park, as well as the Mesolithic site used for manufacturing flints on the Tatton Estate. These finds date from the early Stone Age.

Turn west towards High Legh. During field walking and excavations by South Trafford Archaeology Group on the Romano-British enclosure, next to the water tower at High Legh, more finds of various flint tools came to light. This site shows distinct signs of being moated especially on aerial photographs. Twenty flint tools and an axe were also recovered by Manchester University archaeologists from the enclosure sites at Legh Oaks farm.

Warrington Museum are currently displaying a Stone Age perforated axe-hammer found at Swineyard Hall Farm, High Legh (find 109'977) and another prehistoric stone tool was recovered from the area of Badger's Croft Farm. Hill Cliffe has also given up several prehistoric finds and burial mounds listed in Book 3 of this series under the section on Appleton.

The overall evidence suggests long term use of a track through High Legh belonging to the ancient British/Celtic peoples, cleared in ancient times but perhaps not greatly used by the Romans, who chose the North Cheshire Ridge at this point instead. More evidence to follow.

In Domesday the area of High Legh is simply recorded as LEGE held under Hugh Lupus Earl of Chester, by the Norman Gilbert Venables, Baron of Kinderton over the two previous Saxon owners Dot and Ulviet (who also owned Lymm and Warburton). The name HIGH LEGH and LEGE is thought to be derived from the Old English LEDGE meaning a clearing, hence a high clearing'.

The present name of Legh was given to two families in the reign of Henry II (1154 to 1189AD) in honour of their control of the land. The earliest known ancestors are Hamon de Legh of the West Hall family (hall stood south of St John's church) and Efward de Lega of the East Hall (hall stood south east of St John's church), both contemporaries of Hamon de Venables, third Baron of Kinderton and younger son of the Gilbert Venables recorded in Domesday.

As George Omerod noted, Efward (of East Hall) sounds suspiciously of Celtic/Saxon descent, possibly from the Kinderton family. Ulviet is also listed with an 'Edward' as owning Lymm who may, in fact, be the same 'Efward' listed here. Ulviet may have had his homestead at Sworten Heath. The Legh family still live in the area as the Cornwall-Legh family (Lord Grey) but both halls have now been demolished to build a housing estate, the original main road (B5159) moved to the west, where it is now, and no record of archaeological activity on the sites appears to exist.

Recent surveys by South Trafford Archaeological Group may have revealed the remains of a moated site in fields to the west of St John's church and it is hoped that this is the site of Edward de Lega's Norman/Saxon homestead. Only the two chapels belonging to the families remain on the estate, beyond the gatehouse opposite High Legh garden centre.

The East Chapel

The East Chapel from the East Hall was built in 1581AD by Thomas Legh and has always been known as High Legh Chapel. No record of its consecration exists and at some time it was dedicated to The Blessed Virgin Mary.

Before the estate enclosed it it stood next to the ancient Warrington-Knutsford road, and it is thought, from research in ancient deeds, to have been built over the site of the original Domesday church mentioned in 1086AD (although no physical evidence for this has yet come to light). It is recorded that no 'church' existed in Legh in 1280AD, which points to the chapel standing then as the Domesday site and the date for the building of the present chapel (1581AD) matches the date at which the original Medieval Old Hall on the site was demolished and an Elizabethan mansion built to replace it.

A pre-Reformation consecration cross appears to be cut into one of the stones at the west door confirming a chapel here before written records began in 1581AD. The Legh Chapel in Rostherne church was in ruins and without glass just before this date, further confirming the existence of an alternative private chapel elsewhere from Medieval times.

In 1836 a south aisle was added to the chapel and the stone containing the Legh family arms, date and motto was moved from the east wall to above the new west porch (which had formerly been over the original entrance on the south side).

In 1858 the chapel finally took on its present shape under the architect Butterfield, who made it accommodate 200 people. Sadly the ancient giant yew tree which grew on the south side by the south west window was felled along with a second tree at the north west corner.

The Old East Chapel Today (L) and in 1880 (R)

THE WEST CHAPEL

The first West Chapel from the West Hall was constructed by the Leghs (later Egerton-Leghs) of West Hall in 1408AD, and stood until the Hall and associated buildings disappeared in the mid-17th century (about 1650 AD), possibly due to the Civil War.

The present Church of St John was built on the site of the original in 1814 and its records begin in 1817. A fire destroyed the building in 1891 and the present building, the third to stand on this site, dates from 1893. The large glacial boulders, in front of the church, were placed there in recent times after the building of houses, and the present 'well' feature is actually a Victorian water tank.

Remains of ancient burials have been found at various times on the site since 1814, confirming it to be the site of the chapel of 1408AD, but these are not the only remains to be uncovered during building work in this area.......

CROMWELL'S LOST VILLAGE

Originally High Legh developed at the crossroads, between the A50 Roman road from Warrington to Knutsford and what appears to be a Medieval boundary road from Warburton to Great Budworth. This road probably represents the boundary between the lands owned by the Massey family of Dunham/Tatton and the Warburton family of Warburton/Arley, finally established by agreement in the late 1440sAD (see section on Dunham Massey). But the road may well be older than this date. If the East Chapel represents the Domesday church of 1086AD then the old road is probably of pre-Saxon origin.

In the present hamlet of High Legh, the road has moved west to the site of the present village hall. Up to the Second World War the original course of the main road remained, passing through the grand gateway opposite Halliwell's Brow and the garden centre, through the site of the demolished East Hall and East Chapel, passing the front of St John's church (West Chapel) to rejoin the B5159 West Lane just before Mowpen Brow.

Thirty years ago (around 1964) a friend of mine was a junior apprentice labourer on the construction of houses along this old road in the area of St John's church, and remembers the diggers hitting foundations of what he describes as *"a row of Civil War houses with a pub at one end"*. Buildings do appear here on some old maps.

Work slowed down while finds of Civil War swords, guns, pewter plate and various other objects were dug out, mainly from the 'pub' site furthest down the hill from St John's. During this work the diggers also broke through into a tunnel.

A couple of the juniors, including my friend, took torches into the tunnel, which was big enough to walk freely down in single file, in order to discover if it would affect the building operations. It apparently headed off in the direction of the old hall and continued uninterrupted for about a mile, at which point they turned back and returned to the building site.

The artefacts passed into private ownership, the houses were built over the site and the discoveries were never recorded - until now!

AN ENGLISH MAN'S HOME IS HIS CASTLE!

Much debate has raged over the exact definition of a 'castle' so a brief description of their development will suffice at this point. I hope to look at Cheshire castles in more detail in one of the future books.

It is thought that the earliest 'castles' of the Bronze and Iron Age were naturally defendable sites enhanced with the addition of banks, barricades and ditches, the biggest of which constitute the type known as 'hill forts'. In areas of constant conflict like ours, it is thought that even the smallest farms would have had defences of some kind. Archaeological activities on other sites offering no natural defensive potential have shown that the bank and ditch approach was also widely adopted on much smaller sites, which often show up as crop features on aerial photographs. Along the A50 at High Legh, and then along Swineyard Lane from Sworten Heath, there are seven such sites so far clearly identified.

Probably the best examined of these sites is in the field immediately to the east of the Water Tower at High Legh. Field walking on this rectangular Romano-British enclosure produced many finds of prehistoric flints, followed by excavation by South Trafford Archaeological Group, who recovered large quantities of Roman pottery and other finds associated with a Roman farming villa.

Two enclosures lie in fields north of Leigh Oaks Farm and have produced finds of twenty pieces of struck flint and chert, a hammer stone, two Roman pottery fragments and a circular stone 'hut' 12ft 8ins (4m) across. There are also crop marks in the field to the south which show two possible Bronze Age round barrows and in another field, three fields to the east on the other side of Halliwell's Brow. Evidence indicates late Bronze Age and Iron Age farming activity ending as a Romano-British site connected to the A50 Roman road to the north.

Aerial photography by N.J. Higham in 1989 also revealed a sub-rectangular ditched enclosure visible in cereal crops next to Sink Moss (at the back of Swineyard Hall) along Moss Lane. The owner of Swineyard Hall informs me that the excavations which followed revealed pottery and finds on this site from the Roman period.

Over the M6 motorway there are two more settlement features at the north west and west end of the High Legh Ridge by Badgers Croft Farm. One in particular shows evidence of structures within an elliptical outer bank, the other is an oval enclosure, but no finds have come from these sites so far. All these enclosures once lay on the edges of Sink Moss which has been entirely destroyed by farming activities.

The final suspected enclosure lies on a slope overlooking Appleton Moss, Stretton Moss and Whitley Reed, next to Burleyheyes Farm. Once again the ancient mosslands in this area have been farmed away and the only finds recorded are Roman including a third century (200AD to 300AD) coin from the west side of Whitley Reed.

The next phase of 'castle building' probably included the addition of water filled defensive features some time towards the end of the Roman period and the start of invasion by the Angles and Saxons in the fifth and sixth centuries. Many moated sites have given up finds from the 'Dark Ages', such as the detailed excavations on the moat on Altrincham Golf Course, undertaken by South Trafford Archaeological Group over the last ten years, which has produced evidence from the Saxon period and earlier.

The addition of water may have been an accidental consequence of bank and ditch digging in previous ages, but moated sites did develop and were probably established as fortified homesteads by the Danish invasions of the tenth century (900AD to 1000AD) although it is not clear if these were round or square or both!

The first motte (mound) and bailey (enclosure) 'castle' was thought to be built by King Harold II at Dover in 1062AD but it is notable that mounds were in use as meeting places ('moot hills') throughout the Dark Ages, so the design was not entirely new. It can be generally supposed that motte and bailey castles are Norman, and moated sites Anglo-Saxon in origin. Castles then became larger timber and stone structures and moated homesteads took on the characteristic square ditch shape, often with fish and fowl ponds attached.

High Legh can boast at least eight identified square moated sites to date between Rostherne and Appleton along the same line as the earlier enclosures. Not all of these have been surveyed so it is my intention to simply list them with any available details.

1). Denfield Cottage

This is a domestic property built in several distinct phases standing almost next to the A56 Manchester to Chester Roman Road not far from the listed Millington Hall (which has no moat). The earliest standing phase appears to date from the Elizabethan period (1560AD to 1600AD) but is significantly constructed in stone not the usual black and white timber.

Field walking behind the building produced pottery from the Elizabethan period up to date and the surprise find of the Hoxnian axe and seven flints recorded at the start of this book.

A large, enigmatic rise, which resembles a Bronze Age burial mound, also exists on the rear lawn and the property currently houses the pulpit from the old Wesleyan Chapel at Booth Bank, Millington, which was demolished to build the M56 motorway.

the pulpit

Evidence of the moat exists as a north-west to south-east wide stream across the front of the property which turns at ninety degrees to the south-west and ends beyond the property in a square pond of some size. These features may also be Elizabethan in origin but this site remains as a tantalising mystery yet to be fully explored.

the mound

2). hough hall moat

This site has been very briefly excavated but the information has not been made available in published form.

The hall was still standing on the 1805 to 1873 OS Map but had been demolished by some time after the Second World War and remains now only as a fairly impressive set of deep field features partially filled with marsh grass and water.

On a site survey in 1998, the central platform, gatehouse and bridge platform, barn and fish pond from the moat could still be identified on the ground, and the whole site appears of the same approximate age as Denfield Cottage, Elizabethan or early Tudor.

3). dairy farm

This brick and half-timbered property has only recently been restored and is part of the estates belonging to Lord Grey of the Cornwall-Legh family.

Apparently a potential moat feature was located and examined during restoration work on the grounds and a water-filled ditch with a distinct ninety degree bend does exist at the north east corner of the property and just in the field across Halliwell's Brow.

Apart from this obvious feature this site also remains to be archaeologically surveyed.

The water-filled ditch (L) and moat feature (R) at Dairy Farm

4). Swineyard Hall

The oldest find so far recorded on a moated site in High Legh is the Stone Age perforated shaft-hole axe-hammer found at Swineyard Hall Farm, High Legh, some time before D. Longley included it in his *Victoria County History* of 1987. Very ancient finds on moated sites should not come as a surprise considering the example set by the excavation of the moat on Altrincham Golf Course where the oldest organic find to date gave a carbon-date of 41,000BC!

Today Swineyard (or Swinehead) Hall and Farm represents one of the finest examples of a moated farm house in Cheshire. It has a timbered frontage containing Tudor 'ogee lozenge' patterns at first floor level, and heavy diagonal beams in the gable. The house has been extended visibly twice to the west, the centre part is coated in grey exterior rendering and the west wing is Victorian black and white timber and brick.

The present owner remembers a 'drawbridge' structure and a cobbled front court dismantled by her parents (probably early this century), and the well, situated central to the rear of the building, still fed water to the later extension wing up to the 1980s. She felt that the water is probably still drinkable today.

The moat surrounds the front and sides of the house only at present but evidence from building work on the site and the layout indicates that it once continued all the way round, with the "drawbridge" probably where the wooden bridge and front path is today.

The west side of the moat is extensively surrounded by old masonry indicating the existence of more substantial buildings in addition to the dismantled 'drawbridge', probably dating back to

OLD MASONRY FOUND ROUND THE WEST SIDE OF THE MOAT

ownership of the site by Hugh de Legh of East Hall early in the 14th century. The moated site and buildings were evidently already in existence in 1347AD when the site was bought from Matthew de Legh who had obtained the lands of 'Sworten' by inheritance over seven generations from Efward de Lega (also known as Eswald and Oswald) who lived only one generation after Domesday.

This implies that Swineyard Hall dates back beyond the 12th century (1100 to 1200AD), to Saxon ownership under Efward, and may pre-date Domesday, hence the inclusion of 'Efward's Swine Head Hall' in a book about Celtic Warrington.

Richard Legh, lineal descendant of Matthew, the founder of the East Hall Legh family, was living in Swineyard Hall in 1663AD after which time it was sold to Henry Legh of East Hall, a descendant of the present owner. The other hall owned by the Legh family was Northwood Hall situated about a mile to the south east but this survives only as a relatively recent structure and has no moat. Any visitors should report to the house, if they wish to go further onto the property than the animal defence ditch next to Swineyard Lane.

SWINEYARD HALL VIEWED FROM THE ROAD

5). BARLEY CASTLE FARM

I am indebted to Phillip, Jane, Robert and Louise Harrison, who are the present owners of Barley Castle Farm, for their enthusiasm in doing much research and allowing us unruly archaeologists permission to undertake quite detailed surveys of their ancient home. A great deal of what follows has been collected by them over the years.

Although the ordinary reader will not be able to experience the farm at first hand, I hope that this account and accompanying photographs will give a fair picture of a very important local historic site.

In a very similar way to the buildings in the 'hidden village' of Warburton (detailed in Book 1), Barley Castle Farm is a very old building which has been encased inside a later structure at a time when black and white timber framed buildings fell out of fashion. Fortunately only the timber crooks (or 'crucks') from each end of the building have been removed and it appears that these have been reused in building the barns around the same time.

Travelling right back to the origins of the site, the development sequence so far recorded appears to be as follows.

Suggestion One: Probably the oldest (and certainly the most mysterious) constructed feature remaining on site is an 'L' shaped corner of sandstone wall at the centre of the building, over which all other structures appear to have been placed and which has been used to house two later forms of inglenook fireplaces. This wall is of extremely fine workmanship of a type seldom

found even on monastic sites and not generally found before 1066AD (except in Roman buildings).

Therefore the first suggestion is that this corner represents the base of a Roman signal tower, probably constructed between 80 and 380AD, to signal to Winter Hill and Hill Cliffe where other signal stations were known to exist.

The cement, used between the tightly fitting blocks, has broken stone inclusions similar to Roman cement and a 2ins (6cm) inaccuracy in the stone courses has been corrected to the right of the corner with great proficiency. The wall is also perfectly vertical and horizontal indicating the use of plumb lines. The hard sandstone is not found locally and appears to be possibly of Pennine origin, indicating transportation of building materials long distance, at an early date typical of the Romans.

These two corner walls still stand to ceiling height and the termination of the wall at one end has been poorly cut (diagonally) to allow a crook timber to pass over. The other termination once appears to have been the site of a doorway.

Here there are heavy signs of wear in the sandstone blocks which have only recently been revealed when the wall was cleared of plaster. This wear corresponds to impact by the centre hubs of cartwheels of a very early type but no evidence of door fittings or the other side wall of the door has been found so far. It could of course be evidence of knife and tool sharpening in later times.

The rest of this sandstone structure may have been reused in the foundations of the timber over-building and the shape of the centre room may correspond to the extent of the original tower base. A large open doorway formerly existed in the later timber structure almost opposite the worn sandstone door and was probably used as a later front door.

There are six blocks of the same type of sandstone dotted around the garden which appear to have come from the external top of the structure as they have been weather-worn into 'loaf' shapes over the centuries and have two carved 'finishing' lines along the outside edge. The prominence of the bottom two courses of sandstone as defence

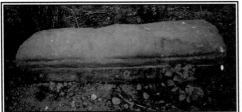

against the weather also appears to point to the external base of a structure like a signal tower but may just indicate that it was once an external end wall.

The relationship of this site to the apparently Roman moat structure lost under the Guinness warehouses on the industrial estate to the south and other Roman features in the area is also worth considering. Possible timber structures have also shown up on ground radar which may indicate Bronze/Iron Age, Romano-British, or Anglo-Saxon building activities but this study is still on-going.

Suggestion Two: The second theory of the wall's origin is that it represents the remains of a castle constructed on the site by the Norman invaders between 1070AD and 1190AD. Was this the site chosen by the first Norman overlords Hamon de Venables, third baron of Kinderton, and his father Gilbert Venables of Domesday, on which to build their castle in 1086AD? If so - why? (Were the Celts or Romans here first?)

Archaeologists from South Trafford Archaeological Group noted that chisel marks in the stones were of a type similar to those used in Norman times (although only faintly visible) and that very early split timbers had been reused during the later building phases. (Timbers cut using saws and axes were only used in later medieval buildings).

It was thought that the original Norman buildings may have been partially destroyed by fire between 1150AD and 1210AD resulting in the conversion to domestic use after the Norman

Conquest had been completed.

Further support for this theory comes from the existence of a small 'moat' feature to the front left side of the building and the discovery of a wide trench filled with dark soil deposits during building work about 30 yards (28m) to the north, behind the farm. This could represent two sides of a moat and the remaining sandstone walls may have been the gatehouse facing an old road.

In both of these possible ancient origins for the sandstone structure, the local Celtic population would have seen the distinct image of a Roman or Norman 'castle standing in the barley fields' possibly giving the place its name as BARLEY CASTLE.

South Trafford Archaeological Group took samples of the oak crook timbers from the house in order to establish the date these trees were cut down using a method of matching local tree ring growth known as Dendrology. The results came back as something of a surprise giving the very early year of tree felling as 1211AD (±50 years). It is one of these crook timber uprights that has been set up over the sandstone wall probably dating the wall to before 1200AD.

More archaeological work undertaken in 1998 and 1999 confirmed that some timbers showed growth ring sequences dating the felling of the trees to about 1207AD. Excavation of the floor inside the 'L' shaped wall revealed various original levels, the lowest interpreted as possibly Saxon, which placed the sandstone wall in the late Norman period once again. Sadly no datable finds were recovered from the lower floor levels.

The crook timber house frame was then infilled with wattle and daub which still exists in great quantities on the site as a mixture of animal hair, mud and blood over woven willow wattles. The sandstone wall became the central fire place, which would originally have been open with smoke leaving through the thatched roof, and one smoke window of four openings

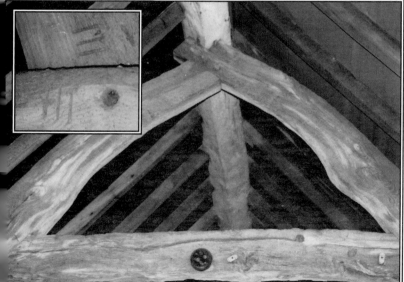

remains blocked up at ceiling height in the north wall of the Dining Room (where the fire place is now). This timber window structure has never been rebated for glass.

Timbers removed from this early building phase have been reused in the barn and show builders marks but no sign of the original medieval thatched roof remains.

The four fields in front of the farm (to the south across the old road) were recorded on the 1765AD estate map of Appleton as Castle Croft (x2), Higher Castle Croft and Castle Field, and the remains of buildings

THE AERIAL PHOTOGRAPH SHOWS BARLEY CASTLE FARM (BOTTOM L), AND BRADLEY HALL (TOP R)
INSETS: TIMBER FRAME CONSTRUCTION FEATURES FROM INSIDE BARLEY CASTLE FARM

of uncertain age have been detected under the near side of these fields and by the road over the years. One local tradition makes these 'sandstone castle foundations', but another story remembers them as later farm buildings, either of which may be true.

In a publication *Cheshire Village Memories* produced by the Cheshire Federation Of Women's Institutes the following appears under 'Barley Castle':

"On the outskirts of the village (of Appleton), bordering High Legh, stood an old thatched cottage dated 1401AD and demolished between the world wars. Originally it was one of those known as Barley Castle - because it was a beer house approached by rather steep stone steps and with a large cellar underneath for storage. A later tenant kept his cow there. ....

On the opposite side of the road were two more cottages, and a descendant of one of the inhabitants says that her Great Grandfather had a weaving shed by the side of his home. Near Barley Castle is a Tanyard Farm with a tan pit surrounded by cobble stones still in the yard. Another tan pit was in Pepper Street and when buying skins the owner brought home some gazelles from South America. The change of climate cannot have suited them as they died soon after, in 1880, and were buried under a cherry tree."

Here is a clear suggestion that no 'castle' ever existed, rather a Tudor pub serving 'barley' beer that proved as difficult to enter as any castle!

Six buildings (which must include the pub) are shown in the 'Barley Castle' group on the

Appleton Estate Map of 1765AD, four on the 1805 OS Map and two (obviously minus the pub) on the present OS Map, and still standing today. The missing buildings showed up again on a geophysical survey undertaken by archaeologists in 1997 in the field opposite the front of the farm and across the old road as it is today, but no trace of any castle structures were found.

In Barley Castle Farm the room now used as the lounge appears to be a Tudor extension made from reused timber added about 1450AD, constructed using box framing which has later been infilled with brick. The largest visible base timber may have come from a ship (which was common practice at this time) and the other timbers may indicate the remains of earlier timber buildings on the site which were dismantled to extend the house.

In the 1998/1999 excavations the early Tudor brick hearth foundations were found under the floor inside the 'L' shaped sandstone wall, in front of the present fire place. This has probably always been the location of the 'hearth' since the timber construction of 1200AD but, sadly, a location for this was not found.

Over the next few hundred years the building was extended into a yeoman's cottage by the addition of what is now the kitchen, bathroom and pantry on the ground floor (built entirely of bricks), and the addition of a first floor for the storage of provisions. Husks of oats and barley still fall from the floor cavities on windy days and it is thought that the well was hidden somewhere under what is now the pantry floor.

At some point between 1550AD and 1650AD the house was completed to its present layout but appears to have then been reduced to a ruin as large parts of the building from this period are missing, especially two walls and the roof at the front and side of the east end.

It is recorded that a 'Yeoman', Gabriel Knowles, lived here at this time and it is likely that he sided with King Charles I during the Civil War resulting in the destruction of his property after Cromwell's victory at Warrington. Troops marching from Latchford into Cheshire would have passed very close to here on many occasions and may have partly reduced the house to ruin if they met with any organised resistance. The 'New Model Army' were renowned for acts of 'vandalism'!

6). BRADLEY HALL

The Danyers family of Grappenhall are recorded as living at Bradley Hall moated site in the 13th and 14th centuries. The family almost certainly came from France with William the Conqueror after 1066AD when their name was De Angers suggesting they came from the Anjou region of western France near Nantes.

The family can be traced from 1294AD, and by 1339AD Thomas Danyers had become a leading light of local society, returning to France to fight at Crecy under the 'Black Prince' (son of Edward III) in 1346AD and rising, on his return, to become the Justice of Chester, then Sheriff of the County of Cheshire by 1350AD. The name went through various changes from D'Anyers, Danvers, Danyell, Danyers and had become Daniels by the 16th century (1500AD to 1600AD).

Today the site has been extensively examined by the now discontinued Liverpool

University Field Archaeology Unit, who found that the platform on which the present house stands had been heavily constructed on in recent times, the last time to build a complex of greenhouses with brick foundations which had destroyed all earlier features. Nothing significant was found. The possibility of material remains beyond the moat, and the obvious relationship to the North Cheshire Ridge Roman road, remains to be explored, and strongly hints at an older Celtic character for the site.

There are various parts of the house standing which may possibly date from Medieval times but they are all encased in internal and external cladding to give the building a uniform character. The oldest feature on the site is a gigantic glacial boulder at the farm end of the drive which was pulled off the field immediately to the south by a team of shire horses in the 19th century.

7). The LOST STRETTON MOAT

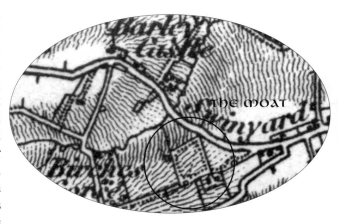

Much research has been undertaken towards identifying this site by archaeologists at Manchester, since the shape shown on Victorian OS maps bears more than a passing resemblance to a Roman military fort of some considerable size. The bad news is that it was seriously affected by the construction of Stretton Air Field during the Second World War, and recently built over with warehouses, before the site was identified. Such banks and ditches as remain (and they are few, and getting fewer) have been periodically examined by Mike Nevell's team from Manchester, who have concluded that it was probably a Roman military enclosure or settlement site of some kind, which has now most likely been lost.

An elderly local resident remembers playing on the site as a little girl, finding "red pottery" and losing a little dog down a hole into old foundations. Was this the original 'Barley Castle'? Sadly we may never know.

At this point Swineyard Lane becomes Barleycastle Lane as it crosses the M56 motorway and terminates at a small traffic island. The next site is straight across on the far corner of the first road on the right.

8). OLD REDDISh hALL MOAT

Here lies three surviving sides of a square moat in a field at the junction of Broad Lane (formerly Hall Lane) and Cartridge Lane, Grappenhall, next to Reddish Hall, which is now a farm.

There is no doubt that this moat dates back to early Medieval times. This was the former home of the Boydell family who were responsible for much of the work undertaken at St Wilfrid's church in Grappenhall during the Medieval period. About the same time as commencing work on the church they built for themselves a fortified manor house surrounded by a moat with a bridge across.

Unfortunately the Medieval Boydell family of Grappenhall died out in the male line and the property passed through heiresses to the Reddish family of Caterich in the late 16th century (1500 AD to 1600 AD). Later still it passed to the Marbury family of Marbury and, at some as yet undefined time, the Hall fell into ruin, and was demolished, according to maps produced after 1800 which show only the present small house.

The complete moat is still shown and labelled as Reddish Hall on the 1873 OS Map but the Hall was probably replaced by the large farm building opposite about this time. To date I can find no record of archaeological activity or finds on this site.

The next set of sites may come as something of a surprise in a list of those possessing moats, and leads us nicely into Arley.

Return to the traffic island, go straight across and take the next right into Grappenhall Lane (B5356) towards Appleton Thorn. Here we take our last detour and turn left just after the pub, and before the Church, down Arley Road. Stay on this country road for about two miles and it leads straight into the gates of Arley Hall. Here turn right at the first crossroads to park and visit Arley Hall, or left down Back Lane  towards the final picturesque Cheshire village in this book, Arley Green. The road comes to a logical end at the village and you should park considerably bearing in mind that this is a private estate. Footpath routes should also be strictly adhered to and continue on along the road and over fields as marked.

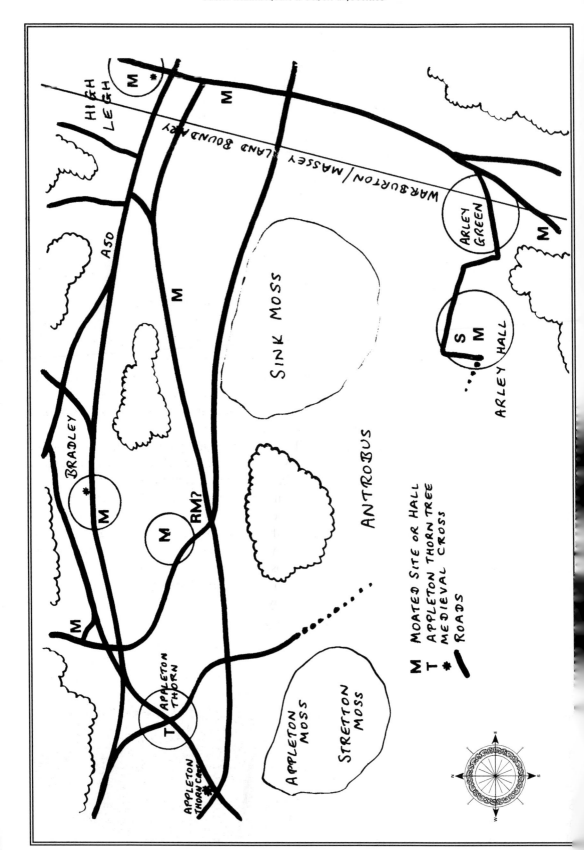

ARLEY HALL AND ARLEY GREEN

COUNTRY OF THE RHYMING SIGNPOSTS

*No cartway save on sufferance here, For horse and foot the road is clear,
To Lymm, High Leigh, Hoo Green and Mere.*

Without any doubt it is worth making a detour from our circular route to visit the present Arley Hall with its superb gardens, and the picturesque neighbouring village of Arley Green. But having spoken at length to the present 'Estate Historian', Charles Foster, it appears that little existed here in Celtic times other than a vast, wooded, deer forest. However some elements of interest to the Celtic traveller remain. A maze of twisting back lanes reach out into the Cheshire plains between the Mersey and the Roman A556 'Watling Street'.

I do not propose to cover this area in detail but hope to highlight the major discoveries up to Medieval times as far south as the Arley Estates and Arley Green. This area was long known as the 'Country of the Rhyming Signposts' because of the activities of Rowland Egerton Warburton, squire of Arley Hall. Apart from writing the lilting poetry in his book of Hunting Songs which has always been popular in Cheshire, he turned his talents to producing information in verse on local buildings and sign posts, such as that which begins this section and the photo on the previous page. At the time of writing the *Arley Hall Guide Book,* in 1982, when the house was first opened to the public, Charles Foster observed three of Rowland's sign posts still standing on the estate, along with the gravestones to his favourite hunting horses, located in the 'Fish Garden' of the hall, and similarly written in rhyme.

9). ARLEY HALL

The founder of the Warburton family was Adam de Dutton, great-grandson of Odard the Norman, recorded in Domesday as the owner of Aston, part of Weston and a third of Dutton.

Unfortunately the present magnificent Arley Hall is outside the time frame set for this book but is certainly worth noting historically. Some authorities believe that the house was begun in the 14th century (1300 to 1400AD) and Sir Geoffrey de

Warburton subscribed a land charter here in 1347AD. It is known for certain that Piers Warburton relocated his principal seat here in 1469AD from the ancient Celtic settlement of Warburton (see Book 1). He constructed a moated, 'U' shaped house, later to be improved to a complete square with a third storey in Tudor times (about 1570AD). This is why the present house qualifies as a moated site despite the absence of an identifiable moat today.

Because of various rebuilds over the years, only the magnificent tithe barn remains complete out of all the structures associated with the first house, and it was probably erected no later than 1470AD. There also survives a completely submerged Medieval well in the pond on the edge of Dairy Wood/Marlfield to the north of the chapel.

Why he chose this site for his new house, so far south of Warburton and in the middle of a wooded deer park, remains a mystery - except

THE 'ROOTERY' (OR ROOTREE) CREATED BY JAMES BATEMAN FROM THE RUBBLE OF THE TUDOR HALL. HE ALSO CREATED THE 'SHRUBBERY' AT BIDDULPH GRANGE IN STAFFORDSHIRE.
INSETS: TWO BEASTS FROM THE WINGS OF THE HALL, WHICH WERE DEMOLISHED IN 1968, COPIED FROM THE VATICAN GARDENS.

perhaps that a ley line appears to run directly through this new hall site if the 'three barrow cluster', Mersey ford and former house and Burr at Warburton are linked up. There may also have been some ancient features here which made the site attractive, one remaining being the enigmatic Arley Green standing stone.

Seldom in my travels over the north-west region have I encountered a stone remaining from the great period of prehistoric monolith building when Avebury and Stone Henge came into being, but this monolith is one exception. To reach it continue some distance along the road through Arley Green, which takes a ninety degree bend to the left, and the small stone appears first on the right followed by the monolith just before the estate gate.

Standing about 4 feet 6ins (1.5m) with two sides about the same square and ends about half as wide, this ancient stone shows signs of the farming practice of 'scalding and breaking' which was inflicted upon these monuments after the Puritan attitudes of the Civil War took hold in the 17th and 18th centuries. A bonfire would be piled up around the 'Pagan monument' and set on fire, then cold water would be thrown on to the heated stone which would crack and be attacked with hammers. The resulting stone fragments were then used as convenient building material and many prehistoric sites suffered from this appalling fate.

The Arley Green stone is badly cracked and discoloured which shows it may have been very much taller than it is now before scalding and breaking. A local story also states that the giant standing stone once stood closer to the now demolished mill but the sheer size of the stone makes a move to the present site unlikely, and it was close to the mill anyway.

The other giant glacial boulder I have recorded along the road on the same side as the monolith, set into the base of a very old tree, may have existed as a track or boundary marker in ancient times before the advent of distinct roads.

Like a great many archaeological mysteries, just when a concrete identification looks like it has been made an element of doubt enters the equation. The Warburton family erected three stones as boundary markers between themselves and the Massey family lands at Dunham Massey in 1446AD and these may represent other examples of this practice, dividing Arley lands from Tatton.

THE NOW DEMOLISHED MILL AT ARLEY GREEN AND THE GARDENS AT ARLEY HALL IN ABOUT 1910.

10). THE MYSTERY MOAT OF ARLEY

Two fields to the south, and hidden in a forest, is a fascinating water-filled moat and pond feature about which virtually nothing is known. It has a central platform, moat, bank and ditch, square pond, four yew trees and an access road, all overgrown. The yew trees are probably no more than 500 years old and the forest has only taken hold over the last 150 years, but no signs of any structures remain except for two vertical oak gateposts with iron hinges at the field boundary,

which look about 350 years old. This moat in Alder Edge Wood was deserted by the date of the 1805 OS Map.

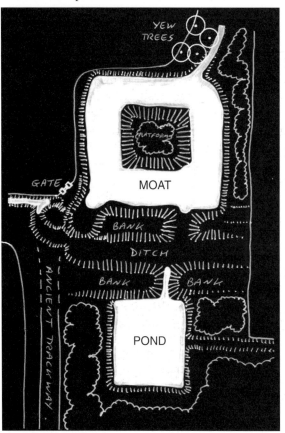

Charles Foster remembers a small scale archaeological survey which took place on the site about ten years ago which itself only reached vague conclusions. A resistivity (or geophysical) study of the platform found no clear underground features, ruling out a moated house site. Examination of the banks, ditches, moat and pool, combined with estate plans showing the area as 'Alder Hedges', led to the opinion that the platform may have housed a late Medieval bird shooting hide for wildfowl, a view supported by the evidence from my own survey and plans of 1998.

Also absent from this area of the Arley Estate is the mill mentioned on Rowland's rhyming sign post which was demolished early this century. Two of the millstones are preserved in the brick floor of the tithe barn, laid there in 1976.

However, there remains a magnificent variety of buildings clustered along the foot paths of Arley Green and Arley Hall which include: the Old Smithy, School House, Cow House Farm, The Ashes, Litley Farm, The Lodge and Arley Hall, all of which I recommend are visited, but please remember that they are privately owned and only the Hall and designated footpaths are open to the public.

Striding over the open estate you may be walking in the footsteps of Arley's most famous guest, Louis Napoleon III, who spent the winter hunting season here from 1847 to 1848.

Return to the car, leave Arley down the roads by which you came, and Arley Road should carry you back to Appleton Thorn.......

APPLETON THORN

The final site, and a fitting conclusion to this book, is the semi-legendary area of the Appleton Thorn and Thorn Cross. Both items exist here in the form of the actual Appleton thorn tree next to the church and the ancient socket cross at the junction of Pepper Street, Stretton Road and Cann Lane, about a quarter of a mile down Stretton Road (B5356) if you turn left.

BAWMING THE THORN

In Appleton Thorn village there is the revived custom of 'barning' or 'bawming' the thorn tree which stands on the crossroads here, outside the church boundary wall. BAWMING as a word is thought to derive from the Saxon BAWM meaning 'tree', and BALM is a healing substance derived from a tree. In modern terms 'bawming' means 'adorning' and the tree is decorated with red ribbons and garlands by the local school children in June every year. The dedication plate currently below the tree reads: *"This thorn tree is an off-shoot from the famous Glastonbury thorn in Somerset. A thorn tree has stood here since the 12th Century when, according to local historians, the original tree was planted by a Norman knight, Adam de Dutton. He was returning from the Crusades c.1178 when he made a pilgrimage to the abbey, bringing an off-shoot of the famous thorn back with him to plant on this site as a thanksgiving for his safe return. Over the centuries the custom of 'Bawming the Thorn' grew up. 'Bawming' means decorating the tree*

THE THORN AS IT IS TODAY
AND, LEFT, AS IT WAS IN
BATEMAN'S PAINTING OF 1880

with flowers and ribbons. This is done to the singing of the Bawming Song written by R.E.Egerton Warburton, a local Cheshire poet of the 19th Century, after which the village children dance round the tree. This unique ceremony was revived in 1973 and since then is held annually on the third Saturday in June. This tree was presented to the village by Appleton Thorn Women's Institute and planted in 1967."

The original thorn was said to be a cutting from the much celebrated 'Holy Thorn' at

Glastonbury, brought from Palestine by Joseph of Aramithea in the form of his staff, which was planted at the foundation of Glastonbury Abbey. The legend goes something like this:

> At some point in Jesus' unrecorded boyhood his uncle, Joseph of Arimathea, brought Jesus to Britain and introduced him to various sites and leading Godly men of this country. Years later, after the Crucifixion, Joseph helped to bury Jesus and left Palestine with a small band of followers bound again for the British Isles, which he also knew through earlier tin trading activities with Cornwall. Joseph and his followers walked into Glastonbury where Joseph stuck his staff into the ground and it immediately took root and blossomed. Later Glastonbury Abbey was built on this site and cuttings were taken from the original thorn tree before it died many of which still survive in the churchyard at Glastonbury.

Apparently the way to identify these thorn trees is by their blossoming twice a year, once at Old Christmas time in early January and again in May - which may be the association with Sir Gawain's Cheshire (the 'Hawk Of May') that caused Adam de Dutton to select a May flowering thorn. A spray of the Glastonbury Thorn still traditionally decorates the Queen's Christmas dinner table every year and the Appleton Thorn is in full flower by June.

Local legend adds that Adam brought an offshoot of the Glastonbury Thorn to his manor at Warburton in 1178AD and erected the Appleton Thorn cross in thanks for his safe return from the second Crusade (1145AD to 1189AD - and something of an extravagant failure as far as Crusades go). The present socketed cross base is not this cross as it is likely to be 300 years too recent, but it does bear a striking resemblance to the cross base at Warburton (see Book 1).

A NEW PICTURE OF THE THORN

In 1880 R.E. Egerton-Warburton combined forces with the Italian Renaissance style painter of the Royal Academy, Robert Bateman (exhibited 1871 to 1889), to produce a giant painting with poetry commemorating possibly the most important recorded chapter in the history of the Appleton Thorn. Written on the painting are the following verses in this manner:

> THIS.THORN.IN.THE.YÈAR.1880.WAS.SET.
> BY.THE.WARBURTON .HEIR.AND.HIS.BRIDE.ANTOINETTE.
> MAY. BLESSINGS.ON.BOTH.BE.ABUNDANTLY.SHED.
> AND.MAY.ALL.THOSE.WHO.BAWM.IT.AS.HAPPILY.WED.

> THIS.THORN.WHICH.SUCCEEDED.THE.OLD.ONE.BLOWN.DOWN.
> STOOD.FOR.55.SUMMERS.IN.APPLETON.TOWN.
> THERE.EACH.JULY.AS.THE.WENCHES.DANCED.ROUND.
> IT.WAS.BAWMED.WITH.FRESH.FLOWERS.AND.WITH.GARLANDS.WAS.CROWNED.
> AT.ARLEY.(WHENCE.BROUGHT.IN.1825).
> ONCE.MORE.MAY.IT.FIRMLY.BE.ROOTED.AND.THRIVE!

From this it can be deduced that a thorn was brought to Arley in 1825 and planted in the old town of Appleton, where it stood for 55 years before being blown down in 1880. At this point another thorn was planted on the spot and commemorated by the painting which strangely shows three trees. The tree on the left has white flowers/berries and two wood pigeons on top, the large middle tree is the thorn and it has been 'bawmed' with garlands and roses, the right tree has different leaves, red flowers/berries and four crows on the branches. Below the left tree are the tiny brown faces of a 'Green Man' and a 'Cernunnos' head (disguised as a fleur-de-lis) and under the right tree are three crossed arrows, both designs having Roland Egerton's verses above.

Either side of the central tree are the figures of a dancing maid to the left and piping boy to the right. The whole presentation points towards fertility in the land and marital relationships.

From 1880 the next we hear of the ceremony is in 1933, 53 years later, when the tree still stood, but the ceremony had ceased following the unruly and drunken behaviour of the reveller at that time. This tree is then lost to history for 34 years until the local W.I. purchase the present tree which has stood for 32 years. This gives the thorn a total written history of only 174 years.

The site of the original Medieval thorn tree and any surviving relatives has now been entirely lost over the preceding 647 years. It is equally possible that the original thorn was planted somewhere in Warburton, Appleton, Arley or Appleton Thorn, but there is a chance it may yet be found if you ever find a thorn tree flowering in mid January!

Some authorities maintain that the present tree is probably close to the original site noting the name of the church (St Cross) to be possibly derived from Adam's 'cross erecting' activities. The close proximity of the pre-Roman North Cheshire Ridge Road has also been suggested as a possible site for a Pagan/Celtic cross close to the present church in ages past, and a later Cheshire socket cross still exists a short way further west up the present B5356 Stretton Road.

APPLETON THORN CROSS

Here on the right, at the crossroads junction of the ancient Pepper Street, Stretton Road and Cann Lane, once stood this socket cross which probably marked a major junction in Medieval times. For the first time I reproduce here an extremely rare original photograph taken in the 1880s which shows the cross in its original position before it somehow became buried by road improving activities. In 1973 it was excavated and moved 4metres north west to its present position when the roads here were widened.

It is believed to have been a late medieval wayside or preaching cross with a wooden cross

SARAH GRIFFITHS

APPLETON THORN CROSS IN ABOUT 1860 (R), AND AFTER BEING MOVED, TODAY (L).

inserted into the socket in the tradition of a great many Cheshire 'socket crosses'. A single coin found under the lowest layer of stones during excavation dates the erection of the cross to around 1400AD to 1420AD, although it may have been erected about fifty years later as part of the building work undertaken in the area by Piers Warburton when he moved his manorial seat here to Arley from Warburton in 1469AD. The same type of cross base also once existed at High Legh and Mere.

Returning back east along Stretton Road to Appleton Thorn village, the small village hall appears just on the left before the church. This is my recommended end to our travels, an award winning real-ale pub appropriately named the Appleton Thorn Village Hall. As Dr Samuel Johnson once said: *"There is nothing which has yet been contrived by man through which so much happiness is produced as by a good tavern or inn."*

The End

CHRONOLOGY OF PRINCIPAL TIME PERIODS USED IN THIS BOOK

Time periods are often referred to in the text by name only (although the centuries are numerically defined) so I feel that a reference list of the approximate periods being referred to would be a helpful appendix to this volume in the series. Please remember that the older the dates given, the more open to debate are the periods as defined.

THE ICE AGES:
500 000 BC - 480 000 BC:	Cromerian (Interglacial Warm Spell).
480 000 BC - 400 000 BC:	Anglian (Ice Age).
400 000 BC - 380 000 BC:	Hoxnian (Interglacial Warm Spell)
380 000 BC - 350 000 BC:	Wolstonian 1 (Cold Spell).
350 000 BC - 320 000 BC:	Wolstonian 1/2 (Interglacial Warm Spell).
320 000 BC - 270 000 BC:	Wolstonian 2 (Ice Age).
270 000 BC - 200 000 BC:	Ilfordian (Interglacial Warm Spell).
200 000 BC - 150 000 BC:	Wolstonian 3 (Ice Age).
150 000 BC - 90 000 BC:	Ipswichian (Start of Modern Climate).
90 000 BC - 10 000 BC:	Devensian (Start of Stone Age Man).

THE STONE AGE:
35 000 BC - 30 000 BC:	Palaeolithic Period (Old Stone Age).
30 000 BC - 25 000 BC:	Aurignacian Period (Old Stone Age).
25 000 BC - 15 000 BC:	Gravetian Period (Old Stone Age).
15 000 BC - 10 000 BC:	Magdalenian Period (Old Stone Age).
10 000 BC - 2 000 AD:	Flandrian (Start Of Modern Man).
10 000 BC - 5 000 BC:	Mesolithic Period (Middle Stone Age).
5 000 BC - 2 000 BC:	Neolithic Period (New Stone Age).

THE BRONZE AGE:
4000 BC - 1300 BC:	Revised Copper Age (Early Bronze Age).
2000 BC - 1100 AD:	Revised Celtic Age. Duration of 3000+ years.
1900 BC - 1500 BC:	Beaker Invasions (Early Bronze Age).
1500 BC - 1300 BC:	Wessex Invasions (Early Bronze Age).
1300 BC - 900 BC:	Urn & Barrow Culture (Middle Bronze Age).
900 BC - 500 BC:	Halstatt Culture (Late Bronze Age).
600 BC - 200 AD:	Phoenicians in Britain.
500 BC - 100 BC:	La Te'ne Culture (Late Bronze Age).

THE IRON AGE:
400 BC - 50 BC:	Greeks in Britain (Iron Age).
200 BC - 50 BC:	Belgic invasions (Iron Age).
55 BC - 410 AD:	Romans invade Cheshire (Iron Age).
300 AD - 410 AD:	Picts & Scots invade. (Iron Age).

THE DARK AGES:
410 AD - 795 AD:	Welsh Britons invade Cheshire.
450 AD - 570 AD:	Saxons invade Cheshire.
570 AD - 790 AD:	Angles invade Cheshire.
790 AD - 900 AD:	Vikings/Norse invade Cheshire.
860 AD - 1066 AD:	Scandinavians/Danes invade Cheshire.

MEDIEVAL TIMES:
1066 AD - 1200 AD:	Normans invade Cheshire.
1090 AD - 1250 AD:	Early Medieval Period.
1095 AD - 1290 AD:	The Crusades (1-8).
1250 AD - 1350 AD:	Middle Medieval Period.
1350 AD - 1500 AD:	Late Medieval Period.

MODERN TIMES:
1480 AD - 1600 AD:	Tudor Period.
1550 AD - 1600 AD:	Elizabethan Period.
1600 AD - 1700 AD:	Stuart Period.
1648 AD - 1660 AD:	English Civil War.
1700 AD - 1830 AD:	Georgian Period.
1720 AD - 1900 AD:	The Industrial Revolution.
1820 AD - 1900 AD:	Victorian Period.
1914 AD - 1918 AD:	The First World War.
1938 AD - 1945 AD:	The Second World War.
1945 AD - 2000 AD:	The Technological Revolution.

FOR BIBLIOGRAPHY SEE BOOKS 1 AND 3